This is the true story of one ma
lead mine, across thousands o
until he reached Persia.

J. M. BAUER

As Far As My Feet
Will Carry Me

Translated from the German by
Lawrence Wilson

PANTHER
Granada Publishing

Panther Books
Granada Publishing Ltd
8 Grafton Street, London W1X 3LA

Published by Panther Books 1966
Reprinted 1967, 1968, 1969, 1975, 1984

First published in Great Britain by
André Deutsch Ltd 1957

Copyright © Josef Martin Bauer 1957

ISBN 0-583-12506-9

Printed and bound in Great Britain by
Collins, Glasgow

Set in Intertype Times

As Far As
My Feet
Will Carry Me

AUTHOR'S NOTE

It was a strange encounter when in the late autumn of 1954, the Munich publisher Franz Ehrenwirth introduced me to a man who claimed to have escaped from Soviet captivity after travelling for over three years from East Cape through the whole of Siberia. The man talked of almost every topic under the sun except the one I wanted to discuss. His conversation hovered between anger and fear. He would lose his temper, count up his wounds, curse Soviet justice, and become explosive with fury at all that had happened to him, complaining that he was a useless cripple, unfit for life or regular employment. Only now and then was it possible to glimpse something of the enormity of his experience. He was afraid of being compromised.

For a long time both he and I considered whether we ought to set about recording his experiences in writing, and it was not until 2nd January 1955, that we came together again. Even then it was some time before he began to piece his story together, in roughly chronological sequence, on a tape-recorder. Often, he lost track of time and place, particularly once we reached his escape, and it was difficult to arrange the episodes in their proper order.

I had no means of testing his accuracy and he grew angry when I expressed doubts or persisted in querying some of his statements. We had our first sharp clash when he spoke of tall, fully-developed trees on the Anadyr, and I told him flatly that it was impossible for trees of any kind to grow there. I thought I knew something of Russia, having soldiered right over the Caucasus and as far as the Leningrad area, but when I sought expert advice, I found that he was right, not I. The whole story was so nightmarish, the incidents and situations he claimed to be true so incredible, that I kept on raising doubts, yielding only to the stubbornness with which he stuck to his story or to corroboration from other sources. Time and again, when I did turn elsewhere for corroboration, his story was confirmed.

As the work went on, my determination to get this book written increased. I maintained as high a literary level as possible and told the story as graphically as I could. As he wished to remain anonymous, I gave him the name of 'Clemens Forell'. To the events and characters which he supplied in outline I tried to give flesh and substance in the form of dialogues and reflections, building up atmosphere and

7

giving the characters thoughts and feelings such as seemed appropriate to their situation.

On 10th May 1955, I delivered the complete script. It remained largely unaltered after 'Forell' had read it, even towards the end where I had condensed a good deal from the mass of material recorded on the tape. Fraught with danger as they were, the experiences in the later stages of the escape were largely a repetition of situations which had occurred before. 'Forell' had, to a certain extent, adapted himself to circumstances and had developed a greater resourcefulness which helped him on his way. That resourcefulness was not particular in the expedients it suggested, so that more than once he asked me: 'Do you intend to mention that in the book?' The change which had taken place in him, understandably enough, in the third year of his escape seems to me sufficiently implicit in the text to explain why I decided not to cover a further hundred pages with a mass of extra detail.

'Forell' himself is satisfied with the book as I have written and concluded it.

FORELL TALKS ABOUT HIMSELF

Based on a conversation recorded in Munich on 26th May 1957. (The questions put to him by his publisher which elicited this information have been omitted, and Forell's answers linked up, but otherwise left unchanged.)

Starting in 1935, I was really no more than a boy then, with nothing but foolishness in my head. I was supposed to be learning the business of photo-reproduction and, in fact, I did learn it, more or less, and passed my exams. I had every hope of setting up in business on my own sooner or later.

Then came my time in the Army. I was called up for Labour Service in the spring of 1938, and did my military service that autumn with the Alpine Troops. After a time I discovered that the *Gebirgsjäger* didn't appeal to me much —mountain climbing and so on—so I volunteered for the paratroops and was sent to Stendal. There I took my jumping tests—three jumps—and got my so-called Jumping Badge. Then I waited for things to start moving.

When the war began we, of course, went into action straight away as what we called the 'Fire Brigade'. That wartime expression meant that they used us wherever there was danger of an enemy break-through, or in places where our own forces were so weak that the normal units could make no progress. We were what were called 'élite' troops.

We were specially trained. Every one of us could handle at least ten different kinds of weapon, apart from the normal infantry weapons. I, for instance, was trained in the machine-gun, the rifle, the pistol and the usual short-range weapons such as the hand-grenade and the bayonet, and in addition I was trained in the 3.5 PAK (the anti-tank gun), the 5.5 and the 88 millimetre ack-ack. I was also trained in the double-barrelled gun, and as a signaller, in morse. We almost all knew the morse code.

As paratroops were dropped in Rotterdam and Eben Emanel, and then in Crete. I was wounded on the last day of the Crete operation: a bullet in my knee. I have had a silver knee-cap in my left leg ever since.

After a short time in hospital and at home I was sent to the Eastern Front. I had been promoted Second Lieutenant in Crete, and on the Eastern Front I was promoted Lieutenant and got a Company—not as Company Commander, but as Company Leader, because with us, at that time, only a

Captain could be a Company Commander. I was dropped behind the Urals with part of my Company—or rather, with the whole of it, but its numbers were much reduced by that time. We were flown over in four Ju 52s. Marching back from the Urals towards the front, we blew up quite a number of bridges, depots and so on, some of them just damaged and some of them blown sky-high.

On the march back we ran out of food and explosives. Ammunition was getting low, too. One day a Russian Cossack unit spotted us—probably we had been careless in some way —and encircled us. We formed the so-called 'hedgehog', which is a circle facing outwards so that you can fire in all directions. Our ammunition ran out and when the Russians had got into a better position they plastered us with their machine-guns and grenades and so on until there was just nothing left of us.

After that—it may have been two or three days later or it may have been the same night—I was picked up by these Russians and taken to a partisan hospital. I had got a head-wound in that affair—a shot through the mouth. The bullet is still in my cerebellum somewhere and gives me attacks of giddiness even today. My eyes play me up, too, in all kinds of ways and I get bad pains in the head. The bullet has been encapsuled now, and I am partially colour blind, but that comes chiefly from working in the lead mine. Lead poisoning.

When I'd been discharged from the Russian partisan hospital as more or less fit I was taken to a transit camp for officers, and after that to various other camps: works camps and officers' camps again. Until 1945 we were not allowed to work because the Russians said that German officers were protected by the Geneva Convention. 'On that point,' they said, 'we recognize the Convention. The officers will be fed, and they mustn't work.' It would have been much better if we could have worked.

They started passing sentences in the autumn of 1945. For some months we had noticed that there were informers in the camps, but we could never prove anything against them. Sooner or later these fellows managed to piece together information we'd withheld from the Russians: our units, where we'd been employed, and so on. It would come out in our talk among ourselves, and they would report it to the NKVD for extra break or a dollop of kasha or something.

Then they collected us together—it must have been between twenty and twenty-two thousand men, though I can't remember exactly—and organized the famous march through Moscow. For two and a half days and nights we were marched back and forth through Moscow, and the people didn't give us exactly a friendly welcome. They howled and

10

screamed and spat and threw stones and filth—anything which came to hand. I remember strips of fencing being hurled down on us. The soldiers just watched and did nothing. Or rather, they did sometimes ward off some of the stuff from themselves, and bawl *'Davai! Davai!'* at us, but that was all.

After that we were put in the Lublyanka, the remand prison in Moscow. We were there for some months, and not exactly well treated. I was struck a few times and still have scars from it.

In the autumn of 1945 we were sentenced. I myself got twenty-five years penal labour in Siberia. Some had longer terms, some shorter. The longest I knew of was a Colonel who got sixty years. One boy of about eighteen got twenty-five years simply because he was alleged to have stolen a few potatoes.

That's about all.

Immediately the train stopped, the guards started yelling. After twenty-six days, the German prisoners had learned to pick out the key words in the torrent of raucous sound and they knew what to do: first of all, lay out the dead, then stuff the stew-pot with snow and collect wood from a nearby pile for the stove—only an armful for each truck, but enough to give some warmth after nine heatless days.

As the guards flung open the doors, a clear sky appeared, flushed faintly by the dying sun. The train had stopped at a junction and was standing amid a wilderness of rails. The men who had died since the last halt were lifted out and placed side by side on the neighbouring embankment, then the survivors collected wood and snow. And then they had eyes for the town. Beyond the railway lines, the sugared domes and pinnacles of Omsk stood roseate beneath the softly glowing sky. A great tall fellow with an armful of wood pointed towards the town.

'A lovely sight!'

'That pile of wood is what I call a lovely sight,' said Leibrecht. 'Shall we try for another lot?'

'I'm too tall; they'll spot me!' laughed Forell. Unnoticed at first by the guards, he rejoined the queue and awaited his turn. He was on the point of helping himself when a stream of epithets broke from a nearby figure cocooned in furs. Even without knowing a word of Russian, Forell could have gathered the gist; no more fuel for Truck Eight. When he returned to the truck, he found Leibrecht gazing at the town.

'You're right, Forell. They have certainly got a fine collection of towers here.'

'I spent most of my childhood in the shadow of church towers. My father was a keen botanist. On Sundays we used to go into the mountains and he pointed out the different species of plants, and showed us the finest churches. Do you know the valley of the Et?'

'Vaguely.'

'You ought to see that church. It's lovely. I wish I was there now.'

'Thanking God for your safe return?'

It made Forell wince to hear Leibrecht talk of home in that off-hand, sarcastic tone, when he knew well enough that none of them would ever return. Without a word, he hauled himself into the truck and then gave Leibrecht a hand up. It looked as if they would soon be moving. The guards were coming down the train, thrusting back the prisoners with their tommy-guns, holding them by the barrel like a croupier's rake. But when the human dough had once more been squeezed into its container, no one thought of shutting the doors. So they were going to stay where they were, for an hour perhaps, perhaps until the following morning, even for days. What was the hurry? None of the men had less than twenty-five years ahead of him and every hour of this stop and start and shove-around was a bit off the life sentence, like a spoonful of salt from the sea.

The sky faded from pink to pale yellow and then to a glassy green, till the oriental silhouettes beyond the railway seemed like a fabulous city, buried fathom deep beneath transparent waters. The candid light laid bare the squalor of the trucks and the waxen faces of the prisoners as they waited, listening for the clank of the potato bucket. It was some hours before the potatoes arrived, half cooked and tepid as usual. As the guard tipped them on to the floor of the truck, those standing by the doors squeezed back to leave a space and minimize the risk of someone seizing more than his fair share. The task of equitable division was entrusted by common consent to Leibrecht. Before the war he had been a bank clerk and respect for the sanctity of figures was in his blood. He, if anyone, would divide the potatoes fairly; as it was, there would only be about one each for the eighty-six men in the truck.

Leibrecht was fifty-one now. During the war, he had worked his way up to the rank of captain in the Home Defence Force. In the mass trial in the Lublyanka he had been sentenced to twenty-five years because, amongst others, his battalion had guarded Russian prisoners of war. That he should have to endure this self-same journey in reverse at the age of seventy-six seemed to him unreasonable.

When he had divided the potatoes as justly as he could, Leibrecht made a suggestion. Now that they had fuel again, why not light the drain-pipe stove, boil up the snow-water and steam the whole issue in a piece of cloth so that, for once, they could have something warm inside them? But to the prospect of warm potatoes in two hours' time, the men preferred the reality of cold ones now. No one knew when the next issue would be made. It might be days before they could eat again, and by then some of them might be dead.

It was not until the evening of the following day that the

14

journey was resumed. For a while the train rattled on over the points; then the chill of the open track began to seep in through floor, walls, roof and the pair of narrow peepholes that so far the guards seemed to have overlooked. They seemed to have been bored by some previous inmate of the truck with a blunt instrument, the handle of a spoon, perhaps, or in ghastly patience with the finger nails.

With twice the number of men in the truck that it was supposed to hold, eighty-six instead of forty, there was only enough space for them to lie down if they all lay on their sides, packed in one behind another like tea-spoons. If a man wanted to turn over, he had to wait until the others were ready, and then they all turned together. Sometimes a body would lie still and silent, ignoring the common movement. Then all would have to turn back again and wait till the next stop before they could lay out the corpse. Five times this had happened so far, but with an inch-thick layer of hoarfrost covering the inside walls and growing steadily thicker, the sixth occasion could not be long delayed.

When the train stopped next day, it was Puchta's turn to be laid out on the embankment. At four in the morning, he had remained obstinately on his right side, arms folded and knees drawn into his chest, when the others had tried turning to the left. Because of him, the whole row had been obliged to turn back again. When they laid him in the snow, he was smiling in his sleep like a child.

After a time, Forell began to think of escape. His school knowledge of Russian geography stopped at the Urals. He turned to the weedy Dannhorn. Dannhorn had spent eleven years at the Cartographic Institute in Leipzig: latitude and longitude had long since become superimposed on his brain.

'When do we get nearest to the Manchurian frontier?'

'Another month,' was the surly reply.

'Try and talk sense, man!'

'I'm merely reckoning by the speed we've been going so far,' said Dannhorn. 'You know this town, don't you?'

'Novo-Sibirsk.'

'Yes. The Chicago of Siberia.' Peering through thick-lensed spectacles—Heaven alone knew how he had managed to save them!—Dannhorn inspected the town through a chink in the doors. 'Chicago wouldn't be flattered. . . .'

Sullen in the prisoner-of-war cage, sullen throughout the mass trial in Moscow and now, at the prospect of twenty-five years hard labour, Dannhorn had been consistently ill-humoured since he was first taken prisoner. He had given the Russian interrogators an easy time, willingly answering their questions and telling them how the Army Cartography Branch, in which he had served during the war, had substituted German legends for Russian on vast numbers of captured maps and speedily reissued them to the German troops in place of their own small-scale maps, of which the largest had been one in three hundred thousand.

'Where is Cape Deschnev?' asked Forell.

'Forell, how much schooling did you have? Who was your geography master? How can a Lieutenant be so ignorant?'

Scratching a thin vertical line in the hoarfrost that covered the wall, Dannhorn proceeded to demonstrate. 'Here are the Urals. To the west, Europe, which no longer concerns us. To the east, the River Irtysh. That's behind us. Omsk—also behind us, as you may remember. This is where we are at the moment. Next comes the River Yenesei. And then the Lena. You see? All the rivers flow northwards, to the Arctic. And then, should we ever see it . . .'

The finger scratched on, further and further eastwards, and higher up the wall of the truck, to the north. Dannhorn was using a strip of wood now to reach——

'—the River Aldan—not without charm.'

'There won't be enough room, Dannhorn.'

'We can draw the rest on the roof. That doesn't matter to you. For here, south of Lake Baikal—shaped like this, roughly —is where you will make a move, or in the Yablonovy mountains, choosing the shortest route to the Mongolian frontier.'

'You keep your hands off that sort of game, Forell!' broke in a voice.

Neither of the two men had noticed that their talk of escape had aroused the attention and then the ire of the other prisoners in the truck. Smoothing back the white hair from his temples, Leibrecht now diffidently reinforced the protest, murmuring that if Forell felt strong enough to escape, that proved he could do without half his potato ration.

For the time being, the map remained unfinished and Forell's question unanswered: 'Where is Cape Deschnev?' But at the conclusion of the mass trial in the Lublyanka, Cape Deschnev had been specified as the area where the condemned men were to serve their sentence, and two days later the other men in the truck repeated the question.

Dannhorn surveyed the map he had traced on the wall and explained that there was no room to show it. East Cape was too far East and too far North to be included, unless he continued on to the roof of the truck. And so the map remained uncompleted, demonstrating to the prisoners that the place to which they had been assigned lay beyond the limits of the finite world.

* * *

When the train reached Krasnoyarsk, no potatoes had been issued for two days. Inside the trucks the frost clung inches thick to the walls and searing draughts poured in through the meagre covering of straw on the floors. In Truck Eight four more men had died and there were now six corpses stacked by the doors, ready to be taken out as soon as they were opened. But no one came. Hours passed and still there was no sign of the guards. At last, the men immured in the trucks became desperate and started kicking the wooden walls with savage, rhythmic persistence. They kept it up for twenty minutes and then had to stop because they were exhausted.

For ten hours the trucks had been stationary, locked, with their load of dead and dying. Outside all was silent. The whole train seemed to have been abandoned. In Truck Eight, only Leibrecht, Forell and a man from Franconia named Burger kept up the stubborn battering. The remainder lay still.

Then the guards arrived. As they opened the doors, two of the corpses toppled out. The Russians showed no surprise, but struck up the usual chant: 'Lay out the dead! One man to collect snow! One man to take over the potato bucket!'

Then Forell went mad. The guard had barely let go the bucket than he seized it and tipped the potatoes on to the line.

'Keep your goddamned Kartoshki!'

Inside the truck the exhausted men stood up while their reeling minds tried to grasp what was happening. They had never yet seen any sense in Forell and his cussedness. Then Leibrecht slid down from the truck and, courteous as ever, said to the guard: 'Please keep the potatoes and tell the Transport Officer we would like to speak to him.'

Apparently no one had ever made such a request before and the guard hesitated. Then the officer himself, a second lieutenant, appeared and solved the dilemma.

'Was willst du?' he said, speaking in almost faultless German.

Leibrecht saw a smooth, cold face. 'Some reasonable food for the men. They are starving.'

'A mutiny?'

'No. There was a truckload of food taken on at Samara between the engine and the guard truck. You should have given your prisoners a proper daily ration, instead of feeding them on half-rotten potatoes.'

'What are you saying?'

'That truck was loaded with food. Now it is empty.'

The officer smiled a thin, dangerous smile. 'Get in!' he said.

Leibrecht clambered back into the truck. All along the train, the men had caught the flame of rebellion and tipped their potatoes on to the line. Now, from Truck Eight, they could hear the guards coming down, rolling and padlocking the doors. Once in darkness, they began to be afraid.

At first, nothing happened. They waited in silence—an hour, two hours. Then, early in the morning, the squint holes in the wall of the truck were suddenly pierced with hard white light. The next moment, they heard the guards shouting and banging open the doors at the head of the train. The light intensified as the guards came nearer, leapt to a glare. . . .

Searchlights. A reprisal, the men thought. Some sort of reprisal. Now it was their turn. Hands were fiddling with the padlock. It sprang open. The doors rolled wide. A blinding light. And then from a large, flat tin, a mass of glittering fishes were poured into the truck, like herrings. There were enough for three each.

* * *

The fish were no more than a memory when the train at last reached Irkutsk, twenty miles from the southern end of Lake Baikal. At Irkutsk they received an unexpected gift from their captors—a packet of coarse Army tobacco for each prisoner. No cigarette papers were supplied, but the men still had some odd strips of newspaper that would serve the purpose. And the tobacco was not the only concession that made then remember Irkutsk. That day, the truck doors were left open and the guards hardly bothered to stop the prisoners talking to their friends along the train. The reason? It was Willi Bauknecht, the youthful student from Truck Four, who supplied the answer. He alone apparently knew how many days had passed since the start of the journey, making a scratch on a painted strip of metal for each day with his finger nail. The train had left Moscow on 24th October.

'And this is the sixty-first day,' he said, and waited while the men slowly puzzled it out.

Finally: 'So that's the reason!' said someone.

Yes, that was the reason, though Willi Bauknecht, of course, had to act tough and get rid of the lump in his throat by pretending the tobacco issue was just a coincidence and trying to sound off-hand as he said: 'After all, you can't expect the Red Army to commemorate Christmas Eve.'

Five hundred miles further east, at Chita, the train journey came to an end. Of the ex-Wehrmacht personnel loaded for slave labour on to the train in Moscow, eighteen hundred and seventy emerged. No one could remember what the original total had been, but judging by the mortality in a single truck, it must have been well over three thousand. In Truck Eight, for example, fifty-five survived out of ninety-one.

Never once during the journey had the Russians counted

the living but only the dead whose frozen bodies had been laid out at each halt beside the line. Now, at Chita, all that was changed. Each man was carefully kept alive as though the prisoners who had survived the journey had proved themselves worth preserving. As soon as they emerged from the trucks, they were counted several times over. Then, heavily escorted, they were marched over a level crossing and up towards a formidable jail lowering on a hillside. The Osmita, it was called, 'The Impregnable,' and to build it must have been a task worthy of Asiatic patience. With a gigantic apron wall of cyclopean masonry and double-barred windows—steel, the Russians boasted, not iron!—the building originated in times when that part of Siberia was still a disputed Russian possession and a collecting centre was required for convicts drafted for colonization from further west. But despite the Osmita's reputation for being the safest jail in the world, for the German prisoners it was apparently not safe enough, and as they lay, near to total exhaustion, in the casemates, they could hear the soft footfall of their guards, prowling continually round the dripping walls. Not even Forell entertained thoughts of escape.

The prisoners were kept in the Osmita not a day longer than was necessary to recover from their exhaustion and be able to withstand the rigours of the next stage in their journey. One day a new chill wind began to blow through the casemates. Their future task-masters had arrived. These were the so-called Convoy Soldiers, professional slave drivers, wearing a distinctive flash on their Cossack-type lambskin caps—a green cross on a scarlet background. Most of them were thickset, and their long fur coats, caps and gloves accentuated their stocky appearance. Hanging from a cord round the neck, they carried a Nagan, or Army pistol, over the shoulder a tommy-gun, and in their hands, a whip consisting of a long strand of tough, curling leather.

This manly splendour of fur and fire-power had not been newly invented for the Germans; there had been slave drivers in Siberia for as long as there had been slaves. The ordinary Red Army soldier could only strike a prisoner on the order of an officer, but these men could use the whip whenever they deemed it necessary, and as the prisoners were soon to learn, that meant almost continually. In the Osmita, the Convoy Soldiers were constantly near them, appraising them with their forked, oriental eyes, patrolling up and down outside the casemates, getting to know the fleeced and shivering flock they were soon to herd across the stricken wastes of Siberia. They took good care that everyone should see the whip; then, when their muscles failed them, fear would drive the prisoners on.

One morning, the prisoners were marched out beyond the town to a bare expanse of snow where they were counted and split into groups of twenty. Then from the town, in twos and threes and finally in an endless column, a hundred and twenty-five horse-drawn sledges came trotting out towards them. After more counting, the Convoy Soldiers separated, one to a sledge, between fifteen and twenty prisoners clambered up behind, the supply sledges took their places at the rear, and the whole vast column began to move off across the bare, snow-swept hills.

As the line spread out, the horses began to trot and then the prisoners at the tail of the column saw a grandiose sight: ahead of them, a mile-long train snaking over the glittering waste beneath a cloud of steam and powdery snow flung up by two thousand hooves. In front of them, the vigorous, bearded moujik sat straight-backed at the reins, while twenty yards behind, the horses of the next sledge loomed with swaying chests through the flurries of snow, vanishing sometimes altogether, then appearing again like shadows rising from the ground. Beyond the horses, the men could be seen, bunched high up on the sledge, a grey, mysterious throng, yet somehow comforting for the sense of close support they gave in the scoured immensities of an unknown land.

At the end of each day, the men got down from the sledges aching and weary after their jolting journey in the open air. They were given better nourishment now, and they needed it if they were to survive nightly frosts of thirty-five to forty degrees, let alone be capable of work when they reached their journey's end.

When the long column halted, iron tripods were set up for four huge cauldrons in which soup was made by the moujiks for two thousand men. In addition to the soup, each prisoner was given a large enough bread ration to satisfy him and still leave some over for the following day. The soup was usually *kasha*, that is, millet cooked to the consistency of thick porridge, followed later in the journey by maize, potatoes or soya beans, often flavoured with a little bacon.

Each evening now, when the fires had been lit and the flames were rising steadily into the frosty air, or later·as, warmed and satisfied by their meal, the men lay in their thin-walled tents in some forest clearing, they were comforted by the vast stillness around them and strengthened as, slow but irresistible, the conviction crept into their clouded minds that their bondage was now only to God.

The nights were bitterly cold and some of the men were afraid to sleep in case while sleeping they might freeze to death. One night, Forell found himself next to the youngest prisoner in the column, Alfons Mattern, not quite eighteen.

The men were huddled together for warmth and were quiet, except for Mattern who was unaccountably restless.

'What's the matter?' said Forell. 'Can't you sleep?'

'I wish I could.'

'You're too young, that's your trouble. You oughtn't to be here.'

'I wouldn't have been if——'

'If what?'

'If—if I hadn't stolen some potatoes.'

'After you were captured, you mean?'

'Yes, in East Prussia. They weren't Russian, they were German potatoes!'

'Never mind, you stole! Let that be a consolation to you. I got twenty-five years without stealing a thing! And I wasn't a "war criminal", never guarded Russian prisoners, and they never discovered I'd already escaped from Russian captivity once, in 1942. No. Do you know why I'm here? Because quite incidentally one day, when the Russians were talking to me, I happened to mention that Russian geese tasted no worse to me than German. Whether they really sentenced me because they thought I had stolen a Russian goose I don't know. But from then on, they never questioned me again.'

'For God's sake shut your mouth and go to sleep!' bawled a throaty Tyrolean voice from the darkness.

Forell was already half asleep when Alfons Mattern whispered: 'I stole because I was hungry. You believe that, don't you?'

'Why not? Who isn't hungry at your age?' murmured Forell, in the hope that the boy would be satisfied as long as he got some sort of reply and would then allow Forell to sleep.

'Yes . . . I'm eighteen next month.'

Forell muttered the first thing that came to his mind. 'It oughtn't to be allowed. . . .'

'What oughtn't to be allowed?' came immediately in a louder tone from the young Mattern.

'Putting kids like you in the Army.'

Mattern seized the opening. 'Oh! I shouldn't have been, only I got wounded—a shrapnel splinter—serving in the Home ack-ack. I was just about to be discharged from hospital when all the fit men were weeded out for the Army. I'd been exactly nine days in uniform when I got captured.'

'Too bad.'

'And now I'm on my way to twenty-five years hard . . .'

'Because you stole some potatoes.'

'Officially—yes, I suppose so, but—you mustn't think I'm complaining at my sentence. I'm not. It was absolutely just. I deserve every minute . . .'

'Ssh! Not so loud!'

Mattern broke off and Forell heard him breathing fast with emotion. There was no hope of sleep now and Mattern had half sat up, propping himself on an elbow, in a state of almost hysterical excitement. To help him speak what was on his mind and so recover his self-control, Forell asked:

'Why do you deserve twenty-five years hard labour?'

'Well,' began Mattern uncertainly. 'It would almost atone for murder, wouldn't it?'

Murder? Wide awake now, at first Forell dismissed the possibility as self-dramatization, but as the youth told his story, he began to see that no other word would fit what Alfons Mattern had done. After being taken prisoner, he had admittedly been caught by the Russians in the act of stealing food and they had put him in detention. But they had never tried to make much of his obviously petty crime and it was not that which they wanted to talk about when they came to see him in prison, but an entirely different matter. There was a certain German, by name Heinz Dechant, they said—a sergeant who had commanded one of the platoons in Mattern's scratch company. What did Mattern think of him? They would be most interested to know. . . .

In fact, Mattern had no recollection whatever of a Sergeant Dechant, and said so, at first. But the Russians could see that he was home-sick and longing to get back to his sister in sunny Baden-Baden, and that, on the other hand, he had a terror of being forced to remain in Russia, and they effectively used their knowledge to help refresh the young man's memory. After a while, then, he changed his mind and said 'yes, perhaps after all, he did know a Sergeant Dechant'.

'I didn't realize the game they were playing with me. I said "yes" once or twice too often.'

The Russians were very friendly and as they seemed to know a great deal already about Sergeant Dechant, whereas Mattern knew precisely nothing, they took care to put their questions in a way which prompted the answer they desired, with the result that before long he found himself confirming that this Sergeant Dechant had not enjoyed a good reputation amongst his men. That seemed an innocent enough admission, in return for a promise to be sent home, but in fact it had earned Dechant a sentence of twenty-five years hard labour.

'And Heinz Dechant,' asked Forell, 'the man you—well, to be honest, the man you denounced—what's happened to him?'

'He's here,' said Mattern. 'I wouldn't recognize him if I saw him, but I know that because I heard his name called out when they announced the sentences in Moscow. So he must

22

be here—unless he was one of those we laid out beside the line on the journey to Chita. . . .'

Young Mattern began to weep and Forell tried to think of something to console him, as perhaps others had done when he had told them his story.

'And you didn't even get your reward?'

'I don't want it. I wouldn't accept it. Can't you see that? I don't know anything about Dechant. I've never seen him. I didn't even know he existed. But I informed against him. I don't want to go home until my twenty-five years are up. Eighteen and twenty-five, that's forty-three. Well, at forty-three, I'll still have a good few years in front of me.'

'No,' said Forell slowly. 'No. That's where you're wrong. As you're so young, you may live to work out your sentence and then, with luck, you might become a paid worker instead of a convict. But you'll never get home. You, and all of us, we're here for the rest of our lives.'

* * *

The journey on horse-drawn sledges across Siberia lasted forty days. Then the prisoners were split into two groups and while one remained in a tented encampment, the other, including Forell, set off again, this time on sledges drawn by huskies. Four or five weeks later, having reached wooded, mountainous country, the party stopped and with a small number of Convoy Soldiers left to guard them, waited while the remainder began the return journey to pick up the second group of prisoners.

By that time, Forell and his companions were nearly dead from exhaustion. The load the huskies could pull was strictly limited and only the sick had been allowed to ride on the sledges, the remainder being lucky if they got a lift occasionally on a downhill run. For most of the way, they had toiled on through deep snow after the fast moving sledges, harried continually by the whips of the Convoy Soldiers who knew exactly how much they could demand from their victims without killing them.

It was ten weeks before the second group of prisoners caught up with them, and by the time the survivors had recovered sufficiently to continue the journey, it was early summer and the snows were beginning to soften. The column had to march. Week after week the men were driven forward across the arsenic green of the Taiga, through misted valleys and up rock-strewn slopes; sweating by day and frozen in the chill, moisture-laden atmosphere by night; a skeletal, hollow-eyed band, agonizing in the half-world between life

23

and death. A month went by. Still they went on, more and more dropping dead in their tracks from exhaustion. A second month. A third. When, in the fourth month, they reached their destination, the prisoners had given up hope that their journey would ever end.

It was in the first snow storm of a new winter that, marching in single file, the column of survivors suddenly saw smoke rising above roofs on a narrow plateau ahead of them. It was so dark at midday that the huts themselves only became visible when they were almost on top of them. Here and there, light glowed in a window. It was bitterly cold.

Some Russian soldiers, one or two officers and an Army medical assistant emerged from the wooden huts and the prisoners fell in to be counted. The muster recorded that of eighteen hundred and seventy men who had started the journey from Chita to East Cape, twelve hundred and thirty-six had survived.

After the men had been counted, they were led off in groups, each to a separate point at the base of a large, conical hill. Attempts seemed to have been made to level the ground and for most of the way they were treading on rubble. Then they came to the head of a shaft tunnelled into the hill-side. Following the Russian soldier as he went through the opening, they found themselves in a passageway with a floor sloping gently downwards. As they progressed, the width and height decreased until each was about six and a half feet. Soon they were in complete darkness and their guide started talking loudly to himself so that they could follow.

After a while, the Russian soldier stopped to light a lantern. In the dim glow, the men saw that they had reached a small cave, empty except for a bare table and a stool at one side. Lighting a second lantern from the first, the Russian left one burning on the table and signed to the prisoners to follow him. At the far end of the cave they entered another passage leading to another and much larger cave. Here the guard stopped and, holding up his lantern, indicated that this was to be the prisoners' home. The men gaped. Some of them had imagined they would be housed in the huts they had seen above ground. Certainly none had expected to be thrust into a subterranean cavern and told to live and sleep there by the light of a single flickering lamp. As far as they could see, the place was bare; no furniture, no straw, even, on the rocky floor and the only means of ventilation was the passage down which they had come. There was one compensation—it was warm.

Leaving the lantern with the prisoners, the guard went back up the tunnel towards the smaller cave and, putting his tommy-gun on the table before him, sat down on the stool,

24

facing inwards towards the prisoners. They realized then that the problem of guarding them had been solved in the simplest fashion. Accommodated in the bowels of the earth, close by their place of work, they had only one route to the surface and that could be effectively blocked by one man, or two men, allowing for a relief. If the prisoners had been housed above ground, on the other hand, many times that number of guards would have been needed, together with all the paraphernalia of barbed-wire fences, searchlights and watch towers.

Hours passed while the prisoners gazed helplessly at their new surroundings, then finally a Russian lieutenant came to see them. Speaking in German, he announced that they would not be called upon to work for a month. During that time, they were to recover from their journey and put their clothing in a proper state of repair—how, he did not say. But he mouthed the usual soldierly catch-words: good order, discipline, obedience, hard work. Only one was missing: cleanliness. The prisoners gazed vacantly after his retreating form.

The officer had mentioned something about food, but there was no sign of how or when they would get it.

'Come on, Mattern!' said Forell. 'Let's go and reconnoitre!' And he began to move up towards the guard at his table, followed by the youthful Alfons.

'No silly tricks, mind!' was Leibrecht's parting shot.

Forell turned. 'No tricks at all, I assure you! I've got the bellyache. . . .'

A few minutes later, the men had returned.

'We've seen the bread, anyway,' said Forell. At once the men were all ears. In some the suspicion had been rising that the Russians intended the cave to be their tomb.

'And toilet facilities! It's just too easy! We went up the shaft. Ivan dropped his tommy-gun in our path. We explained our errand, and then he led us a few yards up to another shaft running at right-angles. No chains to pull, but ice is as good as running water, or seems to be! The whole time we were in there, he stood in the main shaft, blocking the route to the surface, which is just a few steps away. A very ingenious system, don't you think?'

'A very sensible one!' said Leibrecht in a lofty tone, smoothing the hair over his ears. 'It gives you less chance to play the giddy goat, Forell!'

'You've got to come here to the end of the world to realize how simple things can be. Two guards for a hundred and eighty of us—just think of that! There are eight of these caverns, so that means sixteen guards in all for twelve hundred prisoners.'

'Where are the other caves?' asked someone.

'Inside here, in this hill somewhere. It's quite a big one, you know. You can smell smoke from a coal fire at the top by the latrine. They are probably doing the cooking now in one of the shafts up there.'

The men were not disappointed. Shortly afterwards, the guard came down and signified that four of them were required to fetch the meal. Forell immediately volunteered, hoping to get a look at the surface, but the cauldron with the barley gruel—enough for two ladles per head—a smaller quantity of *kasha* and heavy, black loaves made of coarse oatmeal were awaiting collection inside the shaft and all Forell got was a tantalizing glimpse of daylight. Ah! Well! There was plenty of time. There would be other opportunities. It was poor consolation, but the food was good.

After they had eaten, the prisoners hovered about, nervy as homeless animals. The blinding snow, even the whips of the Convoy Soldiers seemed better than the muffled desolation of this tomb. The same thought, and the same question were in all minds. Those days with the horses whinnying in the frosted air, the bumping, surging sledge, the pale sun and the red flames of the bivouac fires leaping over a white and silent land —had they been the very last they were destined to spend above ground?

Exhausted though they were, few could find sleep. For as long as there was oil in the lamp, they gyrated like moths round the solitary flame, gazing into each other's faces, talking little, afraid to speak their thoughts.

Next morning five of the prisoners, including Forell, were suffering from dysentery. On the following day, the guard summoned the medical assistant, the 'Vratsch', in the hope, largely, that he could do something to relieve the guard of the irksome duty of escorting the sick men up and down the passageway. But the Vratsch, as it happened, was a man incapable of assimilating the glorious achievements of Soviet or of any other medicine, and while his fellow men of science strode shoulder to shoulder towards a germ-free socialist paradise, he stumbled along the mazy paths of mediaeval alchemy, clutching his panacea, a box of anonymous white tablets tasting remarkably like aspirin.

For some minutes, the Vratsch gazed at the patients, uncertain apparently which of two alternative treatments to adopt: aspirin or no aspirin. Finally, when he could bear the silent scrutiny no longer, Forell said in German: 'We've got dysentery. Do you understand? Dy—sen—tery.'

'*Dag, dag,*' said the Vratsch in a soothing voice.

Forell pointed to his stomach. 'Here! Pains in the stomach!'

'*Dag, dag.*'

Forell tried in Russian. He had learned something of the language during the course of the years, enough to make himself understood, but his vocabulary was small. The Vratsch listened with a detached, professional air, but was obviously none the wiser. However, he seemed to have reached a diagnosis—by intuition, presumably—for, opening the magic box, he now carefully withdrew two tablets and gave them to Forell.

The treatment proved useless; likewise the six further tablets which the Vratsch conceded as reinforcing and maintenance doses. Two days later, in urgent need of an hour's undisturbed rest at his table in the smaller cave, the sentry on duty had the four worst cases escorted by their fellow prisoners to hospital.

Normally Forell would have been pleased to return to daylight, realizing at once the increased opportunity for escape which it offered. As it was, he let himself be conducted across ice, snow and rubble towards the large wooden building below the plateau, sinking with chattering teeth, now right, now left into the arms of his supporters and feeling so desperately cold that he had only one wish—to be back in the warmth below ground. And even when he was lying on a civilized bed and felt a straw mattress beneath him, he still did not realize his good fortune. But gradually, it dawned. Built entirely of wood, the hospital consisted of two storeys with about seven wards on each floor ranged on either side of a central corridor. At the end of each ward was a massive iron stove that gave out a colossal heat and was kept burning all night and most of the day. Moreover, the patients were allowed water, not only for drinking, but also to wash in—a luxury unknown in the underground labyrinth. Finally, the food was tolerable and the treatment reasonably appropriate —sulphonamide from captured German stocks in the form of Prontosil.

The ability to wash encouraged the men to complete the process with a shave. Then sharp-nosed, jaundiced faces appeared, apathetic faces for the most part until it began to penetrate the fevered minds of the ninety or so patients that the hospital enjoyed a yet further distinction, no doubt unique on this outlandish rim of the world: its staff included a woman.

She was certainly no beauty, the sister whose name nobody knew. She wore military boots, her uniform was uncompromisingly severe, in manner and voice she was indistinguishable from a sergeant in the Red Army. Only her hands were well-shapen, and she used them with startling effect. Her main responsibility was to ensure order among the patients— particularly the convalescents—and cleanliness in the wards. The door would fly open and, catching sight of one patient

27

sitting on another's bed, she would pause and wrinkle her brow. The meaning was clear: in a hospital, a man was either ill, in which case he was in bed, or not ill and so could return to work. Head up, chin in, the sister would pass from bed to bed. Now and again her shapely hand would glide with middle finger extended over a head-board; still outstretched, the finger would pass before her eyes, and then, with a look of horror on her face, the sister would utter the one and only German word which she knew: *Spinnwebe!* . . . Cobweb! It was an elegant word, but one of somewhat specialized application. In what circumstances it had reached and imprinted itself on the sister's mind, no one was ever to learn. But it gave her a name.

Thanks to Sergeant Cobweb, cleanliness prevailed in the wards and thanks to self-medication, according to Forell, he gradually got better. Each time the stove was lit in his ward, a small strip of wood soaked in some sticky substance reeking of fish oil was used to fire the coal and after the stove had burnt out, the charcoaled remains of the firelighter would be lying somewhere among the ashes, to be rescued and consumed with evident relish by the tall, eccentric patient. He said he felt better for it, but he hardly looked it. With smudged lips and blackened tongue, he, too, was ripe for a nickname: 'Chow-Chow'.

Before long, Forell was famed, even among the Russians, for his strange addiction to charcoal, and thereby he became one of a select band each of whom was raised out of the rut by some personal idiosyncrasy. Ward Eight, for example, on the ground floor next to the stairs, contained a man who was mentally deranged. All day, he talked of his son in Breslau, the city that had ben overrun by the Russians. His son had buried all the family treasures—old coins, silver, jewellery —and had promised to wait until his father returned. Then they would dig up the hoard together and escape with it to a world where they would have peace to the end of their days. It was a fine story, when the patients first heard it, but they heard it day-in, day-out, until finally it was no more than a threadbare fable. The madman could also sing and when the mood was on him, he could sing open the gates of heaven, and then all was forgiven him until he stopped and started talking again of his son and the buried treasure.

The madman aroused only passing curiosity, but the sergeant on the first floor who was drying out his bread ration on the stove in preparation for escape was a man whom Forell was determined to meet. Officially, visits between wards were forbidden, but the patients quickly learned how to slip from one room to another unobserved. The hospital was patrolled by a solitary soldier who, for two hours until he was relieved, paced slowly down the corridor on the ground floor, up the stairs at the far end, along the first-floor corridor and down a second flight of stairs to his starting point. The guard invariably took his time and thus it was possible for any patient able to move fast to await the moment when the guard was beginning to descend the far stairs and then run up to the first floor starting from the ward nearest the opposite stairs. If the patient did not happen to be in the ward by the stairs on the ground floor or want to visit the corresponding ward above, then he had to reach his starting point and his objective in stages.

In due course, then, Forell appeared in the doorway of the ward where the sergeant was said to be planning escape. He was greeted with laughter: 'Chow-chow!' A visitor helped to relieve the monotony and before long, the men were all talking, asking Forell about his patent 'cure' for dysentery, about Sergeant Cobweb—anything so long as it kept them talking and filled the empty hours. From their faces he tried to guess who was the escaper, but finally he had no alternative but to ask outright.

'Who do you think?' growled a man in his forties. 'Him there, in the corner bed!' Forell saw a tough-looking, dark-haired man grinning over at him. He had been one of those who had yelled 'Chow-chow' as soon as Forell put his head round the door.

'So the whole ward knows what you are going to do!' said Forell, going to the sergeant. 'The next thing is, the Russians will hear about it.'

'Let them! I don't mind who knows. The more the better! Then no one will believe it!'

'You're serious about escaping, though?'

'So serious that I'm going to do it,' said the man grimly. Then in a lighter tone: 'I gather you're toying with the idea?'

'Yes, but I wish I knew how.'

'From the hospital, man! That's how! Once you're back in the mine, you've had it.'

'What about barbed wire? An apron fence. Are you sure there isn't?'

The sergeant propped himself up on an elbow and before replying gazed shrewdly and steadily at Forell. Apparently he was satisfied with what he saw, for he then began to talk of the information he had gathered during his stay in hospital. He had spent some time at the window of his ward, watching movement in front of the camp office and trying to form some idea of the Russians' daily routine. It had come as no surprise to see an aerial above one of the huts—he had expected them to have a wireless transmitter. He also noticed a huge pile of coal, or coke, stacked in the background on the opposite side to the lead mine. The sea was not visible, but at the most it could only be a couple of miles away. Presumably the coal had been brought by ship, unless there was a mine somewhere in the immediate neighbourhood. Unfortunately, the view from the hospital was limited in all directions by the lie of the ground and the plateau on which the hutted camp was sited was surrounded on three sides by high cliffs. Though no other signs of development were visible, it might be that the area round East Cape was being worked for various minerals. If that were so, the whole region of the Chukchi Peninsula might be thickly populated. That the German prisoners and their guards were not the only inhabitants of a vital strategic area was obvious. Equally obviously, other prisoners had been there before them. How, otherwise, had the whole vast labyrinth of caves and passages been dug out of the solid rock?

'The longer you talk, the more I like the sound of you,' said Forell.

'Well, as I haven't got a map, I've got to find out all I can before I start.'

Then Forell remembered Dannhorn. 'We've got a tame cartographer in our cave—a gloomy individual, but he knows the map of Siberia by heart.'

The sergeant pursed his lips. 'Um. . . . But the map changes very quickly, you know,' was all he said.

So as not to arouse suspicion, Forell waited four days before slipping upstairs to call on the sergeant again. He found him with a high temperature and inclined to ramble in his conversation. 'I've got to get home,' he kept on repeating, gazing at his visitor out of bloodshot eyes.

'So have I, and I mean to!' said Forell, and then tentatively: 'Why not let's try it together?'

The sergeant nodded, but cautiously. 'All right. But I think winter's the time, not what they call "summer" round here.'

Forell agreed. Then the sergeant added: 'If I can wait that long'. There was something about the way the man said that, and the look on his face, a look of almost savage determination that suddenly put it into Forell's mind to ask: 'And why did they send you here?'

The sergeant was lying on his back, gazing at the ceiling. 'I'll tell you why,' he said with simmering rage, and he told how he had been interrogated by the Russians, grilled, pressed to admit to crimes of which he had not the remotest knowledge.

'I was a sergeant, a platoon commander,' he said, 'when they caught me. We were in East Prussia. Why they should fix on me, I don't know, but they tried to make me confess to the most astounding things, all pure invention as far as I was concerned. To this day, I don't know where they were supposed to have happened. So of course I wouldn't confess, and even when they got very unpleasant—as they can—I still went on refusing. To tell you the truth, I surprised myself. I didn't know I could be so stubborn. It would have been much easier to give in.'

'And then?'

'Well, then they didn't need my confession, after all, because someone else signed on the dotted line and they took his word instead of mine.'

'How do you mean?'

'The b—— denounced me, saddled me with crimes I'd never even heard of.'

'But why? What had he got against you?'

'They gave him his freedom, chum. That's why.'

There was silence. The sergeant's face was twitching as he lay, sweating with fever on his bed. Suddenly he said:

'Do you know the name Mattern?'

Forell was prepared for that question. 'I'm not sure. Is it a place name?'

'No, no. Mattern, I said! Mattern!'

'Why do you ask?'

'Because that was his name: Alfons Mattern. He's gone home now. But I'll find him.'

'Do you know anything about him?'

'No, except that he's got it coming to him. He can't hide from me. I'll find him. Once I'm fit again, and I've got out of here, I'm going to get back to Germany. I'm going to make him wish he'd never been born.'

So that was the motive for the sergeant's escape—not freedom, not wife, not family, but revenge. The conversation had exhausted him and he was lying now with mouth half open, tossing to and fro and muttering weakly to himself.

'Pay no attention to Heinz Dechant,' said someone on the other side of the room as Forell was leaving. 'He's nuts.'

Forell went back to his own ward determined now that when he escaped, he would go on his own. From every point of view Dechant would be a doubtful asset. Forell also made up his mind not to tell Dechant of Alfons Mattern's presence at the lead mine. He had no desire to be responsible for what might follow.

Copying Dechant's example, Forell started to observe the Russian hutments and the life around them about a quarter of a mile from the hospital. The sole means of transport seemed to be dog sledges and on some days there was a busy traffic in front of the store sheds where supplies of all kinds were unloaded, amongst other things, fir branches destined to serve as bedding for the prisoners in the lead mine.

And then, early one afternoon, a sledge stopped at the camp office and two men got down and went inside. After some minutes they reappeared. One of them lifted a large box from the sledge and then the two of them started to walk towards the hospital building.

The sledge had brought medical supplies and a German doctor from a prison camp in Tomsk. Until his call-up into the German Army, he had been a physician and surgeon in Magdeburg. Captured by the Russians in Breslau, he had been sentenced to twenty-five years imprisonment—exactly the period for which a doctor was required to tend the prisoners at East Cape. What a coincidence!

Next morning a solemn procession entered Forell's ward. First, the doctor, a little, grey-faced man in his fifties, wearing snow-white overalls, then the Vratsch, wide-eyed with bovine astonishment, and finally Sergeant Cobweb. As the senior in the ward, Forell stood to attention and reported the number of sick. The doctor examined each case, but when it came to prescribing the treatment, even he had to shrug his shoulders. The medical supplies that had come with him on the previous day had been selected at random by the Russians and were largely useless.

'You don't look too bad.'

'I tried the charcoal cure.'

The doctor smiled. 'What is your name?'

'Forell. Lieutenant Clemens Forell.'

'Not a very common name. I think I've only met it once before. I beg your pardon: my name is Stauffer. Doctor Stauffer.'

Some weeks later, about the middle of January, Forell was fit to leave hospital and return to the lead mine. He might already have been discharged if the name Forell had not stirred Doctor Stauffer's memory. Where had he met it before? Then a dim recollection revived of a fellow student at Tübingen University.

'That might have been my brother Ernst; he studied medicine at Tübingen. He was killed during the war.'

'Doctor Ernst Forell! That's right!' The doctor smiled. 'And meanwhile, you have not only recovered from your dysentery, but you look aggressively fit. It's most unfortunate.'

For the sake of the other patients, the doctor would have to discharge him. To keep a fit man in hospital might cost the doctor his job, leaving the sick to the tender mercy of the Vratsch again.

Then Fortune smiled. That same day, the interpreter from the camp office asked Doctor Stauffer to name two prisoners capable of withstanding an arduous six weeks' sledge journey. The purpose of the expedition was to fetch blankets and medical supplies for the hospital—or so the interpreter said, and for lack of evidence to the contrary the doctor was forced to take him at his word. After some thought, he named two men: Forell, aged twenty-eight and another patient on the point of discharge who was two years younger, Lothar Eisemann by name.

Before the doctor had time, even, to warn Forell, a Russian guard appeared in his ward and told him to come forthwith to the camp office. Still believing he was on his way back to the lead mine, Forell only realized that something else was afoot when he found himself, together with Lothar Eisemann, being fitted out in the clothing store with the complete equipment the Convoy Soldiers had worn on the march to the camp: jacket, breeches, coat, gloves, cap, boots—everything either faced or lined with fur. The omens were favourable. The items were issued with a noisy good humour, ending with the cossack caps which the storeman dumped on the prisoners' heads, and they were given a good meal before being locked in a small room with barred window. 'Sleep here,' they were told. 'We will wake you when it is time to leave.'

It was still night when the guards woke them and told them to help load up the sledge. Half asleep still and clumsy in the unaccustomed furs, they piled on to the steel-framed sledge whatever lay before them—hard tack, dried fish, an assortment of tinned food and the reindeer-skin tent that was to be their shelter for the next few weeks.

Friendly and colossally busy, with blue, child-like eyes, the guard secured the load with leather straps. Vassily was his name, Red Army soldier. He thumped his chest and introduced himself: 'Vassily!'

Hoya Ho!

Vassily was beaming all over his face as he took the reins and with a wonderful, echoing shout to his team, sent the huskies skidding and scrambling over the snow into the cautious Arctic dawn. The two prisoners watched as the grey plateau and the sinister, cone-shaped hill fell away behind them, finally sinking below the white horizon as though they had never been.

Three men, the tent and their provisions were no more than a reasonable load for fifteen huskies and when, after about eleven hours, they finally halted for the night, Vassily said they had covered a distance of eighty versts, or roughly fifty miles.

The Russian set up the tent with incredibly quick and skilful movements. Then he prepared a meal. In all, he took it for granted that the prisoners were inept at such things and when they tried to help, he merely waved them away with a deprecating gesture: 'It's no trouble; leave it to me.'

When they had eaten and were settled under the warmth of the skins, the three of them were united by a feeling of contentment and mutual respect. It grew without need of words, though, with Forell interpreting, they exchanged an occasional remark. Their objective, said Vassily, was a town by the sea and their purpose in going there, to fetch blankets and medical supplies for their comrades. For wicked fellows like themselves who had earned life sentences for their abominable crimes, it was a mark of honour and distinction to be sent on such a journey.

To show their gratitude for favours bestowed, Forell and Eisemann insisted next morning on packing up the tent, imitating in reverse the motions they had watched Vassily perform on the previous evening. Though the result was only moderately successful and Vassily had to unroll the whole bundle again, showing them how to reduce it to a third of its volume, he seemed to appreciate their goodwill. When they set off again across the smooth, unspotted snow, they noticed that Vassily never consulted a map or a compass. Yet there was no visible landmark and the contours of the undulating country were surely too subtle to be distinguishable. How did he choose his direction? They never discovered, either then or throughout the three weeks that the journey lasted. When Forell asked him, he seemed not to understand the question. Yet Vassily never once had to turn back and never showed the least sign of hesitation, even in the last week when their way led across mountainous country down a number of intersecting gorges and defiles of the kind that were never attempted in Europe without experienced guides.

To Vassily all was simple. You set off from East Cape and in due course you arrived at a town of wooden shacks by the sea.

'How often have you been here, Vassily?'

The raised thumb said: once.

After turning innumerable corners, the sledge stopped at the entrance to a military hutted camp and Vassily produced his papers. Driving through, he finally halted at an administration hut where the two prisoners were hustled roughly inside and placed under an armed guard. After some time, they were taken out again to load up the sledge with blankets and crates from a store. Vassily was a changed man. Under the eye of his superiors, he treated the Germans as the Red Army were used to treating their conquered enemies. '*Davai!*' he bawled, hastening them on their way as they staggered towards the sledge with a load of gear. '*Davai!*' greeted them in the morning as they were hauled out by the camp soldiers after spending the night in the punishment cells. But for Vassily's friendliness on the journey, the harsh treatment they now received would not have struck them as painful and insulting.

'As long as we are prisoners, we're no better than cattle,' said Forell. 'Listen, Eisemann! I'm telling you: on the way back, I'm going to push off!'

'Don't be a fool!'

'Will you come with me? It will be easier for two of us.'

'Inside three days they would have caught us again.'

'So what? Do you think they'd shoot us? Never! They want some work out of us first—five or six years in the lead mine, then they will have covered their expenses.'

But Eisemann was half-hearted and Forell prepared to go alone. He was looking forward to the return journey, not for the thrill of it, this time, but so that he could tell Vassily what he thought of him. The Russian was quick to sense Forell's brooding ill temper and at the first night's bivouac, he did his best to cheer him up, handing round tobacco and cigarette papers, doling out extra food and praising the men for the skill they had acquired in putting up and dismantling the tent. Forell had just enough sense of proportion left to appreciate the gesture. After all, why should Vassily care? He was good-hearted, there was no doubt about that—sometimes.

And then, as Forell remembered the man's behaviour at the depot, his anger rose again and he glowered as the Russian offered him some vodka.

'*Was ist?*' said Vassily, parading his newly learnt German.

'I'll tell you. We're not your dogs. Not dogs! No! It's no good you behaving like this. It's just a silly game, that's all. Everything is fine now, isn't it, because we're alone? But as soon as there's a fourth man, a witness, you're scared to be caught acting like a human being. Now listen to me!' And Forell stared Vassily in the face, to reinforce the threat. 'Watch out, Vassily! If ever I catch you napping in the night, I shall push off, vanish—escape!'

Vassily cleared his throat and spat. He had understood well enough and he was angered. But he had seen how the two men had been treated as dirt and realizing his own fault, he could understand why Forell felt as he did.

From then on, Vassily slept by the entrance to the tent with his tommy-gun between his knees. For five nights, he and Forell played a game of cat and mouse, each determined to stay awake until the other was asleep. On the sixth night, Forell was too tired to keep his eyes open and he slept soundly, consoled by the thought that Vassily would keep on the alert for some hours longer in case the prisoner was

35

feigning. And sure enough, on the seventh night, Forell heard Vassily snoring.

Being comparatively fresh, Forell decided to seize his chance and after waiting some minutes to make sure the guard was soundly asleep, he picked up the sheepskin which had served him as blanket and, cautiously stepping over the sleeping Vassily, crept from the tent. He had pondered carefully the items he would take from the sledge, but when it came to the point, he grabbed whatever came first to hand, tied the things in the sheepskin with the aid of a spare sledge trace and made off, carrying the bundle over his shoulder like a sack.

For a while, Forell ran, but before he had gone more than a quarter of a mile, the deep snow, the load on his back and his wasted muscles forced him to a walk. He continued then, trudging slowly along the sledge tracks in the direction from which they had come, trying to get as far as possible from the bivouac before Vassily started in pursuit. If he could avoid recapture for a few hours, Forell thought it might be four or five days before he was finally picked up. Meanwhile he had no other object in mind but to sniff the air of freedom and forget for a while that he was a slave.

As it happened, it was eleven days before a chance encounter put an end to his excursion. One morning, he was approaching a low, hump-backed hill when a sledge suddenly appeared over the top and came curving down towards him. It was a wonderful sight, the team of huskies scurrying forward trailing a long pennon of powdery snow while the sledge glided on as though airborne among white, summery clouds.

There were two men on the sledge and while still some distance away, one of them shouted something. It sounded like: 'Stop!' Forell waited and soon the driver was reigning in the team. As the men strode up to him he caught a glimpse of army uniforms beneath their furs. They conveyed that they wished to see his papers. As well as he could, Forell explained that he had none. He gave his name and left it to the Russians to guess the rest. Calmly but firmly, then, they escorted him to the sledge, seated themselves one behind another with Forell in the middle and set off on a two-hour journey across the snow.

At last they came to a group of block houses standing isolated in the midst of the great white desert. The place seemed to be some kind of police headquarters. In the building to which he was taken, Forell glimpsed a radio transmitter and two more men, both dressed in military-style uniforms. He was given a bowl of thick, hot soup and when he had eaten, he was asked to tell his story. The Russians listened with the same detached attitude that had struck him on first meeting. He saw no point in trying to tell lies. Yes. He was an escaped prisoner-of-war. A German. From East Cape. That produced an incredulous frown. Were there prisoners in that area? Oh, yes. Twelve hundred of them. That was interesting; obviously the Russians did not know that. When Forell had finished his story, they left him. It was not till later that one of them came back and locked the door. Later that night, the low throb of a generator told him that the radio transmitter was in use.

Apparently, Forell's story had been confirmed, for next day his captors did not refer to it again except to ask one question. Comrade Vassily, the soldier in charge of the expedition to fetch medical supplies could he be expected to return to East Cape in due course, or had Forell and the other prisoner perhaps murdered him?

Forell was kept in the block house for another twenty-four hours while the Russians seemingly awaited instructions from East Cape. Then, accompanied by two different guards, he was ordered into the sledge and the three-week journey back to the lead mine began. During the whole of that time he was closely guarded. On the sledge the man behind him kept a pistol at his back and at every halt, thin chains reducing his stride to no more than six inches were immediately locked round his ankles, and kept there until the journey was resumed. The men never spoke to him except to give orders and he felt no desire to talk to them, for their thoughts revolved in an orbit of freedom, whereas his were on the lonely path leading back to slavery.

Forell's return to camp caused no particular sensation. He was taken to the office. The political officer emerged from his room, surveyed the escaper coldly from head to foot and said with the suggestion of a smile: 'Ah! He's back!' Someone removed the fur jacket from his shoulders and took away the fur cap. 'Quick march! Back to quarters!' said the officer casually.

Pascholl! Na doma! Well, thought Forell, if that's all there is to it. . . .

Two soldiers from the guard company escorted him out of the building and down towards the familiar opening at the base of the cone-shaped hill. It was evening and the daylight was almost gone. As he and his escort drew nearer, he saw that his fellow prisoners were drawn up outside the entrance to the shaft, forming a lane—some sort of concession, he supposed, allowing the men a breath of fresh air after the day's work. But then he saw that they were armed, some with strips of wood, some with trouser belts, some, yes, three—five men with lengths of wire cable. One of them held a curving piece of iron from a cart wheel.

'*Pascholl!*' The guard urged him on, but Forell still stood, gazing terrified at the double line of men, a hundred or more, every one gripping iron, wood, leather, a boot, even—anything to clout him with as he ran the gauntlet, he the trouble maker, the escaper, the cause of Russian reprisals, the man who never said die. Now their mad faces were turned towards him, mouths working as they shifted their legs in readiness for the blow.

'*Pascholl!*'

Forell hesitated, calculating at lightning speed. Once inside the shaft, he would be safe. Keep moving, keep your balance. . . . He started to sprint. But the shaft was sixty yards away.

He saw their eyes, burning with hatred. Then the blows rained down. He had barely gone half-way along the double line when he was staggering blindly. The men thrust him off as he lurched against them and so he was propelled a few paces further. Then a succession of savage blows brought him to his knees. He got up again, ran on, flung his hands behind his neck, yelled, was sent sprawling. At that moment, iron struck his head, splitting the scalp.

* * *

When Forell recovered consciousness, he found himself back in the cave. At first he failed to recognize his surroundings. He was in semi-darkness, relieved by a single oil lamp suspended from the rocky ceiling and the dim light threw no shadows in the almost circular space. Then gradually he remembered the sequence of events: the sledge journey back to the lead mine, the beating-up he had received at the hands of men he had supposed were his friends. He put down a hand and felt German tent canvas above the prickly fir branches. By that much, at any rate, conditions in the cave had been improved since last he was there. He tried to turn on to his side, but as soon as he moved he was racked with pain. He felt a continual throbbing somewhere near his right kidney and his head reeled and swam. He felt round it and touched paper bandages. Then he was sinking into a dark pool full of voices and uncomfortable shapes. . . .

He came up to hear feet going past him towards the exit from the cave, slow, shuffling feet moving in a peculiar rhythm: one, scrape—two, scrape—three. As each pair—or was it two pairs?—passed him, more came up behind. It was like a slow procession along a hill-side. In the background, a woodpecker was hammering spasmodically into soft bark.

And once more he was sinking into the pool; sinking, flowing, falling, fast, faster, down, down into the black warm depths. . . .

A whistle shrilled in his ears, dragging him back to consciousness. He opened his eyes and recognized the cave. The men were there, moving away to the far end. Soon, he heard the sound of picks striking into rock and after a time, some of the men came past him again in pairs, carrying large wicker baskets and dragging their feet under the weight in the way he had heard before. He wondered what the time was and whether it was night or day. Who had bandaged his head? How long had he been lying there? Now some of the men were returning with their baskets empty. One of them he recognized, a thin, lanky fellow with a sharp nose and eyes that blinked like a broody hen's.

'Hey! You! Come over here a moment!'

'Can't wait, sorry. Got to get straight back.'

'I said, come over here!'

The man blinked and glanced nervously round. Then he waddled over, dragging the basket and the man on the far side of it with him.

'First of all, how long have I been here and what time is it?'

'It's after midday now. You've been here since we brought you in yesterday evening.'

'And who bandaged my head? Doctor Stauffer, I suppose?'

'Yes. He wanted to have you in hospital, but the Russians would not allow it.'

'I see——' Forell felt a stab in his chest every time he spoke, but there was something he had to say to this man. 'So when you swung that piece of wire rope at me with the frayed end, you were doing it on orders from the Russians?'

'Oh, no, you mustn't think that! I wish it had been. . . .'

The man came nearer and, fishing a hunk of bread from his pocket, held it out to Forell. 'I've brought you this.'

'To make amends for what you did to me last night, is that it? If the Russians didn't force you, what possessed you, you and all of them, to strike at a man who was utterly defenceless? What have I done to you, anyway? What business is it of yours if I chose to escape?'

'Yes, but——'

'There's no "but"! I know your name, Portschach, isn't it? Simon Portschach——'

Forell broke off, his head reeling with sudden nausea. He shut his eyes and the man, Portschach, started to make soothing noises, said something about 'resting' and 'you've got to take it easy, you know'. At that, Forell heaved himself up

39

until he was sitting and glared feverishly into the soft, heavy-lidded eyes.

'Now, Portschach, listen. I'm going to deal with you. As soon as I can stand on two feet, I'll show you what a mess can be made of a man, without any wire rope, just with the bare hands. That's coming to you, Portschach. I'll teach you to go arse-crawling to the Russians!'

'But I didn't, I haven't, I——'

'Well, someone has, if not you, somebody else.'

'No. None of us have. It was just, well, as soon as they heard you'd escaped, they cut our rations right down. No bread, no *kasha*, just thin barley gruel and not much of that. You try hacking at a rock all day long, or carting the stuff up to the surface on nothing but dirty water and see how you feel!'

'But why should they cut your rations? I didn't escape from the lead mine.'

'No, but rather than waste their manpower and materials in making escape impossible, the Russians prefer to make it so unpopular that no one will try.'

'So it *was* the Russians' idea, this running the gauntlet?'

'No, I tell you. No, it wasn't. The Russians never said anything—directly, that is. But the security officer came down twice a day to the cave, the first time at midday, just after we'd licked the last drop out of the tin and were ravening with hunger, knowing we'd get nothing again for twenty-four hours. Only one issue in twenty-four hours! But twice a day, he told us why; because you had escaped. Then as soon as they heard you'd been recaptured, the Russians suddenly started letting us up to daylight twice a week, instead of only once, as before. By that time, the men were talking pretty wild about what they'd do to you when they saw you again, and above ground there, they found the means to do it—wood and stuff lying around, just what we—just what they needed.'

'And now you're on full rations again, I suppose?'

'Yes, in fact they've been increased.'

'And this wood, and iron, and wire rope, was put out there by the Russians, of course?'

'I suppose so. We didn't stop to think.'

'Well, suppose you think now!'

'It's all very well for you, Forell,' said Portschach venomously. 'You don't know what it is to work in this mine. You've played the invalid ever since the real work started. Fattened yourself up in hospital till you were fighting fit, then wangled yourself a sleigh ride. Then, not content with that, you go and escape. You never gave a thought to us, did you? Never stopped to think what the Russians might do to us?'

'If you got a chance to escape, wouldn't you take it?'

40

'No. Certainly not. It wouldn't be fair on the other men.'
Forell was about to retort, but his head was singing and
throbbing again. Portschach's long nose kept going out of
focus and a red mist was swirling about in the cave. Forell
shut his eyes. 'Go away, Portschach! I'm tired.'

*　　*　　*

Portschach had tried to apologize. He was not even man
enough to bear a guilty conscience. But the other prisoners
preferred to show their contrition by deeds rather than profess
it in words. They brought Forell his food, helped him up the
shaft to the latrine, fixed his bandages when they slipped and
were careful to say nothing that called for the reply, 'don't
mention it'. The Russian guard disposed of the matter with
less delicacy of feeling. There seemed to be a statutory time
allowed for recovery from a beating-up and on the fifth day,
the guard considered it had expired. At reveille Forell was
hustled off to work with the rest of the men. Whether, in fact,
he was capable of raising a pick above his shoulder was of
no concern to the guard, or to anyone outside the gang to
which he was allotted.

The system devised for extracting ore from the lead mine
had a certain grandiose simplicity. The veins of lead-bearing
ore ran at right-angles to the shaft connecting the cave with
the surface, and to reach them, the men had only to continue
it at the far end of the cave, inwards towards the centre of
the hill. No machinery was used, either at the rock face for
drilling or throughout the ever-lengthening route from the
face to the gyratory crusher operated by the Russians on the
surface. The work gangs consisted of four men for collecting
the rubble and lead-bearing ore and loading it into baskets,
another sixteen transporting the baskets by hand from the
cave to the crusher sited close by the exit from the shaft.
The remaining men worked at the face. The only implements
provided were picks for the face workers and the wicker
baskets. The picks were old and blunt and their handles
consisted of untrimmed wood impossible to hold for five
minutes without reducing the hands to a mass of blisters. To
use them at all, the men had to shape them with the aid of
broken pieces of glass from an empty bottle grudgingly
supplied by the Russians. As for the baskets, they were far
too light for carrying a hundredweight or more of rock and
rubble and they quickly wore out. The wastage was colossal,
but new baskets were always available and the Russians
seemed not to mind how many were expended. To the
prisoners it seemed obvious that they were the product of

slave labour. The Germans worked hard and the Russians were apparently content, for though a guard stationed at the top of the shaft counted the number of baskets full of ore brought up for treatment by the crusher, during the whole of the time that Forell was at the lead mine, no quota was ever set as regards the weight of material that had to be delivered each day.

Day after day, Forell hacked at the face, taking his turn with the other men to extend the shaft slowly, a foot at a time, towards the centre of the hill. At first, the protests of his gashed and battered body preoccupied him to the exclusion of his surroundings. He was aware only of his limitations, the sudden twinges of pain as he struck hard at unyielding rock or taxed his overstrained muscles. But as time went on, it was the cave that claimed more and more of his attention —the cave with its perpetual fug and glistening walls, the cave in the morning at five o'clock when the guard came down and wrenched him from sleep. With the man's shouts in his ears, Forell would awake from his exhaustion, forgetting for a moment where he was. A second later, and the sight of the rock-bound world would strike him like a blow. To work in the semi-dark, to sleep in darkness and to awake in the semi-dark again was at first eerie, then depressing, then oppressive, until finally it goaded into madness. The other men had all been through the same experience. 'Mine fever,' they called it.

In time Forell recovered from his claustrophobia for there was, in fact, no danger of suffocation in the cave. There was plenty of air. There was also plenty of lead, and lead poisoning loomed over the lives of the prisoners, the more sinister because the subject was seldom mentioned. When the caves and shafts had been tunnelled in the hill, the operation had served a double purpose: the provision of escape-proof accommodation for the Germans and the extraction of lead-bearing ore. Lead was all around them, at night, on the floor and walls of their cave, by day, when they were at work and in their food, even, when they ate. None of them knew much about lead poisoning except that the first symptom was a loosening of the teeth and loss of sensation in the gums and that in the long run it proved fatal. Twenty-five years would certainly be long enough.

One afternoon, after Forell had been three weeks in the mine, the Russians stopped work an hour earlier than usual. The prisoners streamed back into the cave and then the guard appeared and told them to follow him. In single file they closed up behind the man with the tommy-gun as he led the way to the surface. An hour's fresh air—what a boon! What a favour! Long before the sixty minutes were up, the men were longing to return to the warmth below and, as usual, there was little enough for them to see above the ground but driving snow and an occasional glimpse of the men from the next cave, huddling by the entrance to the hill-side about fifty yards away. A bitter wind was moaning round the hill. There was no sign of the sun. The men swung their arms and stamped their feet to keep warm, inwardly cursing the Russians, their climate and this God-forsaken rim of the world, with its colourless austerity and its forlorn and niggardly soul.

The men had only been half an hour above ground when the guard gave the signal to fall in. To them it was a gesture full of beautiful compassion. Ducking their heads as though fleeing from some nameless terror, they ran back into the dark opening in the hill-side, away from the wind, the cold, and the melancholy Siberian spring.

Paschóll!

Hanging from its strap, the guard swung the butt of his tommy-gun against the arched back of a prisoner lingering outside the shaft to collect snow in a piece of tent canvas. The guard had witnessed this curious ritual before, and the same man performing it.

'Yes! Sorry! Straight away! I beg your pardon.' And the prisoner scuttled into the shaft carrying a sheetful of snow over his shoulder.

Arrived below, Leibrecht gave his men an object lesson. Using the bottom of a broken ore basket as bath mat, he stripped and proceeded to rub himself down from head to foot with the snow, loosening the dirt with the first application and rinsing himself clean with a second.

'There's still some snow left—anyone else?'

But the men merely shivered.

'Alfons?' Mattern shook his head.

'Won't you try?'

'I'd rather not,' replied Mattern, courteous but adamant.

Then Leibrecht was forced to reveal the real reason for his ablutions. 'Look at the atmosphere in here,' he said. 'Look at the walls! Look at yourselves! Thick and grimy with lead! If you leave that stuff on your skin, it will kill you! Have you never heard of lead poisoning?'

The men stared at him. No one spoke. Next day, on their last trip back into the mine, the carriers came staggering down with their baskets full of snow.

*   *   *

At the beginning of summer, the men were allowed up again, this time for a whole afternoon. It might have been a

November day of the kind they remembered in Germany, chilly but not cold, with a promise of sun. Within a hundred yards or more of the entrance to the shaft the guards let them wander where they chose. Dirty snow still lay over the plateau and the whole landscape seemed dead, except for one small patch of green moss peering above the ice. In twos and threes the men came to look at it, until there were fifty of them gazing silently at the emerald wonder. Some of them had tears in their eyes.

Kneeling down, Forell gently lifted an edge of the moss, expecting to find earth underneath, but the roots were bedded in a foot thick layer of ice.

'How can moss grow in ice? How can it live?'

'Well, we're still alive, aren't we? Isn't that just as surprising?'

Eight weeks later, the single patch of moss no bigger than a saucer had spread over the entire plateau. The air was milder and sometimes, on their periodic leave above ground, the prisoners could see a gleam beyond the huts in the Russian compound that some said was the Bering Straits. Thoughts of escape began to revive, smouldering in the mind, until one day they flared abruptly into flame. Beyond the huts, the smoke of a ship was rising, eddying in dense clouds under a slight breeze.

'A ship! There's a ship out there!' Forell could hardly contain himself. Everyone had to have the news and he ran from group to group, compelling the men to share his excitement. 'A ship!'

'Come on, Chow-Chow, stop acting like a kid!' A man taller even than Forell and somewhat broader in the shoulders was gazing at him quizzically.

'Good Lord! Dechant!'

'Yes. Didn't you know about the ship?'

'How should I?'

'I got the details of its schedule when I was in hospital.'

'So you're recovered, at last?'

'Yes, at last. Your charcoal cure was a flop.'

'Well, what about this ship?'

Dechant gazed with savage intensity at Forell. 'You're supposed to be the one that's always thinking of escape, aren't you? And you mean to say you've never really thought of how to get across this little ditch, the Bering Straits?'

'Where's Alaska? Which direction?'

That seemed to goad Dechant into fury. 'Are you a seminarist to ask questions like that? Listen! That ship calls here twice every summer. Brings coal, wood, flour, potatoes, implements and anything else there's room for in a junk of that kind. Those are unloaded, and then it takes on lead.'

'I see. . . .' said Forell dubiously, wondering where Dechant got his information.

'You want to go and have a look at her, that's the first thing. If they call for volunteers for unloading, step up straight away!'

And with that piece of advice Dechant was suddenly off on some purposeful errand of his own.

Next morning at five o'clock, when the guard blew the whistle for the start of work, instead of going back up the shaft with his lamp as he usually did, he came down into the centre of the cave and called for twenty volunteers for work above ground. Forell was employed as a carrier now, paired with Willi Bauknecht, and both of them immediately stepped forward, quickly followed by forty or fifty other men. But the guard passed over the two men and selected the gang from the late comers, on the principle, presumably, that the least eager would be the most trustworthy.

The twenty men were marched off while the remainder started the day's work in the cave. By this time the distance from the face to the exit from the shaft was considerable and the carriers were obliged to take a breather before hauling their baskets up the last stretch. As soon as Forell and Bauknecht had deposited their load, the boy blurted:

'You know what I think they're doing? Unloading that ship! Oh! What wouldn't I give to be there!'

Forell was still struggling to regain his breath. Willi waited, expecting some pearl of wisdom to fall from Forell's lips. When nothing came, he said impatiently: 'Well, what do you think?'

'You may be right.'

'May be! Well, what other explanation is there?'

'Oh, none, of course!'

Willi looked solicitous. Forell must be sick, that was what it was. That was why he could summon only a weary sarcasm when there was a ship out there, just waiting for him to step on board and escape. But in his admiration for Forell Willi was generous. The fact was that his hero was not sick, but just tired and dispirited by the younger man's health and vitality.

'I know what it is,' said Willi. 'I've been a carrier now for six weeks, so I'm used to it. But the first day—oh! You should have seen me! Dripping from head to foot! You'll be all right in a few days. When you get up to the top, you want to breathe deeply, in—out! Like that!'

'I see. Well, let's get to the top, shall we?'

They carried their basket to the surface, tipped the contents on to a wooden chute and then, following Willi's advice, Forell took a few deep breaths of the keen, fresh air. 'The processing is interesting,' said Willi, but Forell's eyesight was not as good

45

as the younger man's. All he could see was smoke, a conglomeration of machinery and further off, before the plateau fell away towards a slag heap, a considerable crowd of Russian workmen. But the guard left them no time to loiter and inside half a minute they were shuffling down the shaft again on their way to fetch another load.

At the end of the twelve hour day Forell was ready to drop. He believed he was totally exhausted, but when the twenty volunteers returned, he found he still had ears for their story.

'What was it like?'

'Hard work.'

'Is there really a ship down there?'

'Yes,' said Dannhorn, and collapsed on his palliasse, in no mood to say more.

'What sort of a ship?'

Portschach replied. 'I don't know,' he said, grinning like a simpleton and blinking his great sleepy eyes. 'Couldn't tell you —I was looking at the grub!'

'What was there? Did you pinch any?'

'Oh, lovely stuff!' said Portschach in a dreamy voice. 'Sacks of flour, about fifty tons of it. Canned food, barley, bacon, meat . . .'

Forell broke in. 'What else did you see?'

'. . . Great red juicy tomatoes! You should have seen the pictures on those labels! Sliced pork, so real, you could touch it . . .'

'But did you see Alaska, man?' Forell's exhaustion had vanished.

Then Dannhorn spoke, in a surprisingly sympathetic tone. 'No, Forell, we didn't, and I don't suppose we could have done, even on a clear day, from where we were. But there was a mist today and we could only see the ship and about a hundred yards beyond—black, still water, shining like ebony.'

'Um. . . .'

Forell expected his grunt of disappointment to provoke some sarcastic comment from Dannhorn, on the theme of men who spent their lives dreaming of escape, but instead, he laughed. 'It's all right, Forell! I know what you feel. No one could have been more disappointed than I. Don't forget, the ship was right there in front of me. If thought could get me across, I'd be in Alaska by now. It's only fifty miles.'

'Too far to swim.'

Again Dannhorn laughed. 'How right you are!'

Sitting close by, Leibrecht noticed there was an eye-tooth missing in Dannhorn's jaw. Surely the gap had not always been there? Lead poisoning——? He would ask Dannhorn about that, as soon as he got a chance. Then Leibrecht suddenly said:

'Can you cook, Forell?'

'Why?'

'Never mind,' said Leibrecht. 'Just a question. . . .'

Next morning, the twenty men again went down to the pier, with Willi Bauknecht, this time, who had been detailed by the guard to take the place of another man who was sick. That evening, the gang returned without him. It was Leibrecht who told the news, with a hint of melancholy in his voice, because the young student had out-trumped them all.

'This morning, when we got to the pier, we saw two ships, a small trawler as well as the one we are unloading. To tell you the truth, I got wind of that yesterday, so it came as no surprise to me. Anyway—there was a good deal of coming and going between the trawler and the camp office and at midday, the interpreter came down to us and asked if anyone could cook——'

'Ah!' broke in Forell. 'So that was why——?'

'Yes. I was expecting that, too. I heard something yesterday about the trawler's cook who had died at sea. It seemed strange that the Russians meant to put a prisoner on board in his stead, but I'd already made up my mind that I couldn't volunteer. I don't know the first thing about cooking. Well, the men were hesitating this morning, wondering, I suppose, what the interpreter was after, when Willi said, yes, he was a trained cook. The interpreter looked him up and down. Then he asked him which of the Services he had been in during the war. "Kriegsmarine," said Willi. Of course, it wasn't true. He'd never been near the Navy, he was at school for most of the war. Still. . . . "Come with me," said the interpreter, and the next thing was, Willi was aboard the trawler—ship's cook, if you please, in place of the man who had died.'

'Lucky devil. . . .' There was a long silence in the cave, until at last Forell said: 'I only hope he takes his chance. Dannhorn! Was Bauknecht ever in your geography class?'

Dannhorn who the day before had been all smiles was now as disgruntled as ever. 'If only he'd told me! Fancy pushing off like that without a word of sound advice! If only he had let me draw him a map! We ought to pray for Willi Brauknecht—if we hadn't forgotten how.'

* * *

The trawler sailed and a fortnight later, after the cargo ship had finished unloading and taken on the entire nine months' product of the lead mine, she, too, slipped away one night and the prisoners returned to their accustomed routine. Twice during August, when they were allowed to the surface, they

47

caught a glimpse of the sun, and during the course of the month, a new concession was won from the guards. Hitherto, the sixteen men in each gang working in pairs as carriers had worked without a break for twelve hours. Now they were allowed to split into two parties, each of four pairs, and work alternate hours. The output was not affected for the rest enabled the men to maintain a brisker tempo.

Then in September, the concession was suddenly abolished. During the whole month and on into October, there was no further leave above ground. In the middle of October, the rations were suddenly cut by half. There could be only one explanation: Willi Bauknecht had indeed taken his chance, and had been recaptured.

Within a week, the news was definite, confirmed by one of the Russian guards. Willi had been brought back to the camp and was being held a prisoner in the Russian compound. As the men's hunger grew, the old symptoms reappeared: hatred for the cause of their suffering, and thirst for revenge. But now Leibrecht warned them that if they made Willi Bauknecht run the gauntlet, he would follow immediately behind him down the double line. Forell, too, was determined that there should be no repetition of his own ordeal. 'We don't need to flog a man to death to get our rations back,' he said. 'It's lead the Russians want, not corpses.'

Then the unexpected happened. One evening, the door at the upper end of the shaft was left open by the guard—something which had not happened for months—and fresh, cool air streamed into the cave. On the following day, full rations were restored. The carriers were allowed to work in alternate shifts again, and if any of them wanted to linger for a few minutes above ground to watch the surface processing of the ore, instead of the usual peremptory order not to loiter, he got nothing but smiles from the guards.

The carriers could see now how the mixture of ore and rubble which they tipped on to the chute was taken first to a diesel-driven rotary crusher. There, the whole mass was crushed into pieces small enough to be handled by the separator, to which it was passed on a conveyor belt. The separator consisted of a rocking grid where the dead rubble passed down a chute to the slag heap and the lead-bearing ore fell through because of its greater weight on to a second conveyor belt which fed it into yet another crushing machine. Here the ore was reduced still further in size before being smelted. For the smelting, the Russians had managed to install two huge cylindrical boilers—how, the prisoners were never able to decide—each measuring six feet in diameter. These were bedded in concrete and heated from below. From the boilers the lead emerged in the pure state in moulds, and after it had cooled, it was taken by sledge in the form of bars to be stored in a shed on the far side of the plateau.

All this could now be seen, thanks to the Russians' amenable mood, and it gave no small satisfaction to the men who worked below ground to learn from the carriers what became of the ore which they hewed. But the prisoners felt uneasy. There was still no sign of Willi Bauknecht. What was the reason for these sudden concessions? Had the Russians relented, or was this some new trick designed to break the last thread of the prisoners' self-control? Weeks passed and the harsh breath of winter was driving frozen pellets of snow over the plateau before they learned the answer. Then late one night, Doctor Stauffer was fetched down to the cave to examine Alfons Mattern who was suspected of having caught pneumonia during an afternoon's leave above ground.

Whenever a man had a high temperature, and showed it, the Russians kept their distance in case he should turn out to have typhus. They had learnt to respect the agility of the typhus louse. This guard was no exception.

'*Fleckfieber?*'

Doctor Stauffer pursed his lips. 'Maybe.' And the guard edged further away towards the exit from the cave, well out of earshot as the doctor bent over the eighteen-year-old Mattern and, after examining him thoroughly went over his chest again with the stethoscope, while Forell and Leibrecht stood by.

'Breathe in. Thank you. Again. And again. Um. . . . Bauknecht was sent to another cave. The Russians were afraid you might be too kind to him. He got badly mauled. . . . Ask some questions about the patient.'

Forell spoke up. 'Will you be taking him to hospital, Doctor?'

'Yes, Bauknecht got to Alaska. The trawler must have been inside territorial waters. He jumped overboard and swam ashore. He had bad luck. He ran into some American soldiers. He thought he was safe, but they told the Russians and they sent an officer to fetch him.' Doctor Stauffer addressed the patient. 'Do you mind turning over again on to your chest, just for a moment?'

Alfons Mattern obligingly turned over and the doctor listened again to his back. 'Um. . . . Yes. We'll have you in hospital, my boy.'

The Russian guard had turned and was watching them.

'Right. Thank you. Over you go.' Then the doctor spoke to Forell. 'Will you help him on with his shirt?'

The patient sat up and the doctor talked to him as he dressed. 'Yes. A most interesting case. They'd never had one

49

like it before. They took Bauknecht to a coastguard station, listened to his story, fed him, gave him new clothes——'

The guard was coming towards them.

'—Then they took him to some headquarters and showed him to dozens of generals. Then the Russian arrived, signed a receipt and took him away. That's all.'

The guard was standing, looking blankly at the doctor.

'Hospital?'

Stauffer nodded. 'Yes, hospital.'

They helped the patient to his feet, Leibrecht and Forell supporting him on either side. 'Gently does it!' said the doctor. 'And by the way, I believe you have a cartographer in this cave. Would he have to invent too much, do you think, if he were asked to draw a map of the Eastern Hemisphere from memory? Hm-hm. . . . That's it. Now, if you two could help the patient to the top of the shaft; we have a stretcher waiting outside.' The doctor smiled, 'It's as well to be prepared, isn't it? And perhaps your cartographer could fall sick, sometime. That would be excellent. . . .'

When Leibrecht and Forell got back to the cave, Dannhorn raised himself on an elbow. 'I heard it all,' he said.

Leibrecht bent down and whispered: 'Did anyone else—I mean about the map?'

'Hägelin, possibly. He's still awake.'

'He would be! Well, we must be careful. I don't trust that man.'

'No,' said Dannhorn, 'neither do I.'

*   *   *

For a fortnight, Alfons Mattern lay in hospital with double pneumonia, while Doctor Stauffer fought to prevent him slipping over the shadowy line between life and death. By the time the patient was able to leave his bed for an hour or two each day, the summer thaw had already started and the first scene that made any impression on his mind was that of the melting icicles outside the window of his ward. One day, a couple of Russians brought wooden spades and climbed on to the roof to clear the snow, and on the next warm day, they started chipping away the ice from the verge so that, as it melted, the water should not seep in behind the weather-boarding.

Once a day, Sergeant Cobweb would appear in the ward and run her fingers along ledges and window sills. Alfons Mattern smiled then, thinking of her name, and also out of gratitude to her for being a woman. But Cobweb never smiled back. It was enough for her to know that he would be in hospital for many weeks yet. Only Cobweb, and perhaps Doctor Stauffer, knew how many nights she had watched over the boy at the crisis of his illness.

When Sergeant Cobweb had completed her tour of inspection through the hospital as her daily contribution to the battle against dirt and indiscipline, she assisted Doctor Stauffer in an operation for appendicitis. The patient had been in hospital before, a dark-haired, powerfully-built man, immensely tall and broad. Cobweb even remembered his name. Dechant. She pronounced the word with a spit on the dentals: D-echant-t. She did not like this fellow, Dechant. He was too clever by far, and too full of bouncing energy. An unruly patient, or so he had been in the winter of '46 when he had been in hospital with dysentery. And when the operation was over, and the appendix lay in a kidney basin awaiting removal, Cobweb knew enough pathology to recognize a healthy organ when she saw one. But then it was the Vratsch who had admitted Dechant and his stupidity was notorious. Cobweb would speak to him at the next available opportunity. And with that, she dismissed the matter from her mind.

If Cobweb had pursued her thought a little further, her dislike of Dechant might have led her to suspect that some of the blame for his admission with an acute appendix was his—that he had intended to come to hospital, in fact, in order to have rest, and quiet and an opportunity to . . . But there her mind would have embarked on a sea of conjecture quite inappropriate to its factual cast, and so it returned to questions of soot, dust and discipline.

The hospital was half empty and there were only two other men in the ward when, an hour after the operation, Doctor Stauffer called to see his patient.

'Not much wrong with your appendix, Dechant; not even sub-acute!'

'I didn't want it to flare up on me when I'm on the way home.' Dechant felt amongst the clothing beside his bed and drew out a German Army watch. 'Have you seen this?'

'Where did that come from?'

Dechant gave a knowing smile. 'You won't find another of these in the lead mine! This is just the compass part. You officers had Swiss watches, didn't you, watertight and demagnetized? But none of them had a compass in the back. I found someone who had managed to save his watch. He only wanted the timepiece, so we split. I got the compass with the housing and he kept the watch. It took me months to build him a new case for it. Now I shall be able to keep my direction—out there.'

51

'And which direction will that be?'

'Westwards, roughly.'

Doctor Stauffer looked at the powerfully-built man in the bed and thought for a moment before saying quietly: 'It's the "roughly" I don't like. It sounds rather frivolous to me. You've gathered a lot of information, I know, and I thought you had everything worked out. Then you talk about "westwards, roughly". That simply won't do, Dechant. . . . I know what I'm talking about. I know the routes, and I'm not saying this lightly, believe me. . . .'

The jovial Dechant now had a heavy frown on his face.

'I can't understand,' continued the doctor, 'how you can amass so much knowledge about the area round here and yet be so vague about your route. It seems to me, you're being too clever, and too abstract. You think escaping from here is an intellectual problem that can be solved by amassing data. Too much cerebration, Dechant, and not enough fire! If you really wanted to get home there wouldn't be this gap in your plans.'

Dechant had been listening with increasing impatience. Now, with flushed face and lips compressed, he broke in: 'If I really want——! Now listen, Doctor, and I'll tell you something. . . .'

Later that night, Cobweb was just about to go off duty when there came an urgent call from Doctor Stauffer through one of the convalescent patients. She was needed at once to help restrain the appendix case. The man had gone raving mad, jumped out of bed and the sudden movement had opened the stitches. . . . Hours later, after the operation wound had been closed again and Dechant was lying once more, heavily doped, in his bed, the doctor found it necessary to have a private word with the Russian sister. Taking care to speak her language considerably less fluently than he was able, the doctor explained that the patient Dechant was mentally deranged and had conceived the idea of murdering one of his younger comrades. A persecution mania. He believed that the young man had done him an injury. Cobweb listened impassively, even when Doctor Stauffer told her that the object of Dechant's lunatic grudge was the nineteen-year-old Alfons Mattern.

From then on Cobweb had a new name for the boy who was recovering from pneumonia, Aljoscha. Aljoscha was better, now that she knew of Dechant's intention. Mattern was a name she had always found difficult to pronounce. But Dechant was too ill now to have intentions of any kind, and by the time his obsession revived, Aljoscha would long since have returned to the lead mine. Cobweb did not know whether to be pleased or sorry. Her face, meanwhile, remained inscrutable.

* * *

Four times during the summer of 1948 the men in the lead mine were allowed for a whole afternoon above ground. The first occasion was towards the end of June. Work was stopped at midday and then the walking shadows filed slowly from the shaft to stand blinking in the unaccustomed light, while a sharp breeze drove water from their eyes and down their dirt-encrusted cheeks. The ice mists were gradually dispersing and as the men walked about, the sun broke through, turning all to gold.

Leibrecht, thinner now and ashen-faced, still exercised a quiet authority over his men and led the way to a hollow where melting snow offered a chance to get clean. He had about fifty converts now to his cleanliness campaign and soon the hollow was full of naked men stamping and splashing about in the ice-cold water. In token of their official approval, the Russians had even issued a few squares of a clay-coloured substance which passed for soap, but in texture was nearer to pumice.

Leibrecht set to vigorously on the nearest man's back, ignoring protests and entreaties until he had produced a lather of a sort—a pink lather. 'That's funny. It's pink.' The victim howled. 'You silly fool! It's not funny at all. You've drawn blood. That's what you've done!'

Closer in to the foot of the hill, some of the men were having a haircut. Here again, the Russians had proved sympathetic and partly, no doubt, for fear of typhus if the men's hair were allowed to grow too long, had provided scissors and cut-throat razors, issuing them on parole to specified barbers who had to surrender them before returning to the mine.

The subterranean caves where the twelve hundred Germans lived and worked were numbered now, from I to VIII. On their half holidays during the previous summer, the occupants of each cave had been strictly segregated, following the Russians' plan to divide and rule. But now, as the afternoon progressed, the guards began to move further off and from time to time a man would dart from one group to another, stay for a few minutes to exchange news and then await his chance to flit back again.

Forell decided to seek out Willi Bauknecht. Each group of men he reached knew the name, and at the fifth group, they pointed to a solitary figure sitting on the bare rock close by the entrance to their cave.

53

'Willi. . . ?'

The man had a broken nose and might have been anything between fifty and sixty. Surely the men had made a mistake? He looked up as Forell spoke and muttered a barely audible: 'What do you want?'

'Willi, how are you?'

But Willi merely turned his head and gazed blankly at a patch of melting snow.

'Willi, don't you recognize me? Forell. Clemens Forell. Remember?'

Still staring at the snow, as though in a dream the man breathed faintly: 'Forell. . . .' Then suddenly tears were pouring down his face. At that moment came a shrill, drawn-out whistle, the signal for the men to fall in by the entrances to their caves.

'Willi, I must get back. Listen, Willi. See if you can't come back to us. Willi, are you listening? Get a transfer back to your old cave. We'll look after you. We're well organized now, and——'

But the man never moved.

'Willi!'

Again the whistle sounded and without bothering to dodge the guards, Forell had to run in order to reach his own group in time. As he ran he looked round and saw that two men had come up to help Willi to his feet. Then the young student began to hobble slowly towards the entrance to his cave.

* * *

Before the summer was out, Alfons Mattern returned, quite recovered, from hospital. But he would have to be treated gently. Return to the lead mine after so long an interval would not have been easy for anyone, and for him, with a severe illness behind him. . . . Unobtrusively, Leibrecht saw to it that the transition was gradual. Mattern needed someone to look after him and befriend him for a while, until he had got used to life below ground, and, ambiguous figure though he was in other respects, Hägelin seemed to Leibrecht to be the right man for the job. When it came to hard work, he did his share and Leibrecht guessed that his perpetual eavesdropping on the other men and his apparent fondness for the Russians sprang in part from loneliness.

So Leibrecht asked Hägelin if he would keep an eye on the young Mattern. 'If you treat him gently, he'll be a genuine friend. Let him work with you at the face. But don't expect him to do much, to start with, at any rate.' Hägelin was visibly touched and his willingness to take Mattern by the

hand was sincere. In the latter's absence in hospital, someone
else had taken the patch of rock where he had slept at night
and Hägelin made room for him beside his own palliasse.
'Here! Alfons! Put your things down here!'

'Oh, I'm not called Alfons now! I've been rechristened
Aljoscha.'

'Russified already?'

'Cobweb did it, to distinguish me from someone else, I
suppose. She was a wonderful nurse.'

Hägelin looked thoughtful, but said nothing.

Heinz Dechant was getting ready to make his escape at the
beginning of autumn. The circle of those in the know was
small and confined to the individuals whose help he would
need. But how many prisoners suspected or had somehow
already got wind of the scheme, none of the initiates dared
guess. Dannhorn, at any rate, had to know, as he was needed
to draw the map. He had already agreed to do so, with the
reservation that he could not guarantee the accuracy of the
scale, even before he was told the name of the man who
would use it. To Dannhorn, that was a matter of indifference.
His own ambition was not to escape, but to evolve some sort
of life for himself at the lead mine. When Leibrecht asked
him what illness he proposed to contract so as to get admitted
to hospital, Dannhorn unwrapped a small pot of cooking salt
from his belongings.

'But can salt make you ill?'

'If not, why do the Russians reserve a savage punishment
for any prisoner caught with salt on him? It gives you a
temperature.'

Not even Forell was told when the time came for Dannhorn
to fall ill. Dannhorn himself continued his normal work up to
the very last moment. But Hägelin, as he worked at the face
applying his strength scientifically in order to spare Alfons
Mattern, approached the subject obliquely saying: 'He'll have
to start moving soon.'

'Who?'

'Heinz Dechant, of course.'

'I wish him luck,' said Mattern uneasily.

'Do you think he'll go alone?'

'I don't know. How should I? I'd be the last person he'd
talk to.' Then, afraid he had already said too much, Mattern
added lamely: 'I suppose I'm too young. People don't confide
such things to me.'

'That's very possible,' said Hägelin and paused in the act
of raising his pick to smirk at the young man beside him.
To Mattern, this was a new Hägelin. Everyone said he was an
unpleasant and even dangerous man, but Mattern had seen a
different side. To him Hägelin had so far shown nothing but

kindness. Now he began to wonder. Was Forell right when
he called Hägelin a blackguard? Forell, of course, knew
Mattern's story. Mattern had told him that night, long ago,
in the tent outside Chita. Leibrecht might know it, too, from
Forell. Doctor Stauffer perhaps would have heard Dechant's
version. But Hägelin——?

Next morning, Mattern awoke at reveille from a furious
dream argument with Hägelin. When the men went to work,
Dannhorn stayed on his palliasse, sweating with fever. Hägelin
was in high spirits, whistling to himself as they groped their
way along the shaft to the face.

'I wonder how Dannhorn managed it! You know what he's
going to hospital for, don't you? To draw the map for
Dechant. That was all fixed long ago.'

'Oh?' said Mattern.

'Yes.' Hägelin was smiling to himself as he fixed a steel
wedge into a rift in the seam and prepared to drive it in with
the sledge-hammer. 'That's right, isn't it?'

'I don't know, and I don't want to know,' said Mattern
desperately. 'Hägelin, please don't talk about this escape any
more, whether it's true or not. Please, I ask you, leave me out
of it!'

Hägelin put down the sledge-hammer and gave Mattern a
searching look. 'If you really want to be out of it. . . .'

Later that morning, after the guard had told him there was
a sick man in the cave, the Vratsch arrived to examine
Dannhorn. Laying the back of one podgy hand on the
patient's collar bone, he solemnly extended two fingers and
proceeded to 'measure the fever'. Forell and Leibrecht had
stayed behind, ready to help the suffering Dannhorn to
hospital. 'A hundred and four point two,' the Vratsch
murmured, hastily withdrawing his hand in case it should turn
out to be typhus. 'Hospital!' Forell and Leibrecht enjoyed
the game of supporting Dannhorn up the shaft and across
the plateau, although the heavy dose of cooking salt had made
him ill enough. Doctor Stauffer was waiting alone at the door
of the hospital to admit him. 'Thank you,' he said impassively.
That was all.

Apart from the periodic leave above ground which all the
prisoners enjoyed, Dannhorn had never yet had a rest in
hospital and it was well earned. The doctor had little difficulty
in reducing his fever and when Dannhorn was ready, he
produced a small pad of paper about the size of an Army
communication sheet. There being no suitable paper available
in the hospital, the doctor had managed to wangle it from the
camp office. Then Dannhorn started to draw his map. There
were few patients in hospital and the only other man in
Dannhorn's ward was sworn to secrecy. The cartographer

finished his map in two afternoons, covering a series of sheets which the doctor then stuck together with surgical plaster, thereby strengthening, incidentally, the completed map and making it easy to fold. The area shown covered the greater part of Asia, including the whole of Siberia, and stretched from the Chukchi Peninsula on the Bering Straits in the east to the Urals in the west, its southerly limit being a line through the Kurile Islands north-east of Japan; Hankow; the Karakorum Mountains bordering Kashmir; and the Aral Sea. The last place-name near the bottom left-hand corner of the map was a town called Novo-Kasalinsk.

'Why haven't you continued the map westwards?' Doctor Stauffer wanted to know.

The reply was typical of Dannhorn. 'Because before he's finished with this map, Dechant will either have crossed a frontier into freedom or be dead.'

Neither of them mentioned the risk to themselves if Dechant were recaptured with the map on him. The surgical plaster would give the doctor away and the Russians' card index would tell them there was only one cartographer amongst the German prisoners. But Stauffer thought the risk worthwhile. He had set his heart on one man, at least, getting home.

'I wonder if Dechant will succeed,' he murmured after a pause. 'If he does, then at any rate Alfons Mattern will be able to die in peace.' A thin smile appeared on the doctor's face. The next second, it was gone.

Now the finished map was safely in the doctor's possession, for issue in due course, to Dechant, he thought it safer to hand over the further treatment of Dannhorn to the Vratsch, and he felt he could do so with a good conscience as, apart from another week in bed, the patient needed none. Dannhorn was content. The other patient in his ward was discharged and for a few days, he was alone. The ill humour which normally concealed his real self from the world could be dropped and sometimes as he passed the door, Doctor Stauffer could hear Dannhorn busily talking, as though to a long-lost friend.

Dannhorn deserved his contentment. Thereafter times would be sad enough.

* * *

So far, since the German prisoners arrived at the lead mine, six had attempted escape: Forell and Bauknecht and, in addition, two men from another cave whose frozen corpses were found not five miles away after they had only been gone forty-eight hours, and another two who had made a feeble effort to get away during an afternoon's half holiday in the summer of 1949. Five of the six attempts had been doomed to disaster and Willi Bauknecht, well—he had proved once and for all that to escape eastwards towards Alaska was worse than a waste of time.

Now, after Dannhorn had returned to his cave from hospital, the men sensed that yet another attempt was to be made. Perhaps Leibrecht and Forell had over-acted the casualness of their hullos to Dannhorn; perhaps it was merely the fact that autumn—the 'escaping season'—was approaching and the men's thoughts naturally turned to the topic. At any rate, they interpreted as best they could the signs and portents and came to the conclusion that the much maligned Dannhorn was planning to escape and as a consequence, they treated him with a new respect.

Only one man reached the right conclusion, Hägelin. From odd scraps of conversation which he had overheard, he had known for weeks that some obscure connection existed between Mattern and Dechant and, hoping to surprise Mattern into admitting it, he awoke him in the middle of the night.

'Aljoscha,' whispered Hägelin. 'When do you plan to go, you and Dechant?'

'I'm not planning anything. Leave me alone!'

'All right. We'll talk about it tomorrow.'

Hägelin was asleep again almost at once; not so, Mattern. For the rest of the night fear fought with his exhaustion and kept him in an uneasy stupor, half-way between sleeping and waking. His mind jerked and wallowed, desperate with dread, now struggling at feverish speed to fathom Hägelin's intentions, now slipping into nightmare, dreaming that his hands were on Hägelin's throat, throttling him while he slept.

Next morning, Mattern was brought firmly back to reality by the whistle at reveille. He glanced at the snoring Hägelin and realized the futility of his dream. It would take someone stronger than he to throttle the man. As soon as he could, he asked Leibrecht if he could transfer to the carriers. If Leibrecht had agreed, the tragedy that now loomed might have been averted. But Leibrecht said no. He thought carrier work too arduous for the young Mattern and the latter dared not admit that he had asked in order to get away from Hägelin.

'Why did you apply to transfer to the carriers?' asked Hägelin quietly when they had reached the seam.

'The work's healthier, I thought,' said Mattern uncertainly.

'Well, why don't we apply together?'

The question was said in such an innocent tone that

Mattern blurted out an emphatic 'No!' without pausing to think.

'Yes!' insisted Hägelin. 'It's a good idea. We would get more time to talk then, quietly, just you and I.'

With every fibre of his being, Alfons longed to refuse, but he was afraid of Hägelin now and he did not dare. So for the rest of that day, they exchanged with two men on carrier work. Hägelin arranged it without consulting Leibrecht. They were on their way to the surface with their first basket of ore when Hägelin stopped for a breather and, as Mattern knew he would, started pestering him with questions again.

'Well now, about Dechant and this escape plan of his——'

'I don't know anything about it!' said Mattern loudly, desperately.

'He's going. It's on, isn't it?'

Mattern was almost whimpering as he said: 'Well if so, let him go, then! What do you want to do—stop him? I can't stop him! I can't argue with him! Why talk to me?' He was in the last stage of distress. He had heard rumours of Dechant's intention and, God knew, he wanted him to succeed, and go soon, before he discovered that the youth, Alfons Mattern, who had denounced him was not in Germany, but a quarter of a mile away, in the same lead mine as himself. And now, here was Hägelin trying to push his nose in, sniffing out the secret that weighed on Mattern day and night, and wouldn't stop plaguing and pestering him . . . Why?

'And when are they sending you off to join him? You're starting soon, I suppose?'

'Me? For God's sake, what are you talking about? Hägelin!'

'Ha! It's all right. There's no need to act innocent surprise. I know you're in with Forell and Leibrecht and those people. It's their job to get you out of the cave, isn't it? And then you and Dechant will have to fend for yourselves.'

'I tell you, it isn't true. Since Willi Bauknecht was crippled like that, I haven't had the least desire to escape.'

'So you say. . . .'

Mattern had reached breaking point. 'Shut up! Shut up!' He yelled. 'I won't hear another word.'

Hägelin had a venomous expression on his face as he said slowly: 'All right. If you won't listen, there are those that will. It's a crime to send a kid like you on this crazy escape, a crime that shouts to high heaven. If you won't listen, I'll do my talking elsewhere.'

Alfons felt his knees beginning to give way. 'What do you mean?'

'I mean I'm going to stop this escape, and I know the way to do it.'

For two days Mattern tried to ignore Hägelin and refused to open his mouth. Meanwhile Leibrecht had noticed his ghastly appearance and, believing it was the carrier work that was proving too much for him, changed the two men back to work at the face. He was in the same gang with them now and on the third day was working close by. It was in the afternoon, about two hours before the end of work, when it happened. They were extending the roof of the shaft, easing the lumps of rock out cautiously so as to avoid a sudden fall. In one place a slight crack had started. Alfons had wedged in a crow-bar and Leibrecht thought he was going to work it gently with his hands. Hägelin was standing just underneath. The next moment, Alfons had seized the sledge-hammer. There was a yell from Hägelin 'Look out! Hold it!' and he made to dodge aside. Then Alfons struck, with all his force behind the swing, and a huge mass of solid rock crashed to the ground and split in two. Hägelin had disappeared, but Mattern was still visible, lying half-covered by one of the pieces.

When a Russian officer and two men reached the scene, the prisoners had just succeeded in freeing Mattern from under about a ton weight of rock. From the knees downwards, his legs had been badly crushed, but the most serious injury seemed to have been caused by the rock as, in shattering, it had grazed his shoulder and then gouged a deep wound in his chest. The officer ordered him to be taken at once to hospital. Then he had the work continued until the crushed body of Hägelin had been recovered from beneath the larger of the pieces of rock. By then, it was past midnight.

Hägelin was dead. Mattern died in hospital on the following morning. The Russians did not allow their fellow-prisoners to bury them and they never revealed the place of their graves. But during the night before he died, Mattern had regained consciousness for a while and Doctor Stauffer had spoken with him. He believed that Hägelin's motive in taunting Mattern was one of outright jealousy: he could not tolerate the thought that anyone other than himself was capable of helping or protecting the youth, and in particular, that Dechant might successfully shepherd him home. If only he had known the truth!

Towards the end of September, Doctor Stauffer conveyed a message through a patient discharged to Dechant's cave that the time was ripe for his attempt to escape. The first step was for Dechant to get admitted to hospital, as it was from there that the attempt would be made. He had already been in hospital twice, first with dysentery and then with an appendix and to avoid the accusation of malingering would be difficult, even if he contrived to have an accident. Accidents were suspect now with the Russians, since the Mattern affair. The best plan would be to have a Russian as witness, or better still, to arrange for a Russian to cause the accident. But how?

The slag heap fed by the separator above ground seemed a likely cause of superficial injuries, if Dechant could contrive to lose his balance and tumble down the side. But the sides were too steep for the damage to be nicely calculated. It might be that in falling he would dislodge a considerable weight of rubble and end up at the bottom buried beneath it. Dechant was still debating the question when, one morning, a Russian worker did him the favour of stumbling at the very moment when Dechant was passing him, staggering along the top edge of the slag heap with a basket full of ore. The Russian flung up an arm, trying to regain his balance, and Dechant seized his chance. Dropping the handle of the basket, he left his fellow carrier to fend for himself and lurched head-on into the Russian, yelled, tottered and slipped sideways on to the sloping rubble.

The fall was more painful than he had imagined. Sharp stones ripped his trousers to shreds, gashed hands, legs and face and left him groaning and gory at the bottom of the slope. Solicitously, the Russians picked him up and conveyed him to hospital, while Dechant satisfied himself that no bones were broken.

'You did it the hard way, Dechant,' said Stauffer when he had finished cleaning the wounds. 'You might have broken your neck with a fall like that.'

'Any serious damage, Doctor?'

'Nothing that three days in hospital won't mend. That means we had better have a talk, just you and I, the day after tomorrow about your further plans. . . .'

Two days later, Dechant had recovered sufficiently to be able to dodge up to the doctor's room on the first floor.

'Is that you, Dechant? Come in and shut the door. Do you still want to attempt this escape?'

'Yes—of course. Why? Don't you think I'm fit?'

'Physically, yes.'

'What do you mean?'

'Sit down, Dechant, and make yourself comfortable. I've quite a lot to tell you, which it is only right you should know now, before you do anything irrevocable. Alfons Mattern is dead.'

'What? . . . How do you know that?'

'A pity it is night time, otherwise I could show you from this window almost the exact spot where he is buried.'

'He was here? At the lead mine?'

'Yes.'

'How did he die?'

'If you'll stop firing questions, Dechant, and be patient, I'll tell you. I'll tell you the whole story. I had a talk with Mattern the night before he died. . . .'

It was daylight before Dechant left the doctor's room. Twenty-four hours later, when he was due to be discharged from hospital, he sent the doctor the compass he had been wearing on his left wrist and with it, a message: 'If anyone can use this, I wish him the best of luck.'

*　　*　　*

During that third summer at the lead mine the men were continually falling ill. Lead poisoning was no longer a subject to be debated in secret; its effects were only too visible, masked though they were by the lack of a standard of strong and healthy manhood by which the prisoners could assess their deterioration. With the tacit approval of the Russians, Doctor Stauffer was admitting anyone now with the tell-tale symptoms of slow pulse, loss of appetite and marked depression, and in effect that meant admitting every man in turn.

Up to the end of July Forell had gone on carrying baskets. Then one morning at the start of work, he found he could hardly stand. The Vratsch found him lying inert on his palliasse, weak and with a high temperature.

'What shall we do with you, Forell?' Doctor Stauffer was standing at the foot of his bed, smiling slightly at the sight of the giant entrusted to his care.

'Anything except make me work.'

'I'll call it pneumonia.'

'I don't mind, as long as I can see daylight for a change.'

After three years Forell's muscles were as strong as ever. It was his brain that seemed to have softened and lost its edge. His mind toyed merely with thoughts, left them uncompleted, felt tired after exchanging a few meaningless banalities with his fellow prisoners. Life slipped past as though in a dream. In sleep he was half awake. In the daytime he dozed off where he stood, waiting to take his turn to work at the face. Now he was content merely to lie still and shut his eyes.

Three weeks later, rest, clean air and the sight of daylight as long as it lasted had produced an astonishing change.

'What size boots fit those flippers of yours, Forell?'

Since midday the sun had been streaming in through the windows and it was warm in the ward. Forell looked down at his feet protruding under the blankets and laughed. The skin under the joints of the big toes was as smooth as parchment from carrying baskets up the shaft in the mine, and clean now as well—Stauffer and Cobweb combined had seen to that.

'Twelves.'

'Um. . . . How do you feel?'

'A bit yellow about the gills, otherwise fine!'

'Yes, I've noticed that jaundiced look in you before. But it's Prontosil that has done that for you this time.'

'A good camouflage in case the Vratsch should want to discharge me!'

'You don't need any camouflage at the moment.'

The two men gazed out through the window into the August sunlight. The plateau was gleaming under a carpet of emerald moss.

'You could swear it was grass, couldn't you?' said the doctor.

'I wish it were.'

'It reminds me of my home in Magdeburg.'

'—Or of the Tyrol.'

Then, still gazing through the window, the doctor said quietly: 'Are you married, Forell?' Oh, yes. Forell was married.

'What's her name?'

Her name was Catherine—a lovely name, a name that suited her. . . .

The doctor and his patient talked on, of jaundice and moss and Magdeburg, till at last the doctor managed to steer the talk back to Catherine. The patient took it up more eagerly this time and for some minutes the doctor listened to him, smiling and taking care not to interrupt. Finally, before leaving the war, he asked again about Forell's size in boots.

Catherine. . . . Forell's drowsy mind was stirring with half forgotten memories. To him the name had always seemed beautiful, and now its beauty was intensified by the melancholy thought that Catherine was beyond his reach. To be with her in imagination was all he could hope for, now that the lead lay heavy on his feet and brain. The distance between them stretched half-way round the world—a gulf that exhaustion could never bridge, only fantasy. Let fantasy run riot then; it was the only faculty that could give slaves a taste of freedom. Catherine. . . . It would have been nice to have seen her again.

While Forell dreamed on in the August sunlight, Doctor Stauffer waited, wondering whether the escape gear intended for Heinz Dechant would ever be used by this slouching giant in the ward below. The doctor was a patient man, but the opportunity which now beckoned would not stay for long. Now, in the autumn, was the time to escape. Another month, and a prisoner cosseted in the warmth of the lead mine would freeze to death out there, almost before he had taken his first breath of freedom. Earlier, and the ground would have been too soft and even rivulets would have been impassable barriers, swollen as they were in summer by the melting snows. Now was the time. And next year, Doctor Stauffer would no longer be there to launch any man on the hazardous path to freedom. In his talk with Forell, he had tried to convey that, but the matter was a delicate one and the patient's mind was too sluggish for subtleties. So Stauffer waited. The next move had to come from Forell himself. If he did not watch the guard, as Dechant had done, and slip up to the doctor's room one evening of his own accord—just for a chat, of course—then the great object on which the doctor had set his heart would never be realized, and not one of the twelve hundred prisoners at the lead mine would ever get home to Germany with news of their fate.

Meanwhile, Doctor Stauffer visited each ward and talked to each patient as usual twice a day. As the days passed and Forell still seemed content to browse and eat and talk idle rumour, the doctor found his duties an increasing strain. If he made a joke, it was a caustic one, and some of the patients said that his words undid what his skill as a doctor repaired.

Then, one evening:

'That looks interesting.'

Anyone but Doctor Stauffer would have started at the sudden voice behind him, but he merely said: 'Is that you, Forell?'

'A wire noose, is it? What's it for?'

'It's a kind of snare I happened to pick up outside—for trapping Arctic hares, I suppose. It's no good to you, Forell. It would only get in your way. And that reminds me: you'll have to be on your way fairly soon now, I'm afraid. I can't keep you in hospital much longer.'

'How long?'

'Another month, at the outside.'

'Then, early in October I shall have to go back to the lead mine?'

'I'm sorry. But you're not the only one, you know. Others have got to get their breath of fresh air as well.'

'Of course. . . .' Forell moved slowly to the door, waited till he could hear the guard mounting the stairs at the far end of the corridor, then slipped back to his ward on the floor below.

So in a few short weeks he would be back in the mine. It might be two years then before he saw daylight again. What sort of a state would he be in? His arm muscles were flabby now from lack of use, but they would tone up again when they'd had some work to do. And then, Forell thought of the work. There was only one kind—hauling, hacking, shoving in the glistening tomb, by the light of a single paraffin lamp. The thought made his stomach turn over. He would never go back to that. No, never again.

*   *   *

Next evening, Forell again crept up to the doctor's room.

'Doctor,' he began. 'About lead poisoning—would you say I had the symptoms?'

Stauffer spoke with impatience. 'Who hasn't in this place?'

'Is it always fatal?'

'Certainly, when there's nothing to treat it with.'

'*Is* there a treatment?'

Stauffer turned in his chair. 'I believe that people working in an atmosphere polluted by lead dust are advised a change of employment. You see, my friend, there's only one cure for lead poisoning: get away from lead!'

'Get away from lead'. . . . The picture of Catherine was fading now, was no more than a soothing memory, and half a world of bitter suffering lay between Forell and freedom, robbing it of its allure. But now, in their stead, there was a new motive for escape, the certainty of slow death by lead poisoning, and a new picture—the dim-lit wall of rock in the mine. It filled the future with terror and before long, it was pursuing Forell even into his dreams, so that on waking sometimes, he could feel from the soreness of his gums how his fingers had been testing his teeth while he slept, for fear they were loosening in their sockets.

'A change of employment'. . . . A few evenings later, Forell was back in Doctor Stauffer's room, telling him he had made up his mind to escape, while the going was good. The bombshell left Stauffer unmoved.

'Better wait till the frost comes,' was all he said. Yet, hidden in the wainscot only a few feet from where the doctor was sitting lay a complete armoury of escaping gear, awaiting the moment when Forell would be 'ripe'. And that moment would be when, abandoning all customary reserve and reticence, dreaming at night of long treks in the snow and re-thinking the dreams by day, on his knees, almost, to the doctor, wild-eyed and burning for the Great Adventure, Forell would beg and implore his aid. Then, so Doctor Stauffer considered, it might be worth showing him the map —for a start.

Meanwhile, Doctor Stauffer's unexpected coolness was

goading Forell into frenzy. Each day the patients in his ward saw his face become paler, till it turned to a sickly, glistening yellow, like wax. The eyes in their bony sockets darted ceaselessly about the room, or else were fixed in a wild and glassy stare. Then Forell would start to chew his lip, flare into a rage over nothing, talk hysterically of lead poisoning, baring his teeth to show how they were rotting; and then suddenly relapse into exhausted apathy. The cause? The other patients exchanged winks—they could make a shrewd guess. And when Forell jumped into life again, railing obscenely at heaven, the Russians and Fate for their triple conspiracy against him, leaving him to rot here till he died, the guess became a certainty: Forell had the wind-up, because soon he'd be back in the mine. As for his companions, listless and weakened as they were by sickness, they could no longer summon the energy even to despair.

On 26th September, with Forell once more in his room, Doctor Stauffer brought out the map. They bent over it together and, for a moment, the doctor almost seemed to be smiling. The next moment, quite clearly he wasn't; he was horrified by Forell's ridiculous optimism. Obviously he hadn't the faintest idea what the map would look like on the ground. He hadn't even glanced at the scale. There he was, totting up the rivers until he reached a dozen or so, and then calmly pronouncing a round thirty miles as the daily distance he could cover! Naturally, at that rate, he would be at the Manchurian border by the spring.

'If,' said Doctor Stauffer with icy emphasis, 'you have the good fortune to reach the River Lena by the end of this winter, it will be due to the direct intervention of the Almighty.'

'I don't know. I've got my strength back. I'm pretty fit now.'

'But have you any conception what this country is like that you'll be crossing?'

'Doctor, I've told you: I mean to get home.'

'Really? Out through the door at the end of the corridor, I suppose, then turn west and keep going until someone speaks to you in German?'

'I tell you, I can't stick it here any longer—I've got to go!'

Then the doctor did smile. The patient was coming along very nicely, he thought. Commonsense, caution, a smattering of Russian—all that was nothing without a prime mover, without this massive determination unalloyed by knowledge of the hazards in store. The iron in the skull, that was what a man needed before he could be called ripe for freedom. And Forell's mind was splendidly literal, thought the doctor. Rivers, mountains, forests—yes, those he was prepared to

meet, because he could see them marked on the map. As for
the inhabitants of the country, they were not marked, so they
did not exist.

'What about people?' asked Stauffer. 'How will you eat
without contacting the inhabitants?'

'I shan't have to contact them. I'll help myself without being
seen.'

'That won't be easy. People go armed in Siberia, and they'll
be better shots than you. Their ears will be sharper and they'll
move quicker in snow.'

'Well, we'll see. . . .'

'We'll see if you don't end up wishing yourself back in the
lead mine!'

'I'm not going back.' The words had a finality about them
that imposed silence. Then Forell said: 'And I'm not going
to oblige by running the gauntlet again—whatever happens.
If it comes to the point, I'll choose my own way out. If I
could have that snare———'

'You mean, the wire noose?'

'Yes, I'd like to have it so that I could choose for
myself. . . .'

'Quite so. I quite understand. I'm glad you thought of that
because that situation is not only possible, but probable,
Forell—you realize that?'

Forell laughed. 'Oh, of course, there's always a chance I'll
be recaptured; that's obvious, isn't it?'

The doctor shrugged his shoulders. 'All right. But I know
something of what's ahead of you, more than you do, because
here in the hospital I've had a better chance to find out. And
I can tell you this: not even the Russians here know what
the country is like to the west. Some of it is unexplored. In
other parts, you'll find more people than you'll want to see.
Make for the unexplored areas, to start with, at any rate
—the blanks on the map, but remember, they may not be
blanks on the ground. Here, for instance'—the doctor pointed
to the map—'there are coal mines—brown coal—you must
watch your step or you'll find yourself in the pits.'

'They won't get me alive, don't you worry!'

'Don't be too sure. You might not get time to pull the
trigger———'

'Trigger?'

'—Even if you had a pistol. Suppose they found you
asleep?'

Doctor Stauffer sat hunched in his chair as though he were
in pain. His face looked drawn and grey. Dyspeptic, thought
Forell, that's what he is, and that's how he talks.

'It's all very well,' the doctor resumed, 'for you to say: "I'll
do this, but I won't do that," and so on and so forth, now,

when you've not the faintest conception what's waiting for you out there. You'll see: after two days, you'll be wishing you'd never set out.'

'That's not likely.'

'Oh, I don't mean you'll give yourself up! Your kind never do. But they'll get you all right, and then—well, you know the rest: you'll run the gauntlet again, again you'll escape, etcetera. Is it worth it?'

'No! no, it's not going to be like that!'

'I hope you're right. I don't want to have to mend your broken body all over again.'

'It'll be broken anyway, won't it, if I don't go now? It will be two years before I get another chance, and what sort of a chance would I have then? You know better than anyone: we're just falling to bits, all of us—rotting, like a heap of leaves!'

'To be raked over occasionally by Doctor Stauffer?'

'Yes, exactly! You said it yourself, didn't you? "Get away from lead." That's the only cure, isn't it? There's nothing you can do? Well, I'm getting away now, while I've still got some guts left!'

'All right, then! But don't blame me, if things begin to look a bit different after your first bivouac in the snow. There's no Doctor Stauffer out there, remember!'

The two men glared at each other and, for a moment, something like hatred seemed to flicker between them. Then without a word, Forell turned and went back to his ward.

* * *

For two days, the doctor seemed to avoid Forell, while the latter seethed with his plans to escape. Then Forell went to the doctor's room again. Outside it was bitterly cold and snowing. Thick flakes as hard as hail-stones were clattering against the window-panes.

As soon as the door was shut, Forell started talking like a madman, alternately pleading for help and accusing the doctor of trying to stop his escape. At times he seemed to be on the point of delirium. Sitting at his table, Doctor Stauffer listened impassively, nodding and pursing his lips occasionally, but otherwise quite unmoved. Then suddenly he spoke:

'All right. When is it to be?'

Dumbfounded by this abrupt change of attitude, Forell could only stammer: 'What?'

'This crazy escape of yours—when d'you want to go?'

'Tomorrow!'

'I think we'd better make it the day after, on Sunday. The

guards are more careless on Sundays, they've got more vodka in them.'

'All right. Sunday.' Suddenly, as often when he was excited, coloured rings began to dance in front of Forell's eyes. He swore inwardly, but made up his mind to say nothing to Doctor Stauffer.

The latter was easing out a section of the wainscot. 'Now let's see what you'll need.' Then, there was no doubt about it, the doctor smiled. 'You've been quite a long time, haven't you, getting up steam for this?'

Forell was not sure what he meant and the doctor did not seem to expect a reply. Perhaps he felt it was all to the good if Forell had not realized yet how he had been playing a game with him, how by reserve, then scepticism and finally by outright mockery and denigration he had been deliberately fanning those first, faint yearnings for freedom until, like some wild beast, Forell now stood, tensed and ready for the irrevocable leap from the cage.

Holding the loosened panel in place, Doctor Stauffer paused before removing it. 'There is just one thing, Forell, which I ask in return for the help which I shall give you. Should you, by some inconceivable chance, ever succeed in reaching home, will you get in touch with my wife for me, and tell her where I am? Magdeburg—can you remember that? I think I had better scratch the address for you on the bottom of your mess-tin. Will you let me have it tomorrow?'

'There's no need,' said Forell. 'I can remember an address.'

'Now, perhaps. But later on——? I'd better have that mess-tin, to be on the safe side.'

Why he should feel momentarily aggrieved at the discovery that Doctor Stauffer had this personal motive in helping him to escape, Forell never bothered to think. He had enough to think about as it was. Returning once more to his ward, he began to ponder how much food he would need for a fortnight on the march. For some weeks he had been saving up the greasy little fish, reeking of train oil, that the Russians issued occasionally to the prisoners. Most of the other patients had been unable to stomach them and had given their ration to him, to be stored in the deep-freeze on the outside window-sill, between the pane and the bars. Once he had got a real marching hunger, they would go down all right, and he had saved enough bread to help them.

So much for food. That was all Forell had been able to devise. But the doctor, he suspected, had some better ideas.

On the Saturday morning, thirty-six hours before he had planned to escape and in thought already far beyond the camp, Forell was suddenly confronted by the guard and told to report immediately to the Commandant's office. Though the guard did not even bother to escort him from the hospital and that fact should have told him it was nothing serious, Forell found himself gripped by a paralysing dread such as he had never known before. When he reached the office and tried to click his heels, his knee muscles refused to obey.

'You're fit for work,' said the interpreter. 'Come with me.'

Forell felt his stomach begin to turn. He could barely stand upright. A clammy perspiration was irrigating his skin. An arm grabbed his to stop him from falling and the interpreter's voice sounded, oscillating in his ear:

'Come with me.'

In the shed which served as clothing store Forell was given a fresh set of equipment as issued, sometimes, to patients before discharge from hospital when their own had become unserviceable—a new jacket, trousers with cotton wool sewn in as padding, underclothes and boots. The felt boots, though worn at the sole, were much better than the pair which hospital regulations had required him to hand in on admission. Slowly, because he still found difficulty in controlling his limbs, Forell took off his old clothes and put on the new. 'Tomorrow is Sunday,' he was told. 'On Monday morning you will return to the lead mine.' Then he was escorted back to hospital.

That evening, Doctor Stauffer listened to his story with amusement. 'If you cave in like that at the first sign of trouble, I only hope you don't meet up with the M.V.D., that's all.'

The doctor spoke indulgently, affectionately almost, as though his own fate were somehow linked with Forell's. 'Seriously, though, you must get your nerves under control. Here is the mess-tin and here on the bottom is my wife's address. The mess-tin is about the last thing you're likely to throw away, and that's why I put it there.'

Stauffer went into the corridor and listened for a moment. Then from behind the wainscot, he drew out a canvas bag, ready packed and strapped so that it could be carried on the shoulders like a rucksack. Forell tested the weight.

'About forty-eight pounds,' said the doctor. 'You'll find a good deal of bread in there and a small quantity of fat. Then, equally important as bread, methylated spirit in tablet form. And then tobacco—to trade with when you come across a likely inhabitant. There are just on four and a half pounds of that. This tinder-box you'd better put straight into your pocket. You know how to use it? Good. Even in wind? Excellent. But don't lose it! Whatever you do, hang on to your tinder-box! Without it, you're sunk. Now, the money —six hundred roubles. Here, put these in your pocket, too.

What you can buy with them, I wouldn't know. Probably nothing. Still . . .'

Doctor Stauffer prattled on excitedly, almost jovial for once. Forell could not keep his eyes off him. 'I'm coming too, you know—at least in spirit,' said the doctor. 'All this stuff was for my own escape. I started my plans before any of you —I was the first!'

Forell was dumbfounded, but the doctor left him no time to ask questions. 'You'd better keep your mind on your own affairs, at the moment. Hop into these underclothes; yes—straight away!'

There was no denying that the clothes were too wide for Forell's lean frame, but it seemed just as well, for the doctor told him:

'You'll need every stitch at night, when you're sleeping in the open, so you'll just have to put up with sweating by day. Leave nothing behind! Throw nothing away! You've got no furs, remember. Take off a few layers at night and lay them loosely over you, so as to leave air spaces, like a tent. And don't forget to cover your ears and nose!'

Then the doctor stretched down behind the wainscot and drew out a long knife in a wooden sheath. *Kandra* was the Siberian name for it. Forell had never seen one before, but from the feel of the supple double-edged blade he could tell it was excellent steel and if the Siberians preferred it to the short rigid clasp-knife, then he agreed with Doctor Stauffer, it would be worth having.

Next, came a pair of lace-up cavalry boots, from under the doctor's bed. Though not as watertight as jackboots, they would be easier to take off when wet, and the trouser legs could be laced inside them.

'Made in the U.S.A.,' said the doctor. 'The Russians have got a lot of these in store and never use them. Size twelve, that's right for you, isn't it? I take nines, but I managed to exchange them—pretended they were too small.'

Forell eyed the boots dubiously.

'They are the right thing for you,' said the doctor. 'Take it from me! I chose this type of boot for my own escape.'

'Then, if you don't mind me asking——' began Forell.

'—What am I doing here? I wanted everything to be just so, and I hadn't got a compass. Dechant was ahead of me there. You'd better have this. You wear it on the wrist, like a watch. Don't expect it to be accurate, and that goes for the map, as well.'

Doctor Stauffer chattered on, dispensing information, advice, encouragement—amongst other things, a vast array of facts about Siberia and its geography. How he had acquired them was a mystery, and Forell would never remember half.

71

But Stauffer was in his stride now, friendly, and at ease in a way Forell had never seen before. From scepticism he had turned to the opposite extreme, to a confidence so whole-hearted that it was almost aggravating.

The doctor had produced a small bottle of vodka for Forell to take with him. 'For emergency only, mind! I'll put it in the rucksack for you. You know that big stone out there, about a hundred yards away? I'll take your luggage out myself and leave it there tomorrow night, so that you won't be burdened with it when you're getting away from the hospital. Leave the building at nine, punctually. Have you got a watch? No, of course not; how could you? I was forgetting. . . . I'll keep the guard in conversation by the front entrance, while you go out by the back. Don't worry about the patients. They won't see you. They'll all be in their wards. By the way, did I tell you, you must sing when you're out there on your own? Talk to yourself. Did I tell you that?'

'Yes, several times.'

'If you see trees, you can talk to them. Otherwise, you may lose your voice.' Suddenly, as though by magic, Stauffer held out a handful of pistol ammunition. 'Recognize it?'

'Good Lord. . . !'

'Well, go on! Take it!'

'It won't be much good to me, I'm afraid.'

'Wait!' And the next moment, the doctor was holding a pistol in his hand. 'This has got to vanish again quickly. You carry it strapped between your legs—like this.' And before Forell could recover from his surprise, Stauffer had pushed the pistol down past his waist band, helped him draw one strap backwards through his legs, picked up the other, pulled it over his chest and buckled the two ends over the right shoulder. 'Sorry! But you've got to be quick! You know what happens if they catch you with that, don't you?'

'How did you manage. . . ?'

'Never mind about that! Now you've got it, hang on to it. It doesn't matter where it came from. I'm sorry there are only sixteen rounds.'

'They'll do!' He would keep eight of them in the pistol, Forell was thinking, ready for an emergency. Flash— detonation—recoil! The very violence of the image gave him a feeling of security and overwhelming power. Now that he had a pistol, the world seemed suddenly drained of its menace. No one would beat him up or push him around any more. He was master of his fate again.

And Doctor Stauffer? He was sorting some papers, meticulous as ever. Even with a pistol and sixteen rounds in his pocket, he had not dared strike a blow for freedom.

Stauffer looked up and gave a twitching frown, as though

he sensed what was in the other's mind. 'You'd better go to bed, Forell; get some sleep. But first—the small service you promised to do me, the message to my wife. I'll tell you now what you should say, because tomorrow there may not be time. If you see her, Forell—no. When you see her, tell her this: tell her I sent you, because I could not go myself. Tell her, I had everything ready for my own escape and I made my first attempt, which was unsuccessful, when we were in Tomsk. I was going to try again from the hospital, and I had made the most meticulous preparations—I think you'll agree there?——'

'Yes, indeed.'

'The most meticulous preparations, and then——'

And then he lost his nerve, thought Forell. Well, why make any bones about it? Why look as if he had to apologize?

'—And then, I realized there was no point, because I'd never get home. Forell, what I'm going to tell you is for yourself alone—do you understand?'

'Yes, yes, yes, of course.' Impatient for sleep, Forell looked stonily at the doctor. The next moment, he was numbed with horror as Stauffer said:

'Forell, I'm dying of cancer. . . . I see the thought distresses you, as it did me, when I first made the diagnosis. That was three months ago. I told myself that even the best doctors are notoriously incompetent when it comes to diagnosing themselves. I told myself that lead poisoning might produce symptoms very similar to those of cancer. But why should I get lead poisoning? I don't work in the mine! Well, that was three months ago. Since then, I have lived with the thought and—yes, I think, even accepted it, and now that I can look at it without fear, of course I know it's the truth.'

'Then what am I to tell your wife?'

'Not what I've just told you. That's not for her, Forell—not on any account. How far had we got with the message?'

'I am to tell your wife this, I am to say to her: I have come from your husband, Doctor Stauffer——'

'Doctor Heinz Stauffer.'

'Doctor Heinz Stauffer. He sent me, because he could not come himself. He tried to escape at Tomsk. He was going to try again from the hospital at East Cape, but——'

'—but he died in the winter of 1949. Then, describe to my wife that piece of ground behind the barracks where they usually bury us. My wife is a Christian, Forell, so remember to say they put a cross on my grave——'

Doctor Stauffer paused for a moment and then continued: 'I think you'd better say: "He died in March, 1950." That will make it sound a little less forlorn. It will be getting on for spring, then, and you can say that the snows had almost melted.'

The doctor was looking down at the table and his face was in shadow. When he spoke again, his voice was barely audible. 'Good luck. . . .'

* * *

Sunday, 30th October, 1949. At 9 p.m. precisely, Forell opened the back door of the hospital. Immediately, the wind slammed it heavily against his body and a pile of snow collected above the lintel fell, partly into the corridor, making it impossible to shut the door again. An icy draught began to tunnel through the building.

Half-way up the stairs at the far end, Doctor Stauffer was engaging the Russian guard in conversation. For two minutes only he had promised to hold him and in that time, Forell would have to disappear. He had a minute left now in which to free the door. He tore off his fur gloves and started to scoop out the snow. Every trace would have to be removed or its presence inside the corridor would show that someone had left the building. But even then the door still would not shut, and he had to scratch away the snow that had meanwhile frozen in the jamb before at last he could cross the threshold and close the door softly behind him.

Once outside the lee of the hospital hut, Forell caught the full blast of the wind. It was still snowing heavily, and bitterly cold. From time to time, a lump of half-frozen snow slapped against his ears, stinging like a wet hand. He started towards the rock where Stauffer had promised to leave his rucksack. Mingled with the storm he could hear the steady hiss of snow and then, from the direction of the guard-house, a burst of drunken laughter came past him on the wind. The next moment, one of his gloves blew off. He snatched for it, missed, and found himself flat on his face. Then the wind caught it and sent it scurrying across the snow. Scrambling to his feet, Forell gave chase. By the time he had caught it, the glove was wet inside, but he put it on nevertheless, knowing that his bare hands would quickly freeze.

He had carefully memorized the position of the rock and as he approached and his eyes became accustomed to the night, he could see the dark mass rearing above the snow. Feeling round the base of the rock, he found the rucksack on the far side from the hospital. Ready packed, with the *Kandra* fixed under the flap, shoulder straps—and then his fingers touched something else, made of wood. Taking off his gloves, he felt the shape more carefully : a pair of Siberian skis—Doctor Stauffer's parting gift.

74

The skis consisted of thin strips of birchwood, each about two feet long and pointed at either end. The points were bent upwards and held in position by lengths of thick catgut stretched between them. In the centre were two straps. The toe of the boot was slipped into one and the other was led up round the heel and fastened over the instep. Forell remembered seeing the convoy soldiers wearing skis like this when they had acted as pace-makers for the marching prisoners.

Forell glanced quickly round. Here and there, a lighted window gleamed faintly through the curtain of snow. All seemed deserted. Setting his route as best he could, he began to experiment with the skis, at first without the rucksack, going a short distance each time and then returning to where he had left it on the ground.

The skis, he discovered, were too short to bend at the beginning of a step, but lifted quite easily with the whole foot. It was thus possible to walk with them, or else slide forward keeping them on the ground. In either case, their tracks were shallow and would soon be obliterated by further snow. They were difficult to get used to, because of their length, which was four feet short of the normal. Twice, Forell tipped forward on to his nose, and once the rucksack landed on his head as well, and the experience could be highly unpleasant, with sharp stones lying just below the surface of the snow.

Getting used to the Siberian skis took time and gained him little ground. After thirty minutes of strenuous exertion he could still see lights glowing dimly behind him. By then, at any rate, he had learned how to place his weight and adjust his stride, finding that best use could be made out of the skis by treating them simply as outsize soles, enlarging the area of his tread.

Forell then took a compass bearing. He could see the lie of the needle, but its halves were of equal length and without a light he was unable to distinguish north. Again, off came the gloves and he delved for the tinder-box. By the aid of intermittent sparks he saw, this time, that he was heading in the right direction, due west. But there were no landmarks to keep him on his route and after half a mile he checked again with the compass. Still due west.

Then Forell remembered what Doctor Stauffer had said. 'Don't become a slave to your compass. Granted your general direction is west, your route, at any particular moment, lies where the going is easiest and there's least danger, even if it means going due south for a while. And to start with, until you're outside the area of search from the camp, all that matters is to keep on the move. Then, when you're no longer

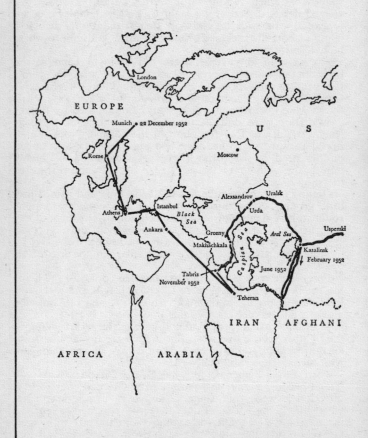

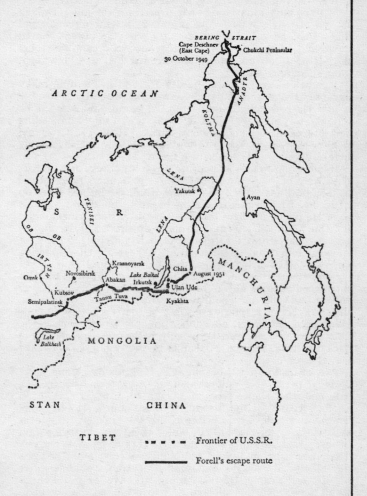

BERING STRAIT
Cape Deschnev
(East Cape)
30 October 1949
Chukchi Peninsular

ARCTIC OCEAN

AMADYR

KOLYMA

LENA

Yakutsk

Ayan

YENISEI

S   S   R

LENA

OB

OB

IRTYSH

Krasnoyarsk   Chita
Novosibirsk   August 1951   MANCHURIA
Omsk   Abakan   Lake Baikal
Kubsov   Irkutsk
Semipalatinsk   Ulan Ude
Tannu Tuva   Kyakhta

Lake
Balkhash

MONGOLIA

STAN   CHINA

TIBET   - - - - -   Frontier of U.S.S.R.

              ———————   Forell's escape route

being driven on by fear of pursuit, let yourself be lured on by the horizon and the prospect of the new country that lies beyond. After six weeks, when you've really got into your stride, you can start thinking about a definite objective.'

New country—that was what drew him on now. Though he had already traversed Siberia in the opposite direction and knew that, as yet, the new country was far distant, Forell could not altogether banish the seductive dream that next day, if he stood on tip-toe and craned his neck, he might glimpse another scene.

Meanwhile, progress was hard work and in the dim, milky expanse around him he could see that the ground was steadily rising. He had noticed that from the camp, and also, as he thought, a sprinkling of massive boulders on stony, undulating soil, but of these there was now no sign. Only an occasional shadow—a spur, perhaps—loomed ahead, to hover uncertainly before his eyes and then vanish again.

By now, the sweat was pouring down his cheeks and his ear-flaps were beginning to trouble him, simulating strange noises as they beat against his jaws in the wind. He pushed them up under his cap. Then frozen snow began to build up round his ears. He pulled the flaps down again and fastened them under his chin. The wind seemed to have dropped a little, though blowing now from his right and then whipping flurries of snow at him from straight ahead, it kept Forell wondering anxiously whether he was maintaining direction.

Sometimes, when the ground fell away from him, the skis threatened to run ahead of his legs. Then he would lean forward and the run would turn into a laborious walk. When the snow began to pile up against him at each step and the going became heavier, he would know he was climbing again. Once, a white wall reared suddenly before his eyes. He flung back his head, put out his hands to shield himself, clutched —nothing but air.

Part of his brain was beginning to long for dawn, and sleep. Twenty, twenty-five miles he should have done by then, a safe enough distance from the camp to justify rest, a good enough record for the first night of his journey to freedom. Twenty-five miles—before dawn. But the night was not over yet, whatever his exhausted body might try to make him believe. And in another part of his brain, he was pleased. That meant, he could still put a mile or two more between himself and the sleighs that sooner or later would set after him from the camp. He felt the urge to have the pistol closer to his hand, then remembered he had promised the doctor to keep it where it was, jolting and scraping between his legs, at any rate for the first two nights. That promise he would fulfil —at least he could do that much for Doctor Stauffer.

Yes, that much—and something more: another few miles before he stopped and made his bivouac. Gathering his ebbing strength, Forell began to count his steps, eyes bent on the few feet of snow ahead. As each foot came down, a number clicked in his brain. One—a hundred—five hundred—a thousand. Again, one to a thousand. And again. And another hundred or so while he was trying to remember whether it was three thousand he had done, or two. Every step, like that, brought its meed of achievement and gradually as he went on counting, peace came to his mind.

At the eight thousandth step—and with his stride that meant he had covered about four and a half miles—Forell stopped to take a bearing. His right hand began to feel for the tinder-box. Then with a shock he realized there was no need. He could see to read the compass without it. With dawn approaching, it was high time to find cover. The storm had slackened and visibility seemed to be improving. Stauffer had warned him that in open country by day, his dark form outlined against the snow would be visible for miles. Moreover, he could take it for granted that his pursuers would always see him first because their eyes would be used to the brilliance of the Siberian snows.

Seeing some rocks ahead of him outlined against the brightening sky, Forell made as fast as he could towards them. Among them was an enormous boulder about fifteen feet high. It looked ideal for his purpose. Blown over the top by the wind the snow was descending on the sheltered side almost vertically and had formed a drift high enough to conceal him from view. Having excavated a trough between the rock and the drift and looked out over the way he had come to make sure his tracks were now buried beneath further snow, he sat down with his back to the rock and rested his aching legs against the side of the mound.

For an hour he waited, not daring to open his rucksack in case he had to move again quickly. The straps had bitten into his shoulders and his leg muscles were twitching continually from the strain of the march. At last, hunger insisting, he took out a crust of bread and began gnawing at it slowly. 'Be hard on yourself,' he could hear Doctor Stauffer saying. 'Remember your food has got to last you a very long time. Ration it out, so much for each day, and then cut the ration by half. . . .' He would have bread only, then, for this first meal—no fat. He took out another crust and began chewing again. Every now and then, he stopped to listen, convinced his crunching could be heard for miles.

By now he was thirsty. The doctor had wrapped the tea in chamois leather to keep it dry, and just as well: if the snow continued much longer, the rucksack would be soaked right through. After listening to make sure the coast was clear, Forell stamped down a patch of snow and set up the cooking stand. With a base no bigger than a cigarette packet and the mess-tin on top, it had to be carefully balanced. To melt the snow which he had stuffed into the mess-tin took more meta cubes than expected; another time, he told himself, he would have to wait till he could find water. But it was worth it. The tea warmed him in a way which marching could never do and as he drank it, Forell realized that this was his first pleasurable sensation since he had closed the hospital door behind him.

It would be eight hours before he could be on the move again and meanwhile, he would have to stay where he was, like an animal gone to ground. With the tea inside him and sheltered in his trench, he began to feel pleasantly warm. It was still snowing and before going to sleep, he stuck the skis vertically into the drift on either side and laid the rucksack across the top to form a roof. Then, to the sound of the wind sighing and moaning over the rock above, the prisoner slept.

* * *

Some time later, Forell awoke in pitch darkness with the sound of a crash in his ears. He had been dreaming he was skiing down a grassy meadow when suddenly a chasm had opened at his feet and he had dropped down—down—to land with a jolt in the lead mine. He seemed to have hurt his face, for now, fully roused, he could feel it throbbing painfully. He put up a hand—and found the rucksack. The skis had toppled over, depositing it on his head while he slept.

And now it was night again. Forell stood up, aching with cold. His whole body was stiff, as though his muscles had lost their suppleness, like leather that has got wet and been dried out again. Groping in his rucksack for a crust of bread, he came upon a small oblong of bacon. For a moment he held it in his hand, undecided; then he put it back, closed the rucksack and started gnawing the crust of bread. Each time he carried it to his mouth, he caught the savour of bacon, till he was forced to put on his gloves, in case temptation became too strong. Tomorrow morning, he told himself, when he made his bivouac, he would eat just one small shaving of bacon. . . .

Forell shouldered his rucksack and, striking sparks from the tinder-box, took a compass bearing, setting his march due west. Then, a lonely figure, he set off into the freezing void. Only once during the whole of that night did any landmark appear to guide him on his way, and then as no more than a shadow looming ahead, slightly to the north of west. Keeping it on his right, Forell made towards it, only to see it vanish on his approach. Some time later, the same, or another shadow, appeared further northwards.

He was finding it easier to manage the skis now, though for some hours going was slow. After a while, he began counting his steps again. That, at least, convinced him he was making some progress and there was no other means of telling, for hour after hour, the world around him remained without contour or colour, while the only sound was the moaning of the wind. The hundreds he counted on his fingers, stretching them out one at a time. Thousands were represented by eight meta tablets, transferred from left pocket to right and then back again.

Some steps were very short and it seemed to Forell desperately important not to cheat and count half-steps as full digits. If he did, there would be no point in counting at all and nothing certain would be left in the world. One step equals one yard equals one digit: that was the key to the Universe. To restore its validity, he decided to count the whole of a long downhill run on the skis as only one step.

There remained the problem of the actual distance in a straight line that now lay between him and the camp. How many deviations had he made from due west, at what angle and what length? It was impossible to guess, so to allow what seemed a generous margin of error, Forell deducted one-fifth from the distance that his steps had covered. That left him within the radius of search still. Stauffer had put the limit at fifty miles, but it might be twice that distance. At any rate, whenever a man had been missing from the lead mine, the Russians had only abandoned the search after seven days, and in that time they could cover over two hundred miles.

For what remained of the night, Forell tramped on, stepping out the tens, the hundreds and the thousands, with some astronomical target at the back of his mind. With the dawn, the total was fifty-seven thousand. He then decided to make it sixty thousand before he bivouacked for the day, partly as a challenge to himself and partly because he was in open country where, if it stopped snowing and visibility cleared, his form would be seen for miles. And so, once again: ten — twenty — thirty — in whatever rhythm his exhausted body could maintain.

And then he came to a down-slope and he stopped counting as the skis started to run over the snow. After a while, as the slope flattened out into a valley, he began to lose speed. Then the skis were bumping over softer snow—coming to a stop —stopping. And suddenly, all resistance to their movement vanished and they were gliding over ice. Forell looked quickly

81

round—he could hear the ice creaking under foot—saw a watercourse, noted steep banks, poor cover for a bivouac, and then, forgetting that if it stopped snowing, his tracks would remain visible for days, started brushing the ice clear with his skis in an attempt to see which way the water underneath it was flowing. Upstream was the right direction for him; downstream would lead ultimately to the sea. But upstream, according to the compass, was due east; not west. Exhausted and baffled, Forell began to slide further upstream to discover the general lie of the river.

Somewhere close at hand, he could hear water moving freely. He stopped to listen. As he did so, he felt the ice shift under his feet. Suddenly there was a loud crack and the next moment, Forell was knee-deep in freezing water.

Instinct prompted him to lay himself flat, but as he leaned forward on to the moving ice, the surface parted, and a moment later, a second time. By then, he was nearing the bank and, scrambling over some boulders, he managed to wade ashore without sinking into the water beyond his knees. Once on the bank, he could see some distance upstream. The river-bed came down in a series of steps and was liberally strewn with rocks, topped, where they emerged above water, with a crust of frozen spray.

Shivering on the bank, Forell realized now that, all the time he had been struggling in the river, his brain had been busy with a ridiculous childhood rhyme:

> 'Papa said, Cyril! I forbid it!
> And yet the headstrong Cyril did it,
> Cyril went out skating on the pond.'

And very foolish, too, thought Forell—very foolish of both of us. . . .

He was beginning to feel mortally cold. He tried to undo the ski-straps, so as to get his boots off, but the water in them had already frozen and they wouldn't move. For a moment, Forell thought of carrying straight on with the march, hoping that the movement would restore his circulation. Then he realized it was impossible; the cotton wool padding in his trousers was sodden with water and however long he walked, it would never dry out by the warmth of his body alone. Not only that, but his energy was almost spent. At the outside, he could only keep going for a couple of hours; then he would collapse from exhaustion and in thirty degrees of frost he would be dead almost before he touched the ground.

For some seconds, while the last vestige of warmth seemed to ebb from him, Forell was incapable of thought or action. A picture came before his mind, a picture of a dog-team, a flurry of snow—a sleigh—two soldiers. How he wished they would come. . . .

The wish recoiled into action. He slipped off the rucksack and laid it on a nearby stone. Then he was tearing the laces from his boots. Boots and skis came off together. Then stockings, trousers, underpants. He put the cap on the ground to stand on, stumbled trying to step in and found his bare feet in the snow. But they felt warmer for it, if anything, so he rubbed them over with more snow, then planted them firmly in the cap. Next, off came the jacket to wrap round his legs, And then, behind a conveniently large boulder, a long and desperate attempt to make a fire of sodden meta tablets with sparks from a sodden flint. It was half an hour before he could produce the first low, flickering flame.

When the meta tablets, piled up like a house of cards, finally caught light, he started to dry his clothes, holding them as close to the flame as he could without singeing them, and so warming his hands as well. He was determined to use what heat there was to the utmost; the tablets were too precious to waste on the Siberian sky.

Meanwhile, wearing only the four shirts he had set out with, his bare feet stuck in his cap and the jacket wrapped round his legs, he was agonized with cold. He began to wonder whether he should break up the skis and add them to the fire. But the trouser legs were actually beginning to show some dry patches by now, and that gave him just enough encouragement to consider what would happen if he did burn the skis. It was quite simple. If he burnt the skis, he would probably be caught; and that would mean a much more unpleasant end than quietly freezing to death, here, by himself in the snow.

One heap of methylated tablets had been consumed, a second, and now the third was beginning to burn low. There were enough left for one more heap, but if they went, so would all possibility of brewing a hot drink. And even if he did come across wood, or twigs in this denuded landscape, the fire would be certain to betray him to his pursuers. Forell felt the stockings—they were still wet, frozen stiff by now, so they would have to go. The underpants, despite being held to the flame till they singed, also refused to dry; they too, would be sacrificed. It was impossible to dry the boots, so at the last moment, before the flame expired, he would warm them a little inside. The trousers, he would put on straight away. That done, he could put the jacket on again.

Having got so far, Forell ate a crust of bread and a small piece of bacon. Then he remembered the doctor's vodka, 'for emergency use only'. This was undoubtedly an emergency and it justified one small sip. The sip turned out to be smaller than intended, so Forell took another small sip. Then he put on his boots, lacing them up with difficulty because of his frozen fingers. Then he felt an urge to talk.

'What a fool!' he said, looking at the pistol where he had left it on a stone. 'Forgotten to hoist in the pistol!'

He noticed his voice sounded strangely harsh; still, it was a comfort to hear even himself talking, as Stauffer had foretold. 'Stauffer!' he said loudly. 'Stauffer-r-!' That was better; that had cleared his throat. Now he could talk to the man. 'Like all doctors, you, Herr Stauffer, are just a little bit too fussy. Surely to God, if I'm going to use the pistol, I'm going to need it quickly? Stands to reason! So why hide it away? No, no, doc-doctor! It's silly! Besides, it's a very fine pistol! From now on, it's going to be in my pocket.'

He picked up the pistol and twirled it on his finger, till the freezing steel began to burn his skin, then, frowning peevishly, he thrust it away. The boots felt like blocks of ice and very uncomfortable. The leather seemed to have buckled in places and was chafing the skin. He decided to cut up a shirt and bind the cloth round his feet. For that, he needed the Siberian knife. He grasped for his rucksack, bawling, 'Kandra! Come here!'

The knife was very sharp and the experience of cutting a shirt off his own back seemed to strike him as funny. He laughed loudly, then once more unlaced his boots, bound up his feet and laced them up again, talking to himself continually. 'Hm! Excellent!' he muttered, as the cloth began to take up the warmth from his feet, then, remembering how near he had been to disaster, said in a tone of sorrowful reproach, 'Oh, you bloody fool. . . .'

Still chattering carelessly away, Forell started stamping round to warm his feet, picking up his belongings as he found them and restoring them to the rucksack. He came on eight meta tablets that must have fallen out of his pocket. They were lying on a stone and quite dry. With an indifferent gesture, he cast them on the fire. . . .

It was time to be going. The snow all round was churned up with his tracks, the site was exposed and before long the daylight would begin to fade. Forell consulted the compass. Due west, if the compass could be trusted, lay straight uphill. All he wanted was sleep, somewhere under cover from wind, weather and Russians where he could lie up in safety until he had regained his strength.

Forell slowly hoisted the rucksack on to his shoulders and stepped out, groaning, on his way. No sleep for almost twenty-four hours, half frozen to death, and now drunk on a sip of vodka, he would never get far. It was all he could do to stand upright, let alone move, let alone count his steps. The bright light was hurting his eyes. Dimly he remembered that

Stauffer had included a pair of makeshift sun-glasses with the gear. They would be somewhere in the rucksack. But the very idea of unshouldering it again and then routing about inside made him feel weak. In any case, his eyes would not be troubled for long, soon they would shut of their own accord.

Forell laboured on, trudging slowly uphill. They way was becoming steeper and there seemed to be rocks all around. Suddenly his foot slipped on a stone and he nearly fell over. He stopped—and realized he could do no more. He was spent, and sinking to his knees.

Slowly Forell moved his head, left, and then right, looking for cover, saw some rocks close together on the same level as he, a few yards away. Now he was groping towards them, climbing in between two of the largest, finding room to lie down, slipping out of the pack-straps, feet out of the skis. A hand dropped to the ground, gripped, and lifted some snow to his gums. Hot tea would be better, better than snow—but better than either was sleep.

Forell awoke in full daylight to the sound he had most dreaded to hear: the shrill yapping of a sleigh team. With lurching heart he scrambled to a gap between the rocks and peered out over the snow. Yes, there they were, a full team —fifteen dogs,—curving across in a foam of white—two men on the sleigh—soldiers—yes, from the camp! The iron sleigh told him that, the kind they had always used. Forell gripped his pistol.

The sleigh was passing out of sight behind a rock as it rounded the base of the hill. If it kept on turning, it would cross Forell's tracks of the previous day, and the soldiers would never miss those. They were shouting to each other in a series of yells—on sleigh journeys, everyone yells—and the sounds seemed to be getting louder. Forell jumped to another gap, keeping them in view. They were below him now, coming towards him. He could see their uniforms, and the tommy-gun slung over the shoulder. In a few moments, they would be almost within range. He was tempted to shoot first, then thought it would be better to wait. If he missed either shot, the next would have to be for himself. But if the men spotted his tracks, or saw something suspicious and came up to investigate, he could wait till they were almost on him and make sure of them both.

The dogs seemed to know their route exactly. Heading towards Forell in a wide, right-handed curve, they came to within about seventy yards and then, of their own accord, suddenly changed direction and made off down the left bank of the river below the hill, missing his tracks by at least twice that distance. Two minutes from its first appearance, the sleigh was only a distant speck trailing a pennon of powdery snow. The shouts of the soldiers were still faintly audible, but soon, as their figures dissolved into the distant horizon, the sounds died with them and silence returned once more.

The soldiers had searched in a wide circle and now they were on their way back to camp, that much was clear. The direction they had taken was therefore approximately east. Feeling that there was no need to wait until darkness before resuming the march, Forell made ready and then set off in the opposite direction. To start with, he followed the sleigh tracks westwards, knowing that the dogs would have chosen firm ground.

Having survived the last attempt that the Russians at the lead mine would probably make to recapture him, Forell felt pleasantly relaxed, almost like a tourist. Instead of keeping them all in the rucksack, he put some crusts in his pocket, so that he could eat when he felt like it on the march. When hunger told him it was lunch-time, he seated himself comfortably on a stone and treated himself to the best picnic meal he could devise, none other than the fat little fish that had tasted so nauseating when last he had tried them in hospital. But they were the ideal food to give stamina and protection against cold, for they formed the staple diet of the sleigh dogs, whose work required a full measure of both.

The sleigh had approached in a wide circle and then disappeared behind him, heading east. To keep to a westerly direction, he had, therefore, to cross the tracks at the proper moment and then diverge from them steadily. When later he checked with the compass, it showed that he had guessed the moment correctly and that he had been marching, as he intended, due west.

That evening, for the first time, he was unable to find good cover for the night. Aware of the danger of having to make it in the open, he prepared his bivouac with the utmost care, not forgetting to eat some more of the little fish, so that their fat should help to prevent him freezing to death in his sleep.

*　　*　　*

'A man can get used to anything,' Doctor Stauffer had said, 'even, if need be, to dying. . . .'

The doctor had spoken from experience and after three weeks on the march, Forell also had learned the truth of, at any rate, the first part of the dictum. By then, he had got used to a lot of things—sleeping in the bitterest cold, for instance, keeping warm enough to avoid frost-bite by forming a tent with his clothes. Indeed, he had got used to so much that he was beginning to be bored. For the sake of variety, then, he altered his routine, sometimes starting from his bivouac long before dawn and continuing until late afternoon; at others, marching only at night, so incidentally making the most of a full moon. But whether he marched by day or by night was entirely a matter of whim. There was no purpose involved, other than to do what pleased him best; making plans, he had discovered, was a waste of time. Where Dannhorn's map showed mountains, it turned out to be moor, and when the compass told him that one point was due west of another, Forell had only to reach the first and take the bearing of the second to find that it lay in any direction but due east behind him.

To allow for this almost universal uncertainty, Forell was content to cut Doctor Stauffer's operation order by a good half. The object to be attained remained, of course, the same. Information regarding enemy troops, as on most other subjects, was nil. The method to be employed in order to achieve the object was simply to march due west, and failing that, to march in any direction except back to the lead mine. That was all, apart from Forell's purely private conviction that in the first three weeks he had covered a distance of well over a thousand kilometres, in other words, six hundred and twenty-five miles.

So far, the march had taken him across forlorn and barren country with hardly a single distinctive feature on which to take a compass bearing. Once indeed, where the ground was more undulating, he had been able to bivouac under trees. They had turned out to be alders, curiously stunted compared with the ones he remembered, with gnarled, wind-swept branches. Still, it had gladdened his heart to see them, and made him feel nearer home.

Two days later he had come upon some willows growing in marshy soil. He cut down and trimmed a couple of rods to serve as supports for his surplus clothing at night, carrying them sticking out sideways under the flat of his rucksack.

Otherwise, the only relief from the universal blanket of snow had been some dark patches near marshy ground, where the first falls had melted in the muddy water and then been congealed by subsequent frosts into lasting stains, like smudges of ink on blotting paper. Plodding on in the lifeless silence, Forell had been content to wear Doctor Stauffer's patent eye-shields which he had contrived to make from the gill-covers of a large fish. The underlying vertical clefts proved excellent light filters. Often enough, though, the 'glasses', combined with optical illusions, had shown him what seemed like dark masses of rock lying on the horizon, until spurred on towards them in the hope of finding a place to bivouac or simply a change of scenery on the far side, Forell had seen the dark shapes dissolve on his approach, leaving nothing but further vistas of blank, monotonous snow.

Day after day that had happened and so when, one afternoon, he reached the top of a rise and saw the familiar dark mass ahead, he failed, for a moment, to recognize it. That was the trouble with these airy nothings—they misled so often that, finally, the eyes refused to see what was really there. But this time, the mirage was not on the skyline but down below, in a valley, spreading for some distance to right and left. Forell pushed up his snow-blinkers and made a careful scrutiny. From where he was standing, there was no doubt about it; the mirage looked remarkably like a forest of trees. With a long stick, cut some time before from the group of willows, he thrust forward into a ski run. Gliding swiftly down, he noticed that the dark shapes were not receding before him, but stayed solidly in position—like scenery in a theatre, he told himself, as he began to distinguish groups of what looked like poplars, or asps, dotted about in the barren landscape with an effect so incongruous and surprising that they might almost have been lowered from pulleys a few seconds before.

Half expecting to see them vanish again skywards, Forell shouted 'Ho!' as he ducked under the fringe of the trees. 'Oh!' came the echo. So they were real trees, in a real wood! He felt the bark and examined some foliage which he found beneath a loose covering of snow and identified the trees as asps.

Though it was still early afternoon—he judged it to be about 2 p.m.—he unshouldered his rucksack, found a more or less dry spot to lay it on, and began collecting firewood. There was plenty lying about under the trees and soon Forell was holding the magnificent eighteen-inch slow-match from the never failing Puschka to an imposing pile of moss, dead foliage and brushwood. As a light wind drove the flame roaring and crackling underneath and the first streamers of grey-black smoke swept up through the trees, he glanced round to make sure he was still alone. It would have been a choice moment indeed to have found a soldier in M.V.D. uniform at his elbow! Then, as the flames began to leap, he stepped back, gazing at them with tremulous joy, like some small boy who has braved authority's ban and plays with fire.

Standing to windward, Forell watched the column of dense smoke rise between the trees and lose itself among the topmost branches. The dead and rotting wood contained a lot of moisture and was hissing and spitting as the flames caught hold. He edged in towards them, standing as close as the heat would allow, turning this way and that to dry out his clothes.

Once properly alight, the fire soon needed replenishing. This time, Forell climbed the nearest tree and hacked with the Siberian knife at some branches as thick as his arm, till, with a sharp crack, the frosted wood snapped and fell to the ground. Cut up into shorter lengths and piled on the fire, the branches were slow to burn and as the ground beneath them thawed and added its moisture to theirs, a gigantic pillar of black smoke went spiralling skywards.

By now it was about four o'clock and the daylight was beginning to fade. He pared down some of the branches he had felled to serve as a bed for the night. Though hard, they would at least keep him off the wet ground and he could sleep, then, close in to the fire. Meanwhile, on a sudden impulse, he decided to treat himself to a kind of sauna bath. Taking off all his clothes, including the four shirts and layer upon layer of underclothing he strung them out on some nearby branches, plunged out from beneath the trees and rubbed himself down with snow. Then, like some apparition from a prehistoric age, he stood with his long hair straggling down his face, and warmed himself before the flames. Again, he dashed out into the snow to wash the last traces of dirt and sweat from his beard and head before returning once more to the fire to dry himself finally and put on his clothes.

Still as close as he could get to the blaze and dressed, now, except for his boots, Forell sat down to eat with the rucksack between his knees—bread, a little fat that Stauffer had salvaged from the skimmings of some dubious concoction, and, to celebrate the arrival of the trees, one of the two last remaining ounces of bacon. Then he smoked a cigarette, rolling it from a page of *Pravda* ready cut into convenient widths and lighting it with a glowing stick from the fire.

After burning for four hours, the fire was down to the embers, but the red hot mass would last through the night and the prospect of sleeping in real warmth was a cheering one. Forell felt contented, no more than usually hungry, and being completely dry for the first time since his escape from the lead mine, he began gradually to take a more sanguine view of things. It seemed possible, after all, that these random wanderings might ultimately lead him, if not to freedom, then at least to a place where he would be allowed to live out his natural life as something better than a slave. He dared not hope for more.

It was a pity, thought Forell, that he had not got a better newspaper than *Pravda*, something altogether more gossipy, with lots of startling pictures. How nice it would be to read of violence and disaster, now that he himself felt so secure —an earthquake, for instance, in Anatolia, or a putsch in San Salvador. And then, as a soporific before going to bed, one or two homely touches about the market price of turnips, and broad beans. Yes, that would be nice. . . .

Forell pushed back the rucksack for a pillow and lay down by the fire. It was dark now all around, but that was in another world. His eyes were on the glowing embers, the white sparks that settled here and there on the red, gleamed and vanished again.

Yes. Very nice to have one of those papers from home. Would there be, he wondered, yawning—would there be a little paragraph in a corner, at the bottom of a page somewhere, about that poor devil who was taken for slave labour by the Russians—who escaped—and who, after long years and many vicissitudes, finally—finally—reached——? But the rest was only a dream.

*　　*　　*

The fire had lasted well. With the daylight, the last embers were still glowing with enough heat to melt snow and boil water for tea. Looking round at the groups of trees, Forell was struck again by their resemblance to a stage set. 'Scene: a glade in the forest.' Only there was no forest, not even a wood, simply clumps of trees in echelon as far as the eye could see, screening the view.

When Forell saw what lay beyond the trees, he stood aghast, horrified by the sight which met his eyes—a smooth, limitless expanse of frozen sea. At one bow, all his hopes and calculations and sense of achievement were shattered. The sea mocked at his careful compass bearings, derided his map, swept away self-confidence and optimism as though they had never been. If this truly was the sea, then nothing would ever be certain again. Forell knew nothing about the sea, except that, for him, it spelt danger. Coast-land, however, inhospitable, attracted people of all kinds, scientists studying erosion, tides, rock formations; geologists looking for surface coal; coast-guards; meteorologists; fishermen; and, of course, the Red Army, guarding its slaves. 'Keep clear of the coast,' the doctor had said. And so Forell had intended. . . .

But was this the sea? Would the sea be frozen over at this time of year? Was it ever frozen completely? Surely the salt would stop it freezing? And it looked very smooth, more like a lake. . . . Questions, doubts, everything he had ever heard on the subject of the sea began to chase through Forell's mind. Whenever, once a week or a fortnight, the prisoners at East Cape had been allowed up into the daylight, the first thing that Dannhorn had always looked at was the sky. Usually it was grey and shrouded in mist, but sometimes it glittered, dazzling the eyes, and then Dannhorn would say: 'The drift-ice is on the move. We shall have cold weather.' Curiously enough, when the sky was overcast, it was warmer, the reason, according to Dannhorn, being that the sky reflected the light off the sea and was darker when the latter was ice-free. Then, thought Forell, if that vast stretch of ice in front of him were really the sea, the sky ought to be bright right up to the horizon. But it was not, therefore——?

But who could believe anything that Dannhorn said? So much that he had asserted as a fact had been quite incapable of proof. Heavy in heart, weak-limbed and feeling totally helpless, Forell got out the map, to gaze abstractedly at the faint criss-cross of lines. Sometimes they indicated mountains, sometimes rivers, and often, apparently, nothing at all. Of sea, or coast there was not a sign. What did it matter? For nearly a month, he had marched, with detours, admittedly, occasionally south and north to avoid some obstacle, or cancel a previous error, but always with west as his general direction, because it was a continent and not an ocean that lay between him and his home. But now the ocean lay before him, what need had he of maps or of the intelligent Dannhorn to know that he had marched in vain?

Folding the map and restoring it to the lining-pocket of his coat, Forell stood, for a moment, inert and with vacant gaze, while his mind adjusted itself to the new necessity. Then his legs were moving again and the first step had already been taken, back inland, away from the sea.

It was towards midday, when the sea was still in full view, that the wind freshened and started to blow inland. The sun was shining and on the distant horizon a layer of haze began to detach itself and rise up the sky in a veil of gold. As it did so, land came into view, with wooded slopes descending to a shore.

Forell's first reaction, on meeting that morning with the sea, had been to get away from it again, even though it meant marching due east. But if he had escaped his pursuers by keeping hitherto to what the compass told him was due west, then to march in the opposite direction would surely lead him back towards them again. Ludicrous indeed! Yet there had seemed no alternative. Now, with land visible on the far side of the ice, the situation was different. Was it the mainland and the ice merely a frozen inlet of the sea? If it were, then Forell might be able to continue his land-march due west again. On the other hand, it might be an island. Forell decided he would have to find out. That meant crossing the ice, and since the morning when he had fallen into the river and nearly died of cold, the mere sight of ice had filled him with horror. But there seemed no alternative.

Retracing his steps, he went down to the verge and then, crawling out as far as he dared, knelt down on his skis, took out the Siberian knife and started to cut through the ice to test its depth. Occasionally, far out, he could hear a dull grinding sound, as though the surface were beginning to shift. Before the first sign of water appeared, the knife had sunk in to a reassuring depth and when it finally broke through and Forell measured the thickness of the ice, he found it was considerably more than the span of his hand. He made up his mind to risk it, and began to walk slowly forward, taking short steps and counting them so as to maintain an even rhythm. The skis he preferred to hold, one in each hand, ready to go on all fours and place half his weight on them if the singing of the ice dropped at any time to a more sinister note. The land approached more quickly than he had expected and soon, intent on what he could see he lost count of the distance covered. Immediately ahead of him was a tree-lined shore, but to right and left, still only ice and sky. It seemed to be an island.

Stepping cautiously off the ice, he followed the shore for a while, going west by the compass. Then as soon as the daylight began to fade, he chose a place to bivouac and built another fire. This time, though the wood was drier than the aspen branches of the night before, it gave out less heat and, to Forell, seemed to burn with a less cheerful flame. At any rate, disturbed by the day's experiences, exhausted, but with nerves still on edge from the perilous journey across the ice, he could find little joy in his bonfire. And not even sleep would come. For a long time he lay, hungry and depressed, watching the flickering smoulder of the logs. All around, outside the firelight, the darkness was complete. If only he could sleep. . . .

Suddenly: 'Hyi-yi!' A long quavering call, from the woods, somewhere beyond the fire.

He sat up and listened. Now there was another sound, a strange shifting and thrusting among the trees, as though something were creeping towards him on innumerable little feet. And then he gave a cry of fear. A horrible face, hairy and angular, had appeared in the flickering firelight, then vanished again.

'Hyi-yi!' The shout again, closer now, and then another voice, echoing further off. When he looked back to the fire, the face was there, gazing at him steadily. Shaggy neck, impassive, glittering eyes—and antlers: a reindeer. . . . Sitting astride over the forelegs was a man, riding the animal like a donkey. The man said something in a strange language, speaking with a high, nasal infection. Forell gathered it was a question.

He stood up, so as to see more of the speaker. 'I am on a journey and made the fire because I don't want to freeze,' he said, speaking in German.

Behind the rider a second man had appeared in the circle of the firelight and was watching Forell with curiosity. He looked younger than the first, and was on foot.

Forell thought it was better to keep talking, say anything rather than be silent. Silence seemed somehow to convey guilt. And it was clear that the men could not understand a word he said. 'Yours are the first faces I've seen for a month. I wonder who you are and what you're doing here?'

Perhaps, like Forell a moment earlier, the rider had caught the inflexion and understood that it was a question. At any rate, he seemed to think it was his turn to speak, and he spoke a great deal, glancing from time to time at his companion, as though urging him to confirm what he said. In conclusion, he took his nose between finger and thumb and gave it a long and energetic blow.

Meanwhile, more reindeer had come up and were standing silently round the fire, their eyes shimmering green in the flickering light. Standing by one of them, the younger man was trying to communicate in Russian. Forell pretended not to understand his words. He had no idea where he was or who these men were that had thrust themselves in on his bivouac, and rather than have to give an account of himself, he felt it was wiser to leave the gulf of understanding unbridged. But as the two strangers seemed to enjoy talking, he would talk, too—in German.

'What you say goes round here, doesn't it? If you wanted to, you could hand me over to the Russians tomorrow. You could. But why should you; can you tell me that?'

For answer, the shepherds began an animated discussion between themselves. What they were saying, it was impossible to guess, so Forell felt there was no harm in pretending he could understand every word.

'Now, friends!' he began, breaking in, again in German. 'Don't let's have any trouble! What's the good of it? What's the point? You go your way, and I'll go mine. And I'll tell you where I'm going—I don't care where it is, but I'm going somewhere where a man can live! I'm fed up with existence on this moon!'

The reindeer men nodded vigorously. Yes, they could understand that, and, even if they could not, they liked to hear him talk. The younger of them smiled encouragingly.

'I'm a prisoner-of-war, that's what I am, and I've a right to be treated as such. I've a right to be sent home, back to Germany, in a first-class carriage, because I'm an officer. But the Russians don't think so. They sent me to the lead mines, to work for them, as a slave. But I'm not. I'm a prisoner-of-war. "*Kriegsgefangener.*" D'you get it? "*Voenna Plenny!*"'

Ah! The words were out. That the shepherds could indeed understand, and they nodded with new and vigorous emphasis.

'*Nyemetz!*' said Forell.

'Ah! Ah!'

'*Germanski!*'

'Oh....' At the revelation, the whole herd of reindeer seemed to become restless. But the elder shepherd, still astride his steed, was highly impressed. He blew his nose and then began to gesticulate with his bare hands, conveying his meaning with such skill that when he paused now and then to reflect, it seemed to be his fingers that were thinking what they should say next.

At the conclusion of his speech, the shepherd bowed courteously, smiled, and then waited to hear what Forell had to say. Anxious not to offend, the latter bowed once or twice in return, and said, 'Ah——!'

He gathered now that the elder shepherd was named Pehtak and the younger, who spoke some Russian, seemed to be called Laatmai. But he could not be sure; the words might not be names at all. Having got off his steed, the elder said something to Laatmai, who now disappeared behind the trees, while Pehtak, using a Siberian knife, swiftly lopped some branches to revive the dying fire. Apparently the men had no intention of moving on with their herd, but were going to stay with Forell—perhaps to take him with them on the morrow and hand him back to the Russians. He put down a hand to feel for his pistol; it was still there.

Beaming as though he had just discovered a vein of gold, Laatmai returned with a skin of tightly stretched leather and urged Forell to drink. Balancing the skin inexpertly as the leather gave under his fingers, Forell felt warmth between his hands. Milk? '*Moloko?*' The reindeer men nodded, smiling, and showed him how to tip the milk down his throat. He swallowed a little for the sake of politeness. Reindeer milk? He set the huge skin to his mouth again and drank deeper this time, noting how much better it tasted than the goat's milk he had once tried at home. Once the skin had been taken up, it seemed contrary to custom to set it down again before it was empty. Pehtak lifted it almost reproachfully from the ground where Forell had deposited it, drank and passed it to Laatmai, Laatmai to Forell, and, well—though the taste had not improved during the round, Forell drank again.

This seemed the moment to offer his hosts some tobacco. At any rate, they would appreciate the gesture. But there was no reason why they should see how much of it he had, and how little food. Without revealing its contents, Forell groped in his rucksack and collected a quantity of Machorka in the hollow of his hand. The stuff looked like chicken feed. The shepherds were delighted. In gratitude, Laatmai seized his right wrist and Pehtak leaned over and placed a hand on his knee and, though Forell could not understand a word, there was so much friendly vehemence in their accompanying speeches that he failed to notice how easily they could have brought down the Siberian knife on the nape of his neck, split the rest of the Machorka between them and still have looked forward to another good kilo from the Russians as a reward for his severed head.

After a lot more talk, neither side understanding what the other was saying, Forell started to make his bed for the night. Roaring with laughter, the shepherds broke in on his preparations. That wasn't the way to do it! And before he knew what was happening, Laatmai had scratched up a quantity of moss from where the long tree-roots sank into the ground and placed it in the hollow fork between two of the largest. 'It's warmer like this,' his smile seemed to say.

Miming his words, Forell tried to discover how the shepherds made their beds in areas where there was no moss to be found. In answer, Laatmai made a sweeping gesture over the countryside. His meaning was clear: there was moss everywhere. And if need be: Laatmai clicked his fingers in the direction of the grazing herd and soon, of the several that had come up, one of the reindeer had settled itself down at his back, where it continued to chew like a contented cow.

So as to be ready with his pistol in case of trouble, Forell had intended only to doze. But the moss was so much more comfortable to sleep on than branches that, in the event, it was the shepherds who woke him next morning with a fresh skin of milk and an invitation to partake of their cheese. Oh! That cheese. . . . By an effort of imagination, he succeeded in getting some of it down. Those black specks, he told himself, were probably pepper; and anyway, why be squeamish? The stuff smelled no worse than a ripe gorgonzola.

The reindeer men looked at the sky. Not much wind; not too cold. The weather seemed set for the day. As they talked, Forell had no doubt of their meaning—they were content to stay where they were. The herd, consisting of about eight hundred reindeer were finding plenty of moss under the snow. In a few weeks' time, so Laatmai succeeded in explaining, they would be joined by two more herds, each roughly of the same size. Then they would set off for the village, for the *kolchoz*. For the first time, the German had heard a word that frightened him. Somewhere, then, there was a collective farm, even for wandering shepherds like these. But, in that case, they were not independent, but a part of the System, outposts, almost, of the Communist Regime, and for an escaped prisoner-of-war who had come in contact with them the consequences might be highly unpleasant.

Forell tried to discover in what direction the shepherds were intending to go with their herd. One of them pointed an arm: over there! And that, according to the compass, was due east.

How far were they going?

Oh, about three hundred versts. . . .[1]

Good. Forell decided he would try to stay with them, for a few days at any rate. By then, he might have been able to discover where he was and which was the best route for his further journey. He pointed to the ice. Was that the sea? Laatmai shrugged, then gestured, meaning, 'if you're asking whether you can come with us; yes, why not?' Though, once mentioned, the word 'kolchoz' seemed to lie like a blight over their nomad, desultory life, and he had no proof apart from their smiling hospitality that he could trust these men, Forell was only too glad to stay with them, for the sake of company. He was beginning to realize now that he had been too long alone.

While Pehtak shouldered a rifle and went off in search of game, Laatmai showed Forell how to fish through the ice. After going some distance from the shore, Laatmai broke open the surface with an axe and trimmed off a neat, rectangular hole, carefully clearing every chip of ice from the water so that it would not immediately freeze over again. Signing to Forell to keep still, he lowered the hooks and lines and then the two men crouched down to wait.

They waited in silence for a while; then, in a mixture of gesture and speech, Laatmai began to talk about women. The drift of what he was saying was clear: he was longing to get back to the kolchoz, to his woman. His high-pitched voice sang on in an even, expressionless tone. Only his eyelids, drooping languidly and puckered at the corners, betrayed the sensual colour of his thoughts.

Forell nodded, showing that he understood. But Laatmai was not satisfied. A nod was not enough. He had confessed his innermost thoughts and now it was Forell's turn. Had not Forell got a woman, a wife perhaps, waiting for him somewhere?

Yes. Oh, yes. . . .

What was she like to look at? What sort of shape? With his hand Laatmai sketched a tentative curve in the air. Something like that?

Yes, something like that.

[1] 187 miles.

'A——!' Laatmai grinned appreciatively. Then his strange, half-oriental face assumed a paternal expression and his outstretched hand patted a small, invisible head. Children? You, too—yes?

Yes. And then Forell had to show how many, and how old and how tall his children had been when last he had seen them. Laatmai seemed satisfied. He could picture them now. There was silence for a moment. Then, he looked puzzled. But where were they? Were Forell's children in a *kolchoz*?

No.

Then where were they?

They were in a town called Munich, almost on the other side of the world.

And Munich was his home?

It had been.

He was a long way from home, then?

Yes.

The young man was sorry, Forell could see that. He put his head on one side, and pouted his lips, and looked sad. . . .

They stayed a long time yet, fishing through the ice and as Laatmai talked on, miming his words, Forell began to admire this young man—he could only be about twenty-eight—who was able to convey his meaning so quickly and resourcefully even in complicated things. Having only a smattering of Russian, Laatmai spoke in his own, incomprehensible language—and he spoke a great deal. But speech was merely an accompaniment to the real talking, which was done by gesture and facial expression. There, Laatmai's vocabulary was immense. He could convey confidence by the lift of an eyebrow, and caution with a smile.

By the time they returned, with six great fish as long as his arm, Forell was aching with cold. Pehtak had put up a tent and was now skinning a small animal of its fur. Of the reindeer, there was not a sign. Seeing Forell's surprise, Laatmai explained that, of their own accord, the animals moved on a little each day towards the village. 'Village' meant *kolchoz*. Forell knew that now. A village he would gladly enter, but not a collective farm. It was difficult to explain, but at last Laatmai's eyes gave a flash of understanding and he hastened to reassure: 'It will be all right; you'll see.'

Forell failed to recognize the animal that Pehtak was skinning but from its stench thought it might be a skunk. From the skunk, Pehtak's hands passed straight to gutting the fish. Forell swore he would eat no supper, but when the fish had been fried over a fire and, following the others' example, he took a piece from the ashes with his fingers, he was surprised to find that it tasted excellent. Yes, a very fine fresh water fish, indeed. . . .

So that vast stretch of ice out there was not the sea, after all! Here was Forell's chance to explain his mistake to the reindeer men, and ultimately he succeeded—ultimately, because they found it hard to believe that anyone could be such a fool as to think a lake was the ocean. But Forell was that fool, and the fact seemed to give them enormous enjoyment. They laughed, and roared, and slapped their thighs —paused to gaze at him in blank astonishment, then laughed and roared again. Even Pehtak, who was more taciturn than Laatmai and seldom given to smiling, finally choked himself with his guffaws and coughed up most of his supper into the fire.

'Lamu', or something like it, was what they called the ocean, and they wanted nothing to do with that. Lamu was bad, through and through, evil-tempered, treacherous—an enemy to man. What did Forell think this was—a lake? And they laughed again. It wasn't even that! It was a river; the river Anadyr! Forell thought they were pulling his leg. He showed them the thin hairline on the map that was marked 'r. Anadyr'. Surely a little brook like that would not be so wide that you could hardly see from one bank to the other? No, said the reindeer men, but who said the map was right? What good was a bit of paper anyway, when the river was there in front of him? Was he saying, they didn't know their own river, the river Anadyr? Their voices rose in shrill protest. Pehtak made a sweeping gesture. Downstream, the river was even wider, but that still didn't make it an ocean! He laughed contemptuously and put a finger to his head: 'The man's a lunatic!' Forell saw the sneer and glowered angrily back. For the rest of the evening he spoke little and made no attempt to offer his tobacco until the others insisted. They had a right to, he realized that, because they had given him food. Otherwise . . .

Anyway, thought Forell, he had learned something from the encounter. But now it was time to go. Pehtak and Laatmai were playing a game with him, dangling him on a string till they had him in the *kolchoz*; then they would sell him to the Russians. While the two men were talking between themselves, Forell strapped his rucksack and made ready to vanish during the night. Meanwhile, it had been getting steadily colder and when the fire began to burn low, the shepherds gestured to him to come with them to the tent. Forell said he preferred to sleep in the open. WHAT? they yelled. The man *was* mad! Then the two of them vied in frenzied entreaty. Did Forell want to kill himself? Couldn't he see what sort of a night they were in for? Did he think they had put up the tent for a joke? Gripping the covering of arched reindeer skins, Pehtak shook them till the whole tent threatened to collapse: that was what it would be like before long! He'd see! Yes, he'd wait and see, thought Forell. This was just another of their dodges, so that they could have him in the tent and keep their eye on him.

But they were right and he was wrong. During the night, the wind rose to a full gale, howling and lashing till the three men had to stand in the tent facing inwards with legs braced and backs arched against the bellying sides to prevent them from carrying away. To Forell, it seemed they would have been better off lying flat on the ground in the open, so offering less resistance to the wind, but that was merely his opinion, and if Laatmai and Pehtak knew hours in advance when there was going to be a storm, they would surely know best how to cope with it when it came.

After about three hours the sustained roaring of the wind dropped to a series of intermittent gusts and at last they could get some sleep. The tent was small and the three men had to lie close together. At any rate, once the covering of skins had been tucked under the left and right sides of the two outer men, it was warm enough and, though Pehtak was not the choicest of bed-fellows, what with the storm outside and the chorus of snoring within, it was not long before Forell was asleep.

In all, the storm lasted for seventy-two hours and for most of that time, it was snowing heavily. The reindeer weathered it out as best they could, standing in twos and threes wherever they could find some slight protection, with feet planted squarely and bodies slanting into the gale. For the men, there was nothing to do except sit in the tent and converse. Talking was pointless, even for the shepherds between themselves, because the storm drowned their words. So once more, they had to depend on gestures and skilled as they were in the pastime of dumb charades, the shepherds waxed visibly more cheerful as the complexities of the game increased. By the time the storm was over, Forell had abandoned his intention of leaving them to continue his journey alone.

*　　*　　*

The storm had left a thick mantle of snow over the tundra and during the following week the search for grazing kept the reindeer continually on the move. At the end of that time, they were joined by another, slightly smaller herd shepherded by three men. The newcomers were quick to note the presence of the stranger and their greetings to Pehtak and Laatmai were cautious and subdued. Who was this man, and what was he doing with the herd?

Pehtak brought forward Forell and told them where he had been found and what account he had given of himself. Looking far from pleased, the newcomers drew Pehtak on one side and began an earnest palaver, casting sidelong glances from time to time at the object of their discussion. Finally, Pehtak shrugged his shoulders, as much as to say: 'Don't blame me, I didn't want him. I'd be only too glad to get rid of the man!' The others nodded agreement.

After all, thought Forell, the reindeer men could hardly be blamed for their attitude. He was a dangerous liability to them. He ate their food and had nothing to give in return but a little tobacco and a lot of trouble. He was unskilled in every aspect of their life, and since he had committed the capital offence of escaping from the lead mine, his mere presence reduced them all to the status of criminals. To bring him with them thus far had been generous indeed.

But Laatmai thought otherwise. He liked Forell. He seemed moved with compassion for this man whose home was on the other side of the world and with respect for him, because he was brave and had once been strong. Laatmai stood up for him, praised his tobacco, obtained the newcomers' grudging tolerance, assuring Forell that their ill humour sprang principally from the fact that during the late summer and early autumn they had lost a large number of reindeer from sickness. Look! He could see for himself. There were the animals' skins!

One of the newcomers was a good-natured, rather bovine fellow, probably in his early thirties, who seemed, if not of pure Russian, then at any rate of mixed Slav and paleoasiatic blood. He had a long, lugubrious face, with a mouth that drooped open when anyone spoke to him. But he was willing enough and seemed to enjoy taking orders from the others, while they treated him with a certain lordly contempt. Perhaps his ancestors had been comparative newcomers to the Arctic regions, whereas the other men were descended from indigenous tribes that claimed to be the original inhabitants. Anyway, he and Forell had something in common in that they were both treated as outsiders, and the Russian began to ingratiate himself—a situation which Laatmai was quick to note and disapprove.

Meanwhile, the two herds of reindeer, now nearly two thousand strong, began to move together across the tundra. As they progressed, the men stopped at intervals to dig their heels into the snow and immediately some of the animals went to the spot and started scratching up lichen. They were approaching the *kolchoz* now, Laatmai explained, and were testing to see if the animals could find enough grazing in the vicinity. Wherever the reindeer saw the men dig in their heels, they understood that they were to seek food, and by watching them, the shepherds could tell whether they were likely to find enough. If the reindeer abandoned the spot, it meant that the snow was too deep, or that early frosts had stunted the growth of the lichens. Then the shepherds would have to leave wife and children again and move further down-river towards the sea. And that would be very unpleasant, for the nearer they got to the sea, the closer they would be to Authority—Authority that stalked about in a peaked cap with a green cloth cover, looking for trouble. . . .

That might be, thought Forell, but things were unpleasant enough already. The news that they were approaching the *kolchoz* had come as a shock. He had intended to leave the reindeer men in good time to avoid it and had only stayed with them until now on the assumption that as the third and last herd had not yet turned up, they must still be some distance away. But it must have gone straight to its destination. Forell realized that it would be impossible to part company on the very outskirts of the *kolchoz*. Nothing would be more likely to arouse the slumbering suspicions of his hosts, or ensure that everything they knew about him, down to the smallest detail, was reported to the nearest Soviet. He would have to stay with them now—and hope for the best.

Though, properly speaking, they were no more than huts, the 'houses' of the *kolchoz* were solid enough and obviously great care had been taken in their construction to make them windproof and warm. The walls consisted of thickly daubed wicker-work and were lined on the inside with hides, of which the smooth surfaces faced inwards and had been decorated with pictures of animals painted in brilliant colours. There were nine of these huts and as the herdsmen approached, the inmates emerged the old men first, then the women, shy and silent, standing on one side until the male greetings were over, and last, a shrill throng of well nourished looking children.

Dismissing the Russian's offer to take Forell into his hut, the reindeer men confabulated for a while on the problem of the stranger. Then Pehtak came forward and said something to the women, pointing to each of them in turn. It seemed that Forell was to be passed round from hut to hut, staying with each family in turn. The first to act as host would be Laatmai. '*Gutt!*' he said imitating Forell's favourite German rejoinder. The reindeer men laughed: and that was '*gutt*', too! From now on, as far as they were concerned, Gutt should be his name.

Laatmai showed 'Gutt' to his hut. Inside, it seemed to be pitch dark. Tripping over a pile of reindeer skins near the entrance, Forell was only aware, at first, of a penetrating smell and what appeared to be innumerable children tumbling about his legs. Then, as his eyes adjusted themselves, he saw the wife whom Laatmai was presenting—or rather, a fur-swaddled figure, whose age, in the dim light, it was impossible to guess. Laatmai was repeating a word that sounded like 'Ankhahta', and Forell took that to be her name. But perhaps that was the number of her children, of whom, as Laatmai's apologetic tones conveyed, they had so far only achieved six.

To be honest, Forell would rather have slept each night in the open than in the greasy hovel where nine lungs fought for what oxygen remained in the fetid, ammoniac air. But to have done so would have mortally offended Laatmai, his host, and Laatmai was something more than amiable; he was a genuine and generous-hearted friend. Laatmai would never betray him, but as long as he stayed in the collective farm, the thought never left Forell that at any moment one of the reindeer men might silently vanish with a message for the nearest commissar. Each day, before they left the *kolchoz* to fish in the neighbouring river, Forell counted the men to make sure there was no one missing, and each evening, when they returned, he counted them again.

After all, he thought, why should they harbour him? They themselves were not free men. Their herds had been taken from them and then returned to be cared for in trust for the State. Though Moscow was four thousand miles away, they had learned to respect decrees that originated from there. Moscow had decreed collectivization and also the banishment into slavery of Clemens Forell. They had not resisted the first; why should they defy the second? Their herds had been collectivized, and so, no doubt, had their conscience. Sooner or later they would surely obey it.

But day after day, nine men went out and nine men returned, and the time came when they invited Forell to go with them. Sometimes they set off in the morning, breaking a hole in the ice and laying their lines in the few short hours of daylight. At others, they would wait till the afternoon, taking torches of tallow with them, which they placed by the holes in the ice to burn there for most of the night with their flickering, smoky flame.

Crouching beside each dark rectangle would be two men, waiting silently with their thin-shafted tridents for the appearance of a fish. Often they would wait for as long as half an hour, both hands gripping the slanting shaft of the trident, motionless as though they themselves had become frozen in a refrigerated world, where the only movement was the thin flutter of the torch flames and the tremulous shadows on the ice. Then suddenly, a trident would streak down into the hole, with hardly a bubble to show where it had cleaved the water. When the man withdrew it again, there, on the short middle prong would be a fat salmon, speared through the middle of its back and held firmly on either side by the two outer prongs. Again, the men would crouch, the fork of the trident pointing downwards, ready to strike. In less than a minute, perhaps, this time, another fish would rise to the surface, attracted by the light of the torch. Then the same process would be repeated, until after some hours, if the catch had been a good one, the men would begin to relax their efforts and slip into a jovial, talkative mood. They would press the trident into Forell's hands. Let Gutt have a try! Go on, man; it's child's play! So Forell would wait, tensed, hands gripping the shaft as the other had done. In a moment, a fish would appear, glinting towards the flame—a strike, and it would vanish, untouched, back to safety below. . . .

To glimpse the fish soon enough as it came up through the water, then to aim off, allowing for the refraction of the light, took a good deal of skill and practice, and Forell never achieved more than modest success. The clumsier his efforts, the broader the grins. The reindeer men were delighted to have found something to put in the scale against Forell's towering six-foot-three. Granted, he had the advantage of them in height, and in a literal sense, no doubt, they had to look up to him, but when it came to handling a trident—and they would smile with charming condescension—why, the man was no more than an outsize child!

But Forell could afford to smile back at them, for he realized full well that his ever growing reputation for amiable incompetence was the best possible guarantee that he would be safe in their hands. But to be a laughing-stock was not enough; Forell also worked in the village. Conscious of his debt to the men who harboured and fed him and, indeed, made this stage of his life worth living, he was glad to give any service he could in return. A large number of reindeer hides from the animals that had died during the autumn required to be tanned and by taking part of this work off their hands, Forell enabled the reindeer men to give more of their own time to providing food.

*   *   *

In January, Forell was still only a few hundred miles from the lead mine. For the whole of February, he stayed in the *kolchoz*. He was safe there, he knew that now, and the word '*kolchoz*' had lost its sinister implications. Here he had at least one good friend and something more than an existence—a life that at times seemed to contain all he could want. And he could stay indefinitely; no one ever suggested him leaving. The temptation was strong—why give up what he already had for the slender chance of regaining a life lost long ago and now hardly even desired?

But then March came, and as the rigours of frost abated and the world began to stir with the first suggestions of spring, Forell began to feel restless and impatient to be gone. The squalor and stench of the tribesmen's huts had not obtruded themselves in the winter, because they offered warmth and protection from the wind. Now, each time he went into one, Forell felt shut in, stifled, like a prisoner, self-condemned. But when he told the reindeer men, through Laatmai, that the time had come to continue his journey, they refused to hear of him leaving. It was out of the question, they said. The winter was not over. When the time was ripe, they would let him know. In due course, it was Laatmai who broached the subject again—Laatmai in a state of hilarious excitement because he had been chosen to convey a quantity of freight 'over the mountains', westwards, in the same direction that Forell would have to go. It was thought that Forell might like to accompany him.

As preparations were made for their departure, the village became the scene of feverish activity. For the time being it was a village, and not a collective farm, there was no doubt about that. There was nothing official about the huge quantities of hides that were loaded with furtive haste on to the big 'nartee', or freight carrying sledge, and no official receiving depot for the products of the farm that lay westwards, inland. On the contrary, legitimate consignments were always sent to the coast, for shipment by sea. Perhaps that was why Laatmai was grinning so much just now.

At first, Forell thought the speed of the preparations showed how anxious they were to see the last of him, but when the time came for his departure and the reindeer men, with unmistakable sincerity, clapped him heartily on the shoulder and loaded him with a profusion of gifts, he realized that they had come to look on him almost with affection. They gave him food in such quantities that he would never be able to carry half of it when he was on his own—fat, cheese, dried fish and a granular substance that tasted something like bread. The finest present of all came from Laatmai, the round-faced grinning friend: a *foffaika*, or coat, made from the warmest part of two reindeer skins and a light sleeping bag that could also be set up as a tent, likewise made of skins. Forell himself had helped in the tanning of these hides and had been amazed to see how hides that were rock hard and cracked by frost could be converted into the supplest leather.

Before they left, the whole village took part in what seemed a traditional leave-taking ceremonial, so devised as to permit the maximum consumption of alcohol. At last, Laatmai climbed on to the driver's seat and took up the reins behind two pairs of reindeer, followed by Forell who settled himself among the freight at his back. The driver wriggled to make himself comfortable, glanced back at Forell, then forward to the waiting antlers, exchanged smiles with the sky, and 'Hyi-yip!' Their journey had begun.

Swaying on his perch, Forell looked back at the village. It would have been a pity, he thought, after all, if he had stayed and made a home with the reindeer men. One day he might have lost altogether the longing he had once had for his own.

* * *

For a fortnight, Laatmai and Forell travelled without incident setting up a tent each night and bivouacking in full style. But on the sixteenth day, Laatmai, normally so phlegmatic, suddenly became nervous. What was troubling him he did not say, but the nature of the danger became clearer when towards afternoon he drew up, dismounted, and told Forell it would be better if he disappeared from view. Forell had no alternative, then, but to help unload, climb back on to the sledge and allow Laatmai to pile the freight of reindeer skins on top of him. Thereafter the journey consisted only of sounds and the jolting movement of the sledge. Five times, at least, he felt it draw up and heard a dialogue between Laatmai and some other men in which the latter seemed to be asking questions. At last, they would move off again and after a few minutes Laatmai would give vent to his relief in gusty snatches of song.

It must have been some hours after sunset when they came to a halt in an echoing stone enclosure. This time, instead of the usual voices, there was complete silence for a moment. Then Forell heard footsteps, and soon after, Laatmai was lifting the piles of reindeer skins off his chest. 'How are you?' he asked solicitously, as he helped Forell to sit up.

And then Forell did sit up. Two men were standing by the sledge, eyeing him quizzically. 'Get a move on!' said one of them—in Russian, '*Pascholl!*'

Pascholl—of all words in any language the most horrible that could strike his ears, the world that stood blazoned over that bestial scene at the lead mine when his fellow prisoners, fellow Germans, had vented their sadistic rage on him and beaten him nearly to death. '*Pascholl!*' Forell shivered, knowing that he had been betrayed.

The sledge was in a court-yard, drawn up beside a lighted window with a door at one side. Forell stumbled to the ground and was hustled unceremoniously into the building, through another door and into a room that was bare of all furniture except for a bench running along one wall. The bench was too high to sit on and the ceiling too low for him to be able to stand upright, and he had to bow with bent back, like a lackey, while the others followed him in and closed the door behind them.

'You are a German?' said one of the Russians.

Out of the corner of his eye, Forell saw Laatmai smiling fatly by the door. He said in a loud voice: 'Yes I am.'

'Then what are you doing here?'

'I was sentenced to twenty-five . . .'

'Precisely. Then what are you doing here?'

'I escaped.'

'Why?'

'Because I want to get home.'

'To Germany?'

'Yes.'

'You're mad,' said the Russian with diagnostic finality.

There was silence for a moment, while the man gave Forell a long and calculating scrutiny. When he spoke again, his voice was insinuating.

'If I help you over the river, shall I have to take your place in the lead mine?'

Forell could hardly believe his ears. He gazed at the Russian and the Russian gazed impassively back. Only the lift of an eyebrow showed that he guessed, perhaps, what was in the other's mind. Forell's relief must have looked rather comic: from the direction of the door came Laatmai's chortling laugh. The Russian never smiled. 'Will you betray me?' he said.

'Why should I?'

There was a pause while the Russian made up his mind. Then: 'All right,' he said, 'I'll take you tomorrow morning'. And in case Forell should embarrass him with thanks, he added: 'I'm not doing this out of charity, you know'. He glanced pointedly at Laatmai. So Laatmai was going to pay him, thought Forell, and it would probably be an enormous sum. The Russian would call himself a 'business man', but the herdsmen would have another name for him. Not content with all he had already done for Forell, as a last gesture of friendship, Laatmai was now going to ruin himself. Forell started to speak, but Laatmai cut him short with a '*Gutt, gutt. . . .*' and a gesture to leave well alone.

From that moment on, as far as the other men were concerned, Forell no longer existed. The skins were brought in from the sledge and the Russians talked a great deal, but in the language of Laatmai's tribe so that Forell was unable to gather more than that payment was to be in kind. The last bale, Forell noticed, was obviously much heavier than the weight of the skins alone and it had to be dragged into the room, whereas the others had been carried. Though his curiosity had been aroused, he could see from Laatmai's deliberately blank expression that the contents of the last bale would remain a mystery. Only his brief '*Gutt!*'—Laatmai's favourite exclamation now—as it was stacked against the wall with the other bales suggested that the weighty whatever-it-was might have something to do with Forell—advance payment to the Russian, perhaps, for acting as his guide.

Then the third man, who so far had spoken little, brought in some cold meat, vodka and bread in the form of flat round cakes, in adequate quantities, but only just, for the two hungry travellers. The Russians barely touched the food and Forell suspected that they had already eaten, perhaps not quite so sparingly as their guests were now called upon to do. 'Help yourself,' said the business man generously, 'there is no payment. . . .'

Reindeer skins were laid on the floor for the guests to sleep on, the Russians preferring to spend the night in an adjoining storeroom. Through the half open door, Forell could see a row of earthenware jars, probably containing wood alcohol, axes, sledge harness and other goods. While the Russians snored, Laatmai chose to talk. For a good hour he lay, hands under his head, speaking in an earnest undertone to Forell, who gathered only that his friend was giving him advice for his future journey. After a while, his voice rose to a more dramatic pitch; he was telling a story, perhaps, a personal experience in illustration of what he had said. Finally he laughed softly—'That just shows you, doesn't it?'—and laid his grubby hands on Forell's face, meaning it was time to go to sleep.

Next morning, half an hour before dawn, when Laatmai said good-bye before starting his return journey to the village, Forell wished he could have spoken his language, if only for five seconds, so that he could have expressed something of the gratitude he felt to this man who had helped and befriended him.

It was not the Russian who had questioned him on his arrival who was going to guide Forell, but his silent companion. The man was ready and anxious to leave and while Laatmai was outside rounding up his sledge team, he and Forell set off towards the river. Hampered by his heavy rucksack, Forell found it hard to keep up as his guide hurried by devious paths through the village in his anxiety to reach the outskirts before sunrise. They marched, then, across open country until, in broad daylight, they descended a steep bank and crossed the frozen surface of a river. In another thirty minutes, after climbing a slight gradient on the far side, the Russian stopped and pointed towards the village, now lying sprawled over the plain below. Forell was surprised to see that it comprised about five hundred buildings.

Then, for the first time, his guide spoke. 'From the village to here is eight versts: that will be two hundred roubles.'

Certainly no man had ever been put on his road with more sombre efficiency than Forell. Whether it would lead him to ultimate freedom or to disaster was another matter, and no concern of his guide's. The man must already have been paid by Laatmai. Still, if he wanted a tip. . . . The notes were of no value in any case, or so Doctor Stauffer had maintained.

Forell took out his roll of bank notes, by now congealed almost to papier mâché, and peeled off two hundred roubles.

'Three hundred!' said the Silent One, eyeing the wealth.

Perhaps they really were of some value; obviously the Russian thought so.

'No, friend! Two hundred—that was what you said!'

'Two hundred and fifty.'

'Two hundred! Here! Take them!'

The man took them. He seemed to bear no ill will, and why should he? Two hundred roubles was the first figure he had mentioned, so probably he had been hoping to get fifty. Included in the price, it seemed, was a rough indication of the line on which Forell should continue his march. The man pointed with his hand to where, below them and to their right, the broad glistening band of the frozen river trailed narrowing into the distance. That was his route. Consulting his compass, Forell found that the direction was due west.

'Make sure you get there,' said the man. 'Don't give in.' And then, as though ashamed of his sudden loquacity, he turned and started back with big, loping strides towards the village. He never looked round.

*　　*　　*

Once more alone, Forell trudged over the still frozen *taiga*, his rucksack heavier by the gifts which the villagers had given him and his muscles soft from long disuse. But even if the going was difficult, he had more and better food with him now and the skins which Laatmai had given him would protect him against the cold. The weight on his back was a guarantee of continued existence, at least for some days.

He had learned a lot in the last few months: the technique

108

of living in the Siberian cold—how to build and maintain a fire of moss scratched from the ground, how to milk reindeer, fish with hook and line through a hole in the ice, how to tan hides, besides a number of small tricks which only the natives, never his own unaided experience, could have taught him. Above all, he had learned that, far from trying to avoid the inhabitants of the country, he depended for his very existence on making friends with them—to replenish his stocks of food, to get reliable information for his future journey and, the key to ultimate success or failure, to renew his strength and refresh his mind by contact with humanity.

For some days, he continued, going west by the compass, the river curling away from him at times until it was lost from view and then returning again, on the last occasion in a rocky gorge where the ice-free waters cascaded down over a series of terraces. Owing to the weight of his rucksack, his daily march was well under twenty miles.

Then he came upon a herd of reindeer. The king stag lumbered massively towards him, more surprised than angry, but from the herdsmen Forell had learned the knack of reassuring a frightened animal and the stag wandered off again, as though to convey to the others that the stranger intended no harm.

The animals were grazing over land where, at its thinnest, the snow was over twelve inches deep and, having partially thawed and then frozen again, it was so hard that Forell could barely break into it with his heel. He wondered how the reindeer managed to find enough food and watched them for some time as they grazed. They seemed to have little difficulty in breaking through the crust of ice with their hooves, but having plucked the moss from beneath it, Forell noticed that they went some distance before repeating the process. In the places which they avoided he tested with the Siberian knife and found that the snow was invariably at its deepest. Once or twice, the reindeer came to investigate the hole which he had excavated, but even when the moss was visible, they would go their way again without cropping it. Why dig two feet down, they seemed to say, when you need only dig one?

For a moment, Forell was tempted by the thought of using a reindeer as a pack animal to carry his rucksack. The possibility of losing everything he possessed, however, if the reindeer took it into its head to cross a river or rejoin the rest of the herd, made him abandon it. As for trying to ride such an animal, with his long legs, it would clearly be out of the question.

It was now nearing the middle of March and though the

snow still stayed, seemingly as a permanent feature of the landscape, and the nights were as cold as ever, in the day sometimes, the veil of mist and cloud would suddenly dissolve, revealing a new world, golden beneath crystal skies.

On one such day of brilliant sunlight, Forell saw ahead of him a group of tents, peering like dark cones above the blanket of white. With the snow piled up all round them, only the tops were visible and he might have missed them altogether if the sound of voices and laughter had not first attracted his attention. As he drew nearer he could see a number of people, among them children, engaged in playing a game of some kind. They nodded to him in a neighbourly sort of way, but did not interrupt their game and he had a curious feeling that they had been expecting him. Now that they had seen him, he could not prevent a twinge of apprehension at the thought that his fate was irrevocably committed to their hands.

The approach to the tents was by a pathway between walls of snow built up to give shelter from the wind. A tall man came forward to greet Forell. With his high forehead, flowing beard and frank, open gaze, he would have looked impressive in any surroundings and from that moment on, Forell thought of him as 'the Tsar'. The Tsar could speak a little Russian. He told the stranger he was expected. Yes, the Tsar could not explain it, but somehow, they had known he would come. With a courteous gesture, he invited Forell to enter one of the tents. As Forell crossed the threshold, the atmosphere struck him like a blow. Compounded of smoke, sour milk, fish, rancid oil, uric acid and then more smoke, it was literally repellent. He stepped back, and as he did so, some children who had been trying to slip past him into the tent became involved with his legs. The next moment, rucksack and all, he fell flat on the ground. Ah-ha! That was splendid! His ears rang with yelps of childish laughter. . . .

Smoke was an evil accepted, apparently, as the inevitable accompaniment of warmth. But whereas in Laatmai's hut it had hovered more or less harmlessly under the flat ceiling before finding its way out through the hole in the roof, here the whole tent seemed to serve as chimney to the fire that smouldered in the middle. Nothing, so Forell told himself, in the whole wide world would persuade him to stay in such a place, let alone sleep there. . . . But of course, he did stay, sleeping in the tent and, though it cost him a struggle, eating there as well, for a fortnight. Under their benevolent Tsar, these people also turned out to be his friends, and because they might be the last, the very last he would ever have, Forell could swallow the food they offered him, could sit on a reindeer skin in the family circle while they ate whole fish with their fingers, right down to the back-bone, gnawing and licking it clean with copious and noisy relish.

Forell stayed with the Koriak tribesmen until the beginning of April. By then, the snow round the tents was starting to melt and each day it was becoming harder to find enough to provide water for cooking. It was time to be on the move. Winter was relaxing its grip and before long would vanish from the land. With cries and endless commotion, the Koriaks prepared to strike their tents and trek across country with their herds. There was a pandemonium of packing and repacking, intermingled with threats, curses and laughter. The tribesmen insisted on examining every article of Forell's clothing to make sure it was rainproof. At last, it only remained to strike camp and find the reindeer. But where were they? So far, Forell had only heard talk of them: apparently no one had seen them for weeks.

The next morning, the herd appeared of its own accord. Forell woke up to find a couple of animals grazing contentedly within a few feet of the tent. Had the Koriaks known all along where they were? Had someone fetched them? Or had the same curious instinct that had forewarned the people of Forell's arrival told them that the herd would turn up on the very day they were ready to leave?

The Koriaks loaded everything they had on to the reindeer, including tents, cooking utensils and Forell's rucksack. Each animal was given only a light load carefully distributed and strapped in position, half over the shoulders and half over the hind quarters. Then they set off, at first uphill in pursuit of the vanishing snows of winter. Their speed was determined by the reindeer and the grazing they could find on the way. Now that the thaw had started, the low-lying ground was becoming marshy and the animals avoided it, preferring the slopes of the hills. Sometimes, when the grazing was scarce, they would move on quickly; otherwise, they would be content to graze near the same spot for several days and then the Koriaks would pitch their tents and await the pleasure of the herd. Forell would gladly have undertaken some work, as a return for the Koriaks' hospitality and to help pass the time, but with his inexperience in everything to do with their life, there was little work he could find, except keep an eye occasionally on the reindeer that were with calf, or search the neighbourhood for game.

After a time, Forell told the Tsar he ought to be on his way. Spreading out his now sorely dilapidated map, he tried to explain to his host how far he believed he had come, and the distance which still lay before him. The Tsar dismissed it all with a snap of the fingers. Perhaps he had understood the map, perhaps he had not. At any rate, he had grasped enough to realize that Forell had set himself a superhuman task, and he now proceeded to lecture him. A man of prudence, he said, only undertook what he might reasonably expect to finish during his lifetime. But in any case, it was ridiculous to want to leave a fine country like that. A fine country it was, with fine people, and the best that Forell or any man could do for himself would be to settle there and get work—hunting, for example. If he joined up with a good Siberian hunter he could make a whole heap of money.

Granted, said the Tsar, the Russians and the Americans, between them—yes, the Americans as well!—had shot the game right out of whole stretches of country, but that was in the lowlands where Russians were two-a-penny—always had been. And furred animals weren't like reindeer. They didn't go down-river each winter, they stayed high up, on the *taiga*, or in the mountains. Admittedly, it was dangerous to seek them out up there, and that was why you didn't find many Russians in the mountains, but to a good man, it was the danger that made hunting worthwhile, that and the money you got for furs—the short furs, of course, not the long ones. But you had to wait till the winter to get your price for them; usually, that was, unless you happened to know a thing or two. . . .

The Tsar smiled and Forell said nothing, for fear it might destroy his communicative mood. The Tsar respected him. To have come that distance up-river with the load he had been carrying was some feat. Moreover, a prisoner who had escaped from the Russians and not been recaptured within forty versts of his starting point had proved himself to be a better man than his former captors. He must have taken a route that no Russian had dared to face.

'Come, *Germanski*! We'll take a walk round.'

The Tsar with a gun over his shoulder and Forell carrying food for them both, they started their walk. It lasted nine days and turned out to be arduous. The last word in the Tsar's description was the only accurate part—they did go round, in a circle, climbing up rocky defiles, past wind-grieved larches whose tall trunks the Tsar seemed to take as pointers for the march. But where were they marching, and why? The object of it all was obscure and more than once Forell tried to take a compass bearing in the hope of discovering some system in the Tsar's seemingly aimless but certainly indefatigable wanderings. But the compass, for some reason, refused to settle down, and the bearings it gave might have been anywhere within an arc of ninety degrees.

The gun seemed to have come with them to lend an air of purpose to the expedition, which in fact had none. Twice only did the Tsar see fit to use it, once to shoot an inedible bird of the crow family, of which, for some unexplained reason, he kept the feet, and the second time, a small hare, or possibly a marmot. With extraordinary detexterity, the Tsar then skinned the animal, removed the entrails and roasted it on a hardwood spit over a fire of twigs and moss, carefully selected to neutralize the unpleasant flavour of fresh game. When seasoned with some grimy salt which the Tsar produced from a leather pouch, Forell agreed that it tasted excellent.

After nine days, they were back at their starting point. All but two of the herdsmen had left, taking most of the reindeer with them. With the remaining men the Tsar talked long and earnestly. They shrugged their shoulders, pursed their lips, their voices rose and fell. It was bad news, apparently, that he had for them, but it seemed they had a plan. The following day they moved off, keeping pace with the grazing herd and taking Forell with them.

About five weeks later, towards the end of May, the Tsar was ready for another 'walk round'. In case it should turn out to be rather a longer walk this time, he suggested Forell should take his full kit with him—everything he had. The Tsar would look after the gun, of course, and he would bring his own food so that Forell would not have to carry anything extra.

This time, the going was even harder. Great patches of gaseous swamp repeatedly blocked their way, even on the higher ground, and the air was full of stinging insects. The Tsar covered his face, neck and hands with an evil-smelling, glutinous substance of which he had brought large quantities carried in a pouch at his side. Forell was prevailed upon to try some and found that, though the mosquitoes and horseflies seemed indifferent to the stench, the stuff in time formed a crust which they were unable to penetrate. Apart from this dubious measure, the two men took care to cover their faces at night. Even so, Forell woke up one day to find his lips had swollen to three times their size and his eyelids had been so badly stung that he could barely open them. It was clear, the Tsar's midge cream was good only to offend the nostrils. No sooner had Forell plastered himself with it than the sweat would wash it away, and then, with a venomous, high-pitched hum, the mosquitoes would descend and burrow joyfully into his neck.

Every day the 'walk' became less of a joke and every day the Tsar less forthcoming about his intentions. As time passed, he began to quicken the pace and to keep up with him in the hot, humid atmosphere, wearing reindeer skins and thick winter clothing and with a rucksack nearly a third heavier than its original weight was an ordeal that Forell found grievous indeed.

113

Moreover, the Tsar was visibly losing confidence in attaining the object, whatever it was, that he had set out to achieve. He would go a mile or two in one direction and then change his mind and go off in another. There would be pauses to reflect and more pauses for rest. The truth was, suspected Forell, that the 'walk round' had proved altogether too ambitious and the Tsar's enthusiasm was beginning to wilt. It finally expired when they came to a fast-flowing river which it seemed impossible to cross. The Tsar sat down, then, and waited for four days, in the hope, apparently, that sooner or later the unruly waters would pass downstream and allow him to cross on dry land.

Meanwhile, Forell announced his intention to bathe. A respector of alien customs, the Tsar was broad-minded and raised no objection. The ice-cold water relieved the itching stings and seemed to diminish for a time the odour of the Tsar's patent mosquito repellent.

Then on the morning of the fourth day, the Tsar became restless, as though he sensed that something was going to happen. After a while, there came a faint drawn-out call from the direction of the river and immediately the Tsar went to the water's edge and looked up-stream. Repeated at intervals, the call was growing steadily louder until finally a raft appeared with three men on it. As soon as they saw the Tsar, they drew in towards him. Half waterlogged and difficult to manoeuvre, the raft gave a final swerve and crashed into the river bank, coming to a stop against the root of a tree. The men clambered ashore and spoke a laconic greeting.

All three of them were Russians. Hollow-eyed, emaciated and bearing plentiful signs of privation, to Forell they seemed villainous-looking scoundrels and their continued existence due only to a fault in the hangman's rope. And yet the Tsar spoke to them and smiled his honest, gentlemanly smile. . . . Anastas, Grigori and Semyon were their names, in order of their importance. Anastas nodded over at Forell. What about him?

'The man's a German,' said the Tsar. 'Will you put him on his way?'

'A *Nyemetz*?' Anastas laughed an incredulous, cackling laugh.

'Escaped.'

Anastas eyed Forell. 'How far do you want to go?'

Forell answered in Russian. 'I want to get home.'

Again the laugh, spiteful, this time. 'Who doesn't?' Then Anastas said to the Tsar: 'I'm sorry—we can't use him. . . .' If he regretted the decision, the Tsar did not show it. He turned to other matters—a little private business.

'We should like to feel we can trust you,' said Anastas and

114

into the Tsar's wide palm he dropped a small wash-leather bag, an extremely heavy bag, judging by the plop it made, despite its diminutive size. 'What have you got for us?'

The Tsar unpacked and proceeded to show them: eight dozen boxes of shot-gun cartridges and more than that amount of rifle ammunition. All that for a little bag of— could it be gold? Forell stretched out a hand and to the Russians' speechless amazement the Tsar dropped the bag into his palm to let him feel the weight. Forell tested it; then to the Russians' even greater surprise handed it back. There was no doubt about it, it contained alluvial gold.

The three Russians had checked over the ammunition and found it correct. There was one more thing which they wanted —the Tsar's handsome American rifle and that, too, he now surrendered.

The business concluded, the Tsar returned to the problem of Forell. 'Look!' he said to Anastas. 'He'd be very useful to you—a good strong walker, an excellent shot and he's got tobacco with him, first quality Machorka.' At the mention of tobacco, the other two Russians pricked up their ears. One of them said something in an undertone to Anastas. Meanwhile: 'It's a fine opportunity,' the Tsar was saying to Forell, striving for a formula acceptable to all. 'You'd have to go a long way to find men like these.' Forell was willing to believe him. 'They know every inch of the *taiga*. You'll be safe with them.' He smiled, and turned as Anastas spoke up for the three Russians: 'Will you bring us some tobacco, next time we meet?'

'Naturally. . . . Of course. . . .' said the Tsar in a faraway voice, then hastened to add: 'If you'll take the German with you. That's agreed, then? That's splendid!' He reeled off his resounding good wishes to the German and then, before the others could recover from their surprise, a hand was raised in dignified farewell and without another word the Tsar betook himself with slow, imperial strides towards the cover of the hills behind them.

As the noble form retreated, Anastas suddenly panicked. '. . . and our very best wishes,' he shouted, 'for the future of the Koriak people, and the Koriak herds. . . .' He watched for a moment to see what effect his words would have, but there was none. Then, with worried countenance, he led the way back to the raft. As they pushed off with long birch poles from the bank, Forell caught his last glimpse of the Tsar. He was standing on the hill-side, smiling as he watched them go.

The three men managed their unwieldy raft with some skill and after about half an hour of turns and twists down the fast-flowing river, they brought it safely in to the exact spot they had chosen where the bank consisted of low-lying sand.

Having tied the four poles together, they left them floating, made fast at each end to some tendrils overhanging the water's edge. Then they set off at a fast speed along faintly discernible tracks, leaving Forell to bring up the rear. For the rest of the day, they trudged in single file, Forell streaming with sweat and tormented by swarms of midges. No one spoke to him or gave the least sign that he was aware of his presence and more than once, when they had left him some distance behind, Forell was tempted to give up the struggle and let them go on without him.

At last, at about ten in the evening, the men halted by a tent of reindeer skins stretched on three sides between trees. While the vagabonds reclined on the grass, Forell did the work: chopping wood (they were thoughtful enough to supply an axe), fetching skins of water from a nearby stream, lighting a fire and preparing a meal. Still no one spoke to him. But the men were watching him all the time, to see what he could do. He was lucky enough to light the fire with the first spark from the flint. Then he cooked a meal, preferring to use his own stocks rather than ask the others for food. It lightened his rucksack considerably, but as far as he was concerned, that was all to the good. Snuffling and drooling at the mouth, the men crammed the food down as fast as it would go. Then they called for tobacco.

'Machorka. Come on, hurry up!' It was Anastas who had spoken; the first words he had addressed to Forell since his curt question nearly twelve hours before. Forell put his hand in the rucksack and felt for the packet of Machorka. Of the four pounds he had set out with, about one pound remained. He had intended to take only a small quantity in the palm of his hand, but seeing the men's malevolent gaze upon him, he brought out the whole packet and laid it before them. They helped themselves, rolling cigarettes from the scraps of paper that Forell supplied.

'So you're a German?' said Anastas.

'I thought you knew that,' answered Forell in the same tough tone of voice.

'You know how to light a fire, and you almost know how to cook. What else can you do? Can you shoot?'

'No worse than you bandits.'

The word was hardly spoken before all three of them had jumped to their feet and were making to spring at him. In case of trouble Forell had been easing up his pistol until he could hold it out of sight between his hip and the ground; now the bandits found themselves staring into the muzzle.

'Oh——!' They had not expected the German to be armed and the cry expressed awe as well as surprise. The man was quick on the draw. He did not waste time, and if he did not

116

waste his bullets either, he was a force to be reckoned with.

Anastas spoke gently. 'Would that be a pistol by any chance?'

'It is.'

'Loaded? . . . No, surely not.'

'Shall I pull the trigger?'

'I thought you said you were a prisoner? They don't issue pistols in prison camps.'

This seemed the moment for a big, hearty lie, of a kind that would impress these men and establish once and for all their already grudging respect.

'No, I helped myself. I was on a working party. The guards had pistols and tommy-guns, of course; all I had was a pick. I laid them out and took what I wanted. I liked the feel of the Sten, but it wasn't so handy. The pistol has come in very useful at times.'

Forell deliberately left the story vague; the details the men could fill in for themselves—the number of corpses, for instance, that stood to the terrible man's account. . . . If only they knew, thought Forell, what an encumbrance the pistol was, how often already he had been tempted to throw it away. In fact, Forell had never once fired it and never did so, at any time, as long as it was in his possession. But the story had achieved its effect and the three scarecrows were visibly impressed.

'Well, put the ruddy thing away!'

'Will you behave yourselves?'

'Yes, yes, of course; we're all chums here, aren't we?'

Anastas gave him his hand, and after him, Grigori and Semyon. Then Semyon said, could he see the pistol, it looked like a make he hadn't come across before? At that, Forell merely grinned and put the pistol in his pocket, on the right side, the side he slept on. . . .

When the four of them set off on the following day, they left the tent of reindeer skins behind. They had enough to carry as it was, and the site was too inaccessible for anyone to find it.

Anastas was skilful in selecting spots for the nightly bivouacs where, no matter how much it rained, they would all remain tolerably dry. And rain it did, in plenty. Under trees, where the heat was moist and stagnant, dense swarms of midges and mosquitoes awaited their prey. As soon as they alighted on their skin, the scarecrows slapped them and smeared the blood over their faces and necks. Thereafter, they were immune from stings, all except Forell, whom the insects drove at times almost to a frenzy.

At last, they reached their destination, a massive hut built into a hill-side, with outcrops of rock forming the whole of the back wall and part of both sides. The three men had made it themselves; it must have taken them some considerable time. The whole site was dry and practically free of mosquitoes, while in front of the hut and below it, the waters of a stream flowed clear and fresh over a sandy bed. The stream had a peculiar importance, as Forell could see.

'So you wash gold here?'

Anastas nodded. 'There'll be plenty of work to do—for everyone.'

The gold-washing plant had obviously been thought out by someone of experience. The stream had been dammed and a cutting made so that it could be diverted from its sandy bed at will. At the moment, the water was flowing through the cutting. At the same time, a sluice had been provided so that a certain amount of water could be let through and 'streamed' over the sand to wash out the gold. All this had been done with timber felled and hewn into shape with an axe. No saw had been available, let alone ready trimmed boards from a saw-mill. The work must have taken years and Anastas showed off his plant with obvious pride.

'*Gelernt ist gelernt,*' smiled Forell, without realizing that he spoke in German. But Anastas seemed to have understood. 'I learned it the hard way,' he said, 'in the gold mines. They gave me twenty years: I did three, then I escaped.' He nodded towards Semyon who was cleaning up some spades in readiness to start work. 'It was his idea. He planned the escape. He was doing a lifer for robbery.'

'And Grigori?'

'Eighteen years. Misappropriating State property, they called it—in plain language, stealing. It was easy for him. He was a *Natschalnik*, an overseer, and lived with the stuff.'

'And you?'

'I told you, I got twenty years.'

'Political?'

'No, I was a member of the Communist Party, an active Komsomol. No. My wife was going with a man: I killed them. They tell you marriage is protected by the State. Well, the State didn't protect mine; so I put an end to it. And the State gave me twenty years.'

Anastas, thought Forell, was the type of man who cuts what he cannot untie. Of the three men, he was the least treacherous and the most predictable. If all other means failed, he could be relied on to resort to violence. And once his blood was up, not even a pistol would stop him, unless he'd heard the click of the safety-catch.

That evening, from a real feeling of being at home again, the three men became talkative—Semyon on the subject of political prisoners.

'I've got no time for "politicals"—they've got no guts. They just lie down to be trampled on. Not one of them dares to escape. When they put me in the mine, I told myself I'd wait just long enough to get a line on this gold-washing, and then I'd beat it—and so I did. Mine work's horrible. Gold-streaming's horrible, but it suits me because you can do it on a small scale, and I'm a small man, always have been, with a small business. But d'you think any of those politicals would work it out like that? Not they! They just sit down and wait for the end. I didn't, nor did Anastas—or Grigori, for that matter, because I told him he was coming along with us. And if I tell Grigori to do something, he does it.'

Forell wanted to know where the gold mine was.

'Does Kolymski mean anything to you?'

'A river, isn't it?'

'No. The river's called Kolyma. Kolymski's the mountains —that's where we worked, and they're Hell; not a hot Hell, but a cold one.'

Forell fetched out his tattered map and, spreading it on his knees, asked Anastas to show him the mining area.

'It's vast! Here—and here—and this is where we escaped from.'

'But that must be close to where we are now!'

'Right. You wouldn't find us here in winter: in the skiing season it gets a bit too close.'

So three hundred miles away there were gold mines, penal colonies, guards, Communists, M.V.D.,—a whole area swarming with people, barring Forell's route. And in winter-time, even the hut where he was sitting was dangerously close to them. 'I'll have to start moving if I'm to get past the gold mines, if I'm ever going to get home!'

'Home?' mocked Anastas with a vicious, jeering laugh. 'Don't make funny jokes! Don't all of us want to get home?'

'I don't,' said Grigori.

Anastas rounded on him. 'You blathering fool! We can't —that's the point, don't you see? Whether we want to or not, we never shall. Remember that, German! Once in Siberia, you stay! And what's your name, incidentally, your first name?'

'Peter.'

'Not very good at lying, are you? Never mind, my name isn't Anastas, either. And these fellows aren't whatever it is they call themselves. You see? I've forgotten, and you want to forget, forget you ever had a name. If people ask, just say: "No. No name. A nobody." Then they'll take you for an honest man. What's the good of calling yourself Pyotr Jakubovitsch? It only reminds you of a life you'll never see again. And a mouthful like that is a terrible waste of time. Before it's out, the other fellow's shot is in—yes, it was only common sense for him to shoot first! He was being on the safe side, that's all. You were quick on the draw with your pistol, but you want to be quicker still in the *taiga*. In the time it took you to draw, you ought to have pulled the trigger. When someone asks you your name, remember: shoot first, then tell him, "Pyotr". That's the right order. Get it?'

'I get it,' said Forell.

'Now give me your map and we'll burn it.'

'No. . . .'

'Oh, yes!' And before Forell could stop him, Anastas had seized the map. In half a minute, it was no more.

'That's better,' said Anastas. 'Toys like that weaken the character. If you can stop acting as though you were still in the nursery, Pyotr, we shall get on all right. Because I like a man that's prepared to risk something to get what he wants. But you're wanting the impossible. Admittedly, you speak quite a fair Russian, but even the village idiot would know you were never born here. And you could be Russian to the last louse in your shirt, you still wouldn't get into a town or out of one without an identity card, a *propusk*—preferably a valid one, but better dated next month than last. As for trains, you can't even look at one without showing your papers. You said that map of yours didn't give enough detail. That's all you know. The more detailed, the less accurate, in this country. Where it put villages, you'd as like as not find nothing. And where there were blanks, meaning open steppe country, or *taiga*, there would probably be a town of ten thousand inhabitants, sprung up in the last eight years. Roads, where you'd hardly expect hare tracks. Anywhere, at any time, in Siberia, you're liable to run into technicians, or workmen. The whole country is being planned, exploited, collectivized. That's life in the Soviet Union today.'

As he spoke of those great and disturbing events, Anastas beamed with pride. The established order had sentenced him to hard labour for committing a double murder, but though he now lived as an outlaw, he was immensely impressed by the fact that existence for him and his kind had been made almost impossible throughout the vast territories that that same order administered. Seeing this, Semyon maliciously started humming the Song of the Komsomols. Anastas listened for a moment, seemingly unaware of any ironic intention, and then softly joined in, eyes turned towards the sunset, and the host of midges that evening had brought to hover like golden mist above the stream.

'There's going to be rain,' he said.

But though, next morning, it was raining heavily, Anastas

had them all promptly at work by six o'clock, one standing by the sluice in the dam regulating the flow of water, while the others, including Forell, shovelled the sand into the primitive washing plant, consisting of a long, inclined board rather like a hen-roost in appearance with boxes let into it at intervals where the finer, gold-bearing sand was retained.

Midday came and went without any pause in the work, until Forell realized that the men were voluntarily imposing on themselves the same discipline that they had been forced to undergo as convicts in the gold mine. In fact, when Anastas at last gave the sign to cease work, they must have done at least twelve hours without a break. Then, dog-tired, they still had to perform the final washing process. In the last washing, the boxes of sand obtained during the day were emptied in turn over another inclined board over which water was slowly poured. As the sand rolled downwards, the grains of gold, grey in colour, were held back with a wooden scraper. After all the sand had been streamed, the final residue of gold was carefully brushed together.

Forell was disappointed at the minute quantity of gold obtained from the first day's work, but the others had expected nothing better. They knew well enough that the yield from this particular stream would be small, but to prospect for gold elsewhere, with all the paraphernalia it entailed for digging deep trial trenches, was impossible for them and even this meagre source would have been missed if Grigori, with his eyes trained to notice such things, had not detected a faint gleam here and there among the sand and recognized gold.

Each day, after the last washing had been completed, the men would shoulder their rifles and disperse to hunt their supper, usually a pigeon or some small animal; in either case, a meagre enough meal for four hungry men. In that particular area wild life was scarce and if nothing could be shot on the wing, the probability was that they would have to go hungry. If they were successful, they shot only what they could eat the same day and whoever fired first would know that as soon as they heard him the other men would unload and make their way back to the hut, confident that the bullet had found its mark. And indeed, bullets were too precious to be wasted. If, on the other hand, no one had any luck, next day Grigori would be taken off gold washing and sent further afield to find something for the larder. He was the best hunter of the three and could be relied on to return, though perhaps only after some days, with a load of venison on his back. The difficulty then was to eat it all before it went bad. There were no fish to be had in the stream and no time to search for fish elsewhere.

Time was short. All summer they washed gold and starved

121

the flesh from their ribs and had little enough to show for it at the end. For four months, Anastas never relaxed his twelve-hour day, until Forell began to wonder why these men had bothered to escape from the gold mine only to continue the same work on the same starvation diet. Occasionally, in moments of solidarity when they were not averse to thinking in communal terms, they would fetch out the pouch of gold to test its weight and gaze at it, trying to convince themselves that it was an adequate reward for their efforts. But nothing could alter the fact that, when converted into ammunition, clothing, salt, or any other commodity, the little heap of gold represented no more than the earnings of four unskilled labourers over the same period of time. The one advantage that could be put on the credit side against a hundred days of arduous toil was that, being gold, it would find universal acceptance even from such disreputable vagabonds as these, whereas a bank note, however genuine, might earn them no more than a bullet between the ribs.

It was a poor result for a whole summer's work and the immediate reason was simple: there was too little gold in the sand and too little sand had been put through the plant. But nevertheless, they worked on through September despite the increasing cold, and on into October, until the first hard frost descended and everything froze. Then even Anastas had to admit defeat, though it was only indirectly that he could bring himself to say so.

'More gold is lost every day in the overflows of the State washing plants than will ever be found in this stream, though we are the first to have worked it. What do you say, we give it a rest? Pyotr, what do you say?'

'What's the alternative?'

'Move on and spend the winter hunting, so we can eat something for a change.'

'I'm all for moving on; you know that.'

'Don't think things will be any easier, they won't. We know, because we've been around here for six years and we've tried everything.'

'Which direction do we go?'

'I suppose you want me to say "westwards, straight to the Fatherland"? I can't tell you where we'll go; we'll go wherever there's game. If we don't find any, we don't live. So if you're coming with us, you can forget about Germany.'

But Forell did not forget about Germany. It was exactly a year since his escape from the lead mine.

Next morning, they barricaded the hut with tree trunks to keep out wild animals and then took an indifferent leave of their home. If they came back, well and good. If they did not, and someone else eventually found shelter there, at least he would find a plentiful quantity of reindeer skins and be grateful to the anonymous donors. The skins were too heavy to take with them and Forell was thankful they had been left behind when, though he had by now become fairly skilful on Siberian skis, he found to his chagrin that the three scarecrows covered enormous distances in a single day and left him struggling far behind.

The men soon became disgruntled at having to wait for him each night and it was easy to tell from Semyon's expression what he was thinking: 'the man's slow, he's holding us back, why wait for him, why don't we leave him to rot?'

Forell realized the hatred he would incur if he continued to make such slow progress. Because of him, the others had to do all the reconnoitring and provide food for the evening meal as well. So far, they had marked the route for him by slicing an occasional piece of bark from a tree, but even so, they had time to make a fire and roast a couple of birds before he arrived. By the third evening, when he was hours late in reaching the bivouac, they had had enough of him.

'We can't go on like this.'

Forell was too exhausted to eat. It was all he could do to wet his gums with a handful of snow. 'Nobody's asking you to!'

'We've done the best we can for you.'

There was no doubt they had, after their fashion. Still. . . . 'What about my map? If you're going to push off, I shall need it, and now you've burnt the ruddy thing.'

'We can't unburn it,' said Anastas dispassionately. 'You can keep the rifle we lent you and you shall have your share of ammunition, as well.' He fetched out the leather pouch, with the gold. 'And you shall have a quarter of this. You're not entitled to it, because you didn't find it and you didn't build the plant, but you shall have exactly one quarter.'

Judging the weight in the palm of his hand, Anastas divided the contents of the pouch into four. He told Forell what he could buy with his quarter share: a sledge with a team of reindeer, or rifles and ammunition, or clothing, or a forged *propusk*, done so accurately that even an M.V.D. man would accept it.

'But where can I get a forged *propusk*?'

The three men burst out laughing. He'd discover that people would do anything to get gold, literally anything. For instance, said Semyon, he might wake up one morning to find his head had come apart from his neck. Semyon guffawed loudly, delighted with his witticism, while before Forell's mind rose a vision of that same Semyon turning back one day to find the German lying exhausted somewhere in the *taiga*, drawing a knife across his throat with compassionate skill and appropriating his share of the gold.

Anastas allowed him to choose his portion. Forell took one, put it back and felt another. Each quarter seemed identical, as though it had been weighed on scales. Then he ate, gnawing the half-cooked flesh from the bone with difficulty.

When they struck camp at the first light of dawn no one said much about the previous evening's arrangement. Semyon and Grigori said 'Good luck!' and with a pitying smile Anastas wished Forell a successful journey home. Then the three men set off, leaving it to Forell to keep up with them for as long as he cared, and then gradually to fall behind. What a waste of good wash-gold! they must have thought, as they saw the last of him. The pouch would slowly rot with the rest of his clothes, the gold would stream out and all that would eventually remain would be a little heap of sand beside a rifle, a pistol and what had once been a man. . . .

But despite all that had been said, one of the three—probably Anastas—still wanted to give Forell a chance to rejoin them and for some hours he kept coming across the familiar bared patches of tree trunk, marking the spots where they had left their previous track, or rejoined it again. He followed the signs, perhaps for five hours or so, because it saved him having to choose a route of his own, but he was in no hurry and when, a few yards ahead, he caught sight of an alpine hare, he decided there and then to accept the offered meal and call it a day. The hare was a fat one and after he had skinned it, Forell saw that it would last him a good three days. But first, he lit a fire so that he could roast the flesh tender, because his teeth were loose in their gums. Having eaten, he stirred the fire and sat gazing into the flames. There was no hurry. No sour looks and reproachful words awaited him by a bivouac miles ahead. He was alone, but he barely thought of that; he was too exhausted to think at all. All he knew was that he was warm, and so weak after the summer's privations that he hardly cared whether he ever got home.

Next day he followed the trail of the men ahead, resting whenever he felt like it and halting early to make his bivouac. The third day it was the same, except that the country seemed to be flattening out gently towards a plain. The going became easier and Forell's only concern was to find trees again when the time came for his nightly fire. Then he came on a wide area of snow that had been flattened by reindeer hooves. He judged that there must be about four hundred in the herd. It was difficult to see which direction they had taken as, grazing in twos and threes, they seemed to have wandered a considerable distance before moving on. The tracks of Anastas and his friends had been obliterated by the reindeer and Forell was not sorry. But somewhere there must be herdsmen—Pehtak and Laatmai perhaps, of odoriferous but joyful memory?

Reindeer herds move slowly and at that time of year there was only one direction they could have taken, namely towards the valley. For four days, Forell continued in pursuit of the herd until, on the last day, the trail took him through a narrowing glade, flanked on either side by closely growing trees. Soon the glade dwindled to a pathway and that, too, was on the point of vanishing when he heard a voice calling to him from among the trees.

'Pyotr!'

Forell raised his rifle.

'Pyotr, come over here!'

Anastas. It would be. . . . Just when he had accustomed himself to being on his own again and was hoping in a few days to catch up with the reindeer men, these furtive gentry had to waylay him!

'Anastas! What's the matter?'

'Nothing's the matter. We decided we didn't want to leave you behind that's all.'

'I was getting on all right. I thought you said I was too slow for you?'

'Let's talk it over,' pleaded Anastas. 'Come over and join us.'

'What do Semyon and Grigori say?'

'They want to have you back, of course!'

'Where are they? Why don't they speak up for themselves?'

'They're here. Can't you see them?'

Forell could not see them. It was a hold-up, thinly disguised. But why here? Why not further back, where the country had been deserted? And why give him the gold at all if they had not wanted him to keep it?

'Are you coming?'

Forell shouldered his rifle and followed Anastas through the trees into a clearing. Semyon and Grigori were sitting round a fire. 'Hullo,' they said, and grinned.

'You're lucky to be alive,' said Anastas. 'We ought never to have let you go off on your own with that gold. We ought to have warned you. You'd have had all the crooks in Siberia after you before long.'

Then Anastas asked for it back—for safe keeping, he said. 'Go on, take it!' Forell handed it over, furious with himself for not having struck out days before on a new trail of his own.

With the gold in his possession, Anastas became talkative. He said there was a herd of reindeer, six hundred strong, about two days' grazing ahead of them. Forell said he knew;

125

he'd seen the tracks. 'Fancy that!' said Anastas. 'He's seen the tracks!' The others sniggered.

'Well what are we going to do about these reindeer?' continued Anastas. 'There are two suggestions. The first is: we could catch up with the herd and then keep behind it for a couple of weeks, helping ourselves to a deer whenever we felt like it. It would be quite easy; there would only be two Tungus herdsmen and the Tungus can't count, though, as someone pointed out, they can tell from the behaviour of the stags when a deer is missing. However, we could take care of them. But we don't want to hurt anybody, it wouldn't be worth it. So that suggestion's out. Now Grigori, that notorious *Natschalnik* and purloiner of State property, suggests——'

But the rest of the sentence was stopped by Grigori who had leapt up and struck Anastas a slanting blow on the back of the neck with the edge of his outstretched hand. Anastas collapsed with hardly a groan. It was a joke—just a joke, that's all, and Grigori laughed. But Anastas, slowly recovering, thought differently. The blow had struck an artery and the pain was agonizing: Grigori should be made to feel it. Anastas began to creep towards him, staggered, then, master of himself again, seized him and began to beat him up systematically. Grigori was powerful, but no match for the other's sinewy strength, and Anastas left him in a sorry state. 'Anyone else?' he said. But there was no one else. There was only Grigori, and he had been dealt with, so what did it matter if murder burned in his eyes?

Anastas calmly resumed. 'Grigori—robber, cheat and coward though he is—has made a more interesting suggestion, namely that we should split off half a dozen or so animals from the herd and take them with us as livestock of our own. That we propose to attempt tonight.'

At that time of year, when moss was still plentiful, two days' grazing meant at the most twenty miles, a distance that could be covered in four hours. By midnight, the four men were near enough to the herd to be able to identify it. Then, creeping in closer, they saw the camp fire and the two herdsmen sitting by it. The stags were now becoming restless and after a while one of the men stood up to have a look round. From the animals' behaviour, he would know that it could not be wolves that disturbed them or they would be in a panic—it must be human beings. In that case, the man seemed to argue, there was no cause for alarm. Sooner or later the strangers would put in an appearance, ask leave, probably, to warm themselves at the fire, offer tobacco perhaps, which offer would be gratefully accepted. . . . The man sat down again.

Closer still now, the marauders were moving towards a

flank where a group of some twenty animals were grazing on their own, apart from the herd. At their approach, the reindeer lifted their heads and stood sniffing the strange scent, uncertain what they should do. Then they began running hither and thither in short, nervous rushes, trying to get past and rejoin the herd. At last, the herdsmen had realized that trouble was brewing and both now left the fire and came towards the stampede. But they were too late. By then the marauders had vanished, driving their booty before them.

For self-defence and as a means of herding the animals, the men had brought long poles with them and Forell tried to prevent the deer from rejoining the main herd by barring their way, holding the pole slantwise. But one of the stags came straight for him and before he could side-step, knocked him over. The reindeer then followed their leader, some of them trampling over the still prostrate Forell, until, badly bruised and shaken, he managed to stagger to his feet and with Semyon's assistance prevent the last six animals from escaping back to the herd.

For the rest of that night, the captured reindeer were so unmanageable that the marauders succeeded in putting only three or four miles between themselves and the herd. With the daylight, they had to reckon with an attempt to recover the animals and after they had managed to hobble the booty together, Forell, Semyon and Grigori dispersed to act as a rearguard, while at his own request, Anastas stayed with the kraal to ensure that if it came to the point, no one on his side would start a shooting match. That at all costs he was anxious to avoid.

Before long the two herdsmen were spotted as they came cautiously up the trail. Evidently the tracks had told them that there were four men ahead, for they were stopping repeatedly to listen, as though they expected an ambush. As they drew closer to the kraal, their pace slackened until finally Anastas saw them halt and hold a brief council of war. Then, with an apprehensive glance at the screen of trees ahead, the two herdsmen turned right about and went back whence they had come.

'Never trust an Asiatic!' warned Anastas, and proceeded to keep an eye on the herdsmen to see whether they moved on with what remained of the herd. Towards noon, they duly departed and then only was Anastas prepared to consider the six reindeer as his own by right of seizure and risk striking a new trail with them and his three companions.

In the event, the four rustlers had little joy of their booty. Animals and men seldom agreed on the choice of route and the latter were too ignorant of reindeer psychology to be able to persuade their charges to compromise. But each day, as

127

they got to know each other better, they covered a greater distance, until they were far enough from the scene of the raid for it to be tolerably certain that the first person they met would not recognize them as the thieves.

After a time, they came on some solid, clean-looking wooden houses. The sight of well-ordered prosperity is not calculated to appeal to any outlaw, and Anastas was no exception. Moreover, the construction of the houses revealed the organizing hand of officialdom, in that the timber had obviously not been found on the site. And officialdom spelt danger. 'Now we're for it!' said Anastas, as they reached the brow of a hill and saw the settlement spread out below. He was tempted to turn back but did not do so, firstly, because it would have looked too suspicious and, secondly, because the six reindeer appeared not to share his inclination, and to have an argument with them under the public gaze would look more suspicious still. So the four men had no alternative but to wander down as nonchalantly as they could in the wake of the browsing animals, firing off an occasional 'Hyi-yip!' and such other cries peculiar to their adopted profession as they could remember.

'Good evening to you, Comrades! Any chance of some shelter for the night?'

Six men looked up from a game of cards to see a rheumy-eyed herdsmen standing in the doorway. Anastas had time to note that an iron stove was roaring in a corner of the room, its pipe not trailing haphazardly out through a hole in the roof, but cemented into a properly constructed chimney—proof positive, to his mind, of the card players' ideological respectability.

The men showed no surprise. One of them—youngish, clean-shaven, suggesting the technocrat—spoke genially. 'Why not? If you don't mind sleeping on the floor. It's warm in here, anyway.'

What, Anastas asked himself, could have induced such people to build their neat, contemporary little houses in this God-forsaken spot?

'Where have you come from?' asked the sleek young man, obviously in the best of moods.

'We're hunters, sir, and trappers, heading down towards the coast; had some bad luck on the way, lost three sledges. . . . Six reindeer and a gun or two, that's all that's left to us in the world.'

'Well, come inside and shut the door. Sit down!' And taking a pack of cards, the young man started to deal.

'Begging your pardon, Comrade, but we were wondering how far it is to the nearest Hunting Base?'

'No idea,' said the young man.

'We want to re-equip ourselves; we can offer a few hides in payment or . . .'

'Amplany!' bawled the young man. 'Get the Comrades something to eat.'

The 'something' turned out to be more than their contracted stomachs could hold. But though the plentiful meal was certainly a proof of goodwill, the four men had an uncomfortable feeling that at any moment the situation might change—and they kept their rifles stacked close by in case of need. From time to time, while they were eating, one of the card players would eye their weapons with furtive admiration. Nice-looking guns! A pity they'd been neglected. . . .

After the meal, they and their hosts began to talk. The clean-shaven young man seemed to be a surveying officer. He and his team had been in the neighbourhood for over a year, surveying an area of several hundred square miles. They had had a good time, he said; then added in a tone which implied that the good time was shortly coming to an end: 'We're expecting Comrade Lederer this evening.'

The card players looked uneasy. Comrade Lederer was obviously a man to be feared. An unholy combination of organizing ability and political fervour, he could be relied on, they said, to act with gusto — inspecting, questioning, admonishing, possibly even ordering the transfer of some luckless half-dozen or so men to more remote and less comfortable jobs, where at any rate one thing could be taken as certain—there would be no trim wooden houses with built-in stoves. . . . Apparently, three men in the surveying team had particular reason for apprehension because they were *Strafniki*, in other words, convicts doing hard labour.

It was clear now, the rustlers could hardly have landed themselves more deeply in the mire. Was there much going on in the neighbourhood, inquired Anastas innocently—farming, for instance, or——? The survey officer gestured vaguely. The nearest *kolchoz* was over a hundred miles away, he said, but there was plenty of development otherwise over the whole area. There was a highway under construction and that took a good deal of labour. Work gangs were dotted about over most of the countryside. . . .

Cheerful news, indeed! At last, the card players broke up and started cleaning out the room in preparation for Comrade Lederer's arrival. Anastas seized his opportunity. Muttering something about keeping an eye on the reindeer, he signed to the rustlers to follow him—yes, all four men would be needed in case the animals had strayed some distance. As though from mere habit, they shouldered their rifles and slouched out of the building. The rucksacks, unfortunately, they had to leave behind.

'Mind you keep your mouth shut!' hissed Anastas to Forell as soon as they were outside. 'If necessary, I'll say you're a deaf mute.' He turned to the others. 'We'll have to face it out here. Better meet this man, Lederer, than run into a gang of convicts somewhere!'

At that moment, they heard the roar of a motor engine, and the next second, a lorry, a Ford six-wheeler, appeared round a corner of a building and headed, lurching perilously, towards the one they had just left. Comrade Lederer, it seemed, had arrived. Now the survey officer had emerged and was hastening across the snow to welcome his superior. Anastas stretched a finger to explore a sudden feeling of constriction round the throat. Now the lorry had stopped and Anastas gazed, lost in admiration, as the great man descended.

On the bridge of Comrade Lederer's quarrelsome nose sat a pair of gold-framed, rimless spectacles, the thick lenses giving his eyes a glittering, ubiquitous look. He walked leaning slightly forward after the manner of some great commander in the field who, when the day is almost won, ascends a convenient hillock, there to order the dispositions that will complete the enemy's rout. That there was no convenient hillock for Comrade Lederer to ascend was clearly causing him some vexation. While the survey officer was making his report, his eyes swept the terrain.

'Those men over there—what are they doing? Who are they?'

'Hunters, Comrade Lederer. They have lost their sledges.'

'Lost them? There must be an inquiry.'

The survey officer led the way indoors, towards warmth and, he hoped, a more cordial atmosphere. Anastas followed, to sit as a silent and admiring spectator, as Comrade Lederer took stock of the work done by the survey team, questioned, admonished, cross-questioned, all with the same thin-lipped, icy precision. What a performance! What a man! Reading the admiration in Anastas' eyes, Lederer gave a curt nod of acknowledgment. Anastas nodded back. The Comrade smiled. Anastas gave an answering beam. Then the voice cut in:

'You've lost your sledges, have you? Disgraceful! You ought to be ashamed of yourselves!'

'It was like this, Comrade Lederer. Can I explain——?'

'You can and will explain to the Head of the Hunting Base. I don't want to hear your story. The cost will be deducted from your earnings. You've been stupid, that's obvious, and stupidity is sabotage—do you realize that?'

Listening to Comrade Lederer, Anastas must have looked stupid indeed. The next moment, the Comrade laughed. Incalculable, thought Anastas. He enjoys making people afraid of him and then laughs at their fear.

'We built the sledges ourselves.'

'A criminal waste of time! Hunting is your job—you're not going to spend half the winter sitting around here. You will draw two new sledges from store immediately. You will sign a receipt for them. And you will remain responsible for them until they are returned.'

There was a pause while Comrade Lederer filled out a form. 'This entitles you to draw your equipment from the Dalstroy store twenty-five miles up-river. It will save you having to go to the Hunting Base and means you can start work sooner.'

Anastas took the form and scrutinized it. He decided to tempt fortune into a yet broader smile. 'Thank you, Comrade —Comrade Overseer,' (that was what the survey officer had called him), 'but there are one or two other things we shall need. We're low in ammunition, for instance, and with the sledges we lost our tent and spare clothing, as well. Axes, too, and shovels. . . .'

'Ammunition? How much?'

'Four hundred rounds of shot-gun and a hundred and fifty rounds of ball.'

Comrade Lederer started filling out a second form.

'Shall we be able to draw those from the store?'

'You will. Here you are. One tent; four axes; four shovels; ammunition! three sets of double sledge-team harness, complete; clothing, and food. My driver will show you the way. And now get out of here!'

'Yes, Comrade! Thank you, Comrade Overseer!'

Then Comrade Lederer delivered his parting shot. 'I shall be calling at the store tomorrow night. Woe betide you if I find you still hanging around!'

Having received food and directions for their journey, Forell and his companions rounded up the six reindeer and set off into the night. Next morning, by eleven, they reached the Dalstroy Depot, a collection of wooden huts and tents, and two hours later, they had everything they had asked for, including a big freight-carrying sledge to be drawn by four reindeer harnessed in pairs and a light sledge for two reindeer in tandem, on the understanding that the equipment was issued solely for use during the hunting season and that its value would be taken into account in the final settlement. It only remained for them to vanish with their booty before Comrade Lederer arrived.

Even with trained animals, it woud have been no simple task to drive a heavily-loaded sledge over ground as yet only thinly covered with snow. As it was, the inhabitants of the settlement were treated to an impromptu circus as the men tried to break in the animals and, at the same time, learn how to drive. First, Anastas was sent flying from his seat as the reindeer galloped over a mound, and then Forell departed on a hectic involuntary tour of the hutments, to appear again at the completion of the circuit, shaken, but still in his seat, amid loud applause.

The onlookers then joined in the performance, loading up the freight-carrying sledge to the maximum in the hope that, if the reindeer could not be tamed, at least it might be possible to tire them. But after the fourth desperate sortie had made no apparent effect on their energies and, for the fourth time, they had left the sledge-load scattered like gifts from a drunken Father Christmas in their wake, those, including Forell, who had some experience of handling reindeer, decided that more drastic measures were called for.

This time, a medium-sized tree trunk was roped to the tail of the sledge. That should do the trick! No reindeer could drag that around for long and preserve a pioneering spirit! Forell climbed into the perch that optimistic persons called a driving seat and gave a subdued 'hyi-yip!' to the team. As the sledge gathered speed, the bystanders noticed that the massive rudder was at least persuading the reindeer to pull in the same direction instead of struggling to make off, each on a private trip of its own, though as the tree trunk went crashing against the corners of the huts, it became obvious enough that it was no specific for the circling disease. However, by the end of the circuit, the reindeer were clearly beginning to tire and, for the first time, showed no particular desire to go anywhere. Quickly, the ropes were untied and Forell gave the animals their head to draw the loaded sledge. They moved off slowly and amiably in a dead straight line.

By then, most of the afternoon had gone and whether the reindeer's good behaviour signified a change of heart or merely a change of tactics could not be put to the test. If the wrath of Comrade Lederer was to be avoided, the party would have to leave immediately. Forell was the man to drive the sledge, said Anastas. Forell had been given opportunity enough earlier in the year to learn how to handle reindeer. He himself had somehow never got on with animals. . . . So the sledge-load was secured, while they discussed the general direction which Forell would take in the unlikely event of the reindeer allowing their driver any choice in the matter. Anastas, Grigori and Semyon would follow with the light sledge, carrying as much of the stores as they could, including some of the essential items in case the big sledge with its load came to grief.

It seemed unlikely that Forell would get far, but at all events he would try and get a safe distance from the settlement, so that the four men could bivouac for the night beyond reach of the man, Lederer. If the others had not caught up with

132

him by nightfall, Forell, if he thought it safe to do so, would light a fire to guide them to the bivouac. All this had to be discussed in snatches, whenever the two men happened to be out of earshot of the depot staff, to whom they remained to the last four sturdy hunters of the Soviet Union.

Luck and his own skill as a sledge driver enabled Forell to cover about fifteen miles in four hours. The reindeer behaved admirably throughout the journey, answering the reins and pulling steadily, for a good deal of the way, uphill. After four hours, Forell stopped and, choosing a suitable spot, lit a fire to guide the others to the bivouac. But it was noon on the following day before they caught up. All three were in high spirits.

'Comrade Lederer is a man of his word,' shouted Anastas, when still some distance away. 'He was there on the dot of seven!' The three men came up and stood gazing at the reindeer, the sledge and its load, as though they had never expected to see them again. 'You've done well, Pyotr. You're quite good at managing reindeer; better than we are, I admit——'

But better than anybody at that and every other task, apparently, was the Comrade Overseer Lederer. To Anastas he personified the vanished ideals of his own Communist youth and Anastas had still not recovered from his last, furtive glimpse of the man and the feelings of nostalgia and awe which it had provoked. To his men, said Anastas, the Comrade was a terror and a scourge. Forell should have seen how the lazy and the inefficient quailed before his rasping admonishments! There was no task, however specialized, that he could not perform, and better than the experts themselves. The way he managed a team of sledge-dogs, or reindeer, was a poem. Throughout the vast district which he administered, he was the supreme authority, the sole source of knowledge and encouragement, whether in road-building, gold-mining, hunting or anything else. 'We couldn't have found a better man,' said Anastas.

'Better, or worse, according to how little or how much he knows about us,' replied Forell.

'All the same, we don't want to outstay our welcome. We'll push on just as fast as we can—westward, Pyotr, the way you want to go.'

They started next morning, before sunrise. The rest had not improved the sledge teams' discipline and some days later, when the men came to an immense river, they were relieved to find that ankle-high snow still covered the ice. They would never have been able to coax the animals across bare ice and as it was, they had difficulty enough in keeping them on the move for no less than eight miles, until they found a spot on the far bank where the ground fell away, allowing an almost level egress for the sledges.

'In the summertime,' said Anastas, 'ocean-going steamers come right up here from the Arctic.' Incredible as the statement sounded, no one dared contradict him, for Anastas had a dangerous temper.

*　　*　　*

The winter with all its severities was now upon them. It was so cold that any sudden movement of hand or arm made the air crackle like thick paper and as soon as they left the camp fire in the mornings the men's boots became as hard as bone. Before they could take them off, or use reindeer skins as a covering for the night, they had laboriously to thaw everything out in front of the fire. The fire, indeed, was the only source of comfort in a frost-bound world, and in its circle of warmth, a man could at least suspend for a while the grim struggle to survive and turn his thoughts to other things.

Owing to the cold and the necessity of allowing time for the reindeer to find grazing, progress was painfully slow and a fortnight had passed before the men were once more in wild and uninhabited regions where the risk of undesired encounters was small. In that time, they had met with three parties of hunters, on each occasion being treated with open mistrust and hostility. What it was about them that aroused suspicion they were unable to define, and to be cold-shouldered without apparent reason was doubly disturbing. Their equipment was correct—that they could see by comparing it with the others'. Their clothing was not unduly shabby. The other men must have sensed that they were bogus, rather than seen any positive evidence. Their manner of speech, perhaps, had given them away, their lack of cordiality, their guilty conscience, or some trick of gait that only a genuine hunter would have or recognize.

By each party, they had been asked the same question: where were they heading for? There were only two possible answers. They could say they were on their way to some recognized hunting ground, or to some new territory where the game was still intact. These were the only answers that Anastas or his companions could give, for they represented the sole alternatives open to men who professed any serious intention of hunting. But in the first case, they might be looked on as undesirable intruders, in the second, as pioneers whom it would be worth joining to exploit whatever opportunities might arise. Yet the truth was that they had only one desire: to avoid the sight of their fellow men and the obligation to give even a false account of themselves to

134

anyone, for now that they were allegedly hunters, they knew from experience how much harder it was to lie convincingly. On one occasion, for example, they had found themselves on a busy main road, far from any possible hunting ground, a prey to the more than idle curiosity of passing M.V.D. men. That experience they were not anxious to repeat.

Their first object, then, was to live and not be seen and only in so far as they had to hunt to stay alive did they pursue their adopted calling. Otherwise their energies were devoted to chasing a strange kind of will-o'-the-wisp. Somewhere, they felt, there must be a region so wild and inaccessible that, once there, they would be safe from all intruders and their worries would be at an end. And so they plodded on. Wherever there was a crag, they would climb it; wherever a jungle, they would laboriously hack their way through. But the refuge of their dreams eluded them. After days of exasperating toil across forlorn and treacherous country, they would seem at last to be on the threshold of a forgotten world, when suddenly the scenery would change, become tamer, and they would find themselves amid ordered domesticity again.

They would turn back, then, to the safety of the wilderness, embittered by the aimlessness of their existence, hating each other, deliberately choosing the roughest and hardest routes, believing that what was difficult must also be worthwhile. But there was little to show for it, no solid achievement in the shape of reindeer skins piled high on their sledges and the sledges themselves and all the splendid equipment that Comrade Lederer, in his folly, had bestowed on them proved merely a liability that hampered movement and gained them nothing in return. Admittedly, they were spared the hunger that had been their gaunt companion during the summer months. They shot a wild sheep and a stray reindeer. Hares were plentiful and sometimes a covey of grey partridges would start up under their feet, to go skimming across the *taiga* in alternate spurts and glides.

And yet, for Forell those days held a unique enchantment —that winter seemed the finest he had spent for a decade.

* * *

The cold, that night, was unusually intense, and in the clearing among trees where they had made their bivouac, the four men were lying huddled in their tight shut tent. Outside, a glacial wind was moaning and, from time to time there came a drawn-out cracking sound, as though the solid earth were slowly disintegrating under the pressure of the cold.

Suddenly, the reindeer grazing in the vicinity could be heard coming closer in towards the tent. The next moment,

135

one of them thrust its head under the laced-up opening. The others came to a halt, their bodies pressing in against the sides, and then their breathing could be heard, shallow and urgent with fear. Anastas and Semyon spoke together: 'Wolves!' All four men grasped for their rifles. Semyon was the first to get outside, and when the others had joined him, they listened silently for a while, their eyes searching the steel-blue haze. Anastas whispered to Forell: 'One of us must stay with the reindeer. It had better be you. Keep them close together, if you can, here, by the tent. The wolves are up-wind of them.' As he spoke, Semyon moved off, a dark form, gliding, halting, gliding on, till it merged and was lost in the void. Anastas and Grigori followed to the left and right of him, in a series of stealthy runs. Then they too became indistinct until all that Forell could see as they stopped some distance away was an occasional glint from their rifles.

By the tent, Forell was trying to pacify the reindeer. With nostrils distended and heaving flanks, the animals were shifting continually as the stench of the wolves came to them, borne on the icy wind. Forell stroked their manes, whispered comforting words and laid a hand over their quivering nostrils to let them scent the presence of a friend. It was all he could do to stop them breaking away, and if one did, the rest would follow and all would be destroyed. Once the wolves had tasted blood, their ferocity and daring would be redoubled and it would be high time, then, for the men to look to themselves.

The reindeer were trembling from head to foot now and glistened with sweat. At intervals, a spasm of fear would run through them like an electric shock. The wolves were coming nearer. Suddenly there was a shot and on top of it, a horrible, piercing howl rang out, stayed for a moment, then fell, choking into silence. Another shot. And then two more.

A few minutes later, the three men returned, grinning all over their faces. They had seen the wolves quite clearly, about twenty of them, lurking among some trees. The first shot had been fired by Semyon. It must have killed the leader of the pack, for the rest had simply turned tail and fled. The men had heard and seen them go and the last three shots had been fired into their tails.

The danger was past, but it was dawn before the reindeer ceased trembling.

* * *

That was not the only occason when the reindeer gave the men timely warning of danger. One day they had been marching long hours in bright sunlight, and as always when the

136

weather was clear, the brilliance of the snow had blurred their eyesight, as though a curtain of grey mist had descended, obscuring the view. And so, until the sledge team began sweating and dancing about, the men failed to notice that with each step they took, they were superimposing their footprints on those of a bear.

The tracks seemed at the most only two days old and, exhilarated by the thought of a valuable bear skin as well as by the thrill of the chase, the men increased their pace to the maximum which the reindeer would allow. After a while they reached a point where the bear had left the pathway and gone climbing up a hill-side. Should they follow, or not? Their combined experience of bears was precisely nil, but it seemed obvious that he would be able to move very much faster than four men, six reindeer and two sledges. Less evident was Grigori's contention that even if they caught up with him, he could still give them the slip. A bear, he said, could thrust a medium-sized sapling from his path as easily as a man might draw a curtain. A bear could literally part the scenery and let it fall into place again behind him.

That might be so, thought the others, but bears were undoubtedly being shot every day of the year by someone— why not by themselves? They would follow, and give Fate a chance to do them a good turn.

So up the hill-side they went, manhandling the sledges up the worst of the slope, eyes glued to the bear tracks and hearts burning with the zeal of the chase. For three whole days the tracks led them on, gradually becoming more clearly defined until at last they seemed only a few minutes old. Then suddenly the men came upon a clearing. In the centre, the ground was a veritable turmoil of foot marks, like a circus arena; or a playground for bears. If any of them had had thoughts that they were wasting their time and that it might be better to turn back, the sight of the bear pit restored unanimity. From now on the four men had a single passion: the bear—at all costs, at whatever sacrifice, and whether they caught up with him this year or next. . . .

By this time, night was coming on. They went another half mile, without further signs of the bear until they came to a dense thicket growing in the shape of a horseshoe. In the centre they made their bivouac, setting up the tent, bringing in the reindeer with the sledge, but reluctantly deciding against cutting poles to bar the exit to their animals, for fear of making too much noise. Silence was the thing, said Anastas, assuming a knowledgeable air; and from then on, they spoke only in whispers. . . . No one felt any desire for sleep, least of all Forell, but because he was the stranger, he was left to guard the reindeer while the other three loaded their rifles with ball and crept off to observe the bear pit.

Alone, Forell saw to the reindeer, then sat down in the tent to wait. At any moment, because he was not there, he expected to hear the sounds of a pitched battle. But there was nothing. All night long not even the reindeer stirred.

Shortly after dawn, Anastas, Grigori and Semyon returned. Waiting motionless for the bear, not even able to stamp their feet, they had been driven back by the cold. They poured some scalding tea down their throats and then Anastas found his voice.

'A wash-out! A complete and utter wash-out! We heard nothing, and we saw nothing, until just now, when it got light —and then, do you know what? Not ten yards away, in the middle of that bear pit——'

Anastas broke off, then barked at Semyon: 'It's a ruddy insult!'

'A bear?' said Forell.

Anastas snorted. 'A pile of droppings!'

Towards midday, after a few hours' sleep, the three men set off again, and searched everywhere, among crags, thickets and dense undergrowth in the hope of coming face to face with their contemptuous opponent. But in vain. At nightfall, another sortie. This time, Forell joined the hunt and Grigori stayed behind to guard the reindeer. As on the previous night, the hunters spread out in a semi-circle within sight of the bear pit.

Meanwhile, Grigori was not sorry to be in the comparative warmth and comfort of the tent. He dozed for a while contentedly, then got up, from long habit slipped his Siberian knife into its sheath at his side, and went out to have a look at the reindeer. They seemed rather restless, but that no doubt was from hunger. The bear hunt had taken priority over their grazing. It was still early, about two o'clock, he thought. He could sleep for a good six hours. Grigori went back to the tent and made himself comfortable under a pile of skins.

When he woke up, it was light. No sign of Anastas and the others; unless—the reindeer seemed to be trampling about a good deal; perhaps the men were coming now. Mechanically, Grigori pulled on his cap, fixed the flaps under his chin, sheathed his knife and went outside, grinning already at the thought of the dejected hunters.

And there was Anastas, muffled in his furs, a few paces away, looking back over his shoulder for the others!

'Well,' said Grigori politely, 'did you have a good time?'

There was no answer. So that's how it was! Feeling a bit peevish, were we? A good hearty slap on the back would soon cure that! Grigori took a pace forward and spoke in a sugary voice, at the same time raising his hand. 'I said, did you have——' But voice and hand remained suspended in mid-air, because at that moment, Anastas went down on all fours. Anastas was a bear.

For a moment, Grigori was paralysed. The shock drained the blood from his brain and if to seize the knife from its sheath had depended on thought, he would have been too late. But the action was instinctive and when the bear, with claws outstretched, aimed a lightning blow at his head, the long, curving blade was already in his hand. . . .

Some time later, when the hunters returned, they found a black bear, stone dead, some four yards from the tent and Grigori sprawled face downwards close by the entrance. The bear was lying in a pool of blood. Blood spattered the sides of the tent and from somewhere beneath Grigori, a dark red stain was slowly spreading out over the snow. But it was surface bleeding, from Grigori's cheek, where the flesh had been ripped by the bear's claws, and as the men lifted him, he opened his eyes. He could remember nothing at first, but when, catching the glint of steel, someone recovered his knife from the snow, he began to recall what had happened.

A split second before he had made to clap Anastas on the shoulder, the realization that it was a bear flashed on his mind. The animal had been standing on its hind legs and as it dropped down to all fours, his hand brushed its head. Immediately, the bear reared up again, exposing its chest and at that moment, Grigori supposed, he must have plunged in the knife. The last he could remember was a searing blow on his face.

No one had ever denied that Grigori had courage and he was given due credit now for having dispatched a bear single-handed, without stirring from the bivouac while his rifle had hung, useless, a few yards away in the tent. But Grigori was not interested in due credit; what he wanted was inordinate and extravagant praise. For several days, while he went about with a torn-up shirt round his face and his ability to speak steadily improved, he devoted himself to rubbing home the contrast between the fruitless vigil of three men with a fire-power to kill twenty bears and the swift slaughter performed by one man with a few inches of curving steel. But Grigori's aura was no sooner established than it was shattered. Within the space of four days, the bag was increased to three.

Though the bears were of no more than moderate size, the skins were in excellent condition, and when they and the choicer cuts of bear meat had been loaded on to the sledges, the equipage at last began to look like a hunting expedition. The winter cold had at any rate one advantage; the meat quickly froze into iron-hard blocks and the hides could safely be carried in the raw state without danger of decomposing.

139

The weeks of arduous and, until latterly, aimless wanderings seemed to have led the party into a region where the wild life was completely untouched. In a matter of days, Forell and Semyon each shot a marten, striped and flying squirrels were plentiful and no less than nine Arctic foxes were killed and skinned. Admittedly, these successes were not achieved without sacrifice of time, labour and progress westwards through Siberia, but to Forell the sacrifice was worthwhile, for these adventurous weeks were filled with a new-found joy of hunting. The higher grew the pile of raw hides on the sledge, the less he was conscious of the cold, the wildness of the scenery, the danger and the essential aimlessness of the life he was leading. If it was not possible to pursue game and, at the same time, a private goal of one's own, then he was content to postpone his efforts to get home.

Anastas, too, was fired with zeal, though in a different sense. 'We are rich men,' he declared one day, eyeing the sledge load of valuable furs. Then he added: 'But we're going to be richer.' And so, because Anastas so willed it, the other three raised no more than a mumble of protest when he decided to continue hunting for another fortnight, instead of making down to the plain to sell the furs they had.

That was late in February, and by then, experienced hunters would have been on the move, away from the wild and inaccessible areas with their thick vegetation and the death traps of rock and precipice which it concealed, so that they could be sure of reaching the plains before the onset of the March storms. But Anastas was not an experienced hunter and so the party struggled on, through dense, snow-smothered forest, across tangled masses of dead branches and fallen trunks, up precipitous gorges and along frozen rivulets, heading always in whatever direction the scenery looked most impenetrable and forlorn.

Once, they found themselves, with night coming on, on a wind-swept height, with no protection, let alone grazing for the reindeer, and barely room enough to set up their tent. Too exhausted to retrace their steps, they cowered in their wind-jostled shelter, while their lips swelled and turned blue with cold and the water from their streaming eyes froze on their cheeks and beards.

On another occasion, after toiling uphill through dense vegetation for several hours, they at last broke out into a clearing, only to find their progress blocked on all sides. Ahead, the clearing bordered on an almost vertical face of rock with a drop of a hundred feet. To their right, the ground rose again steeply, with so little foothold that to attempt it, man-handling the sledges, was out of the question. To the left, the clearing was fringed with an impenetrable mass of giant hawthorn and Arctic bramble. The route by which they had come, though possible uphill, would have been extremely precarious in the reverse direction and to attempt it would have meant abandoning the sledges, with the tent and all their equipment, with the result that they would have frozen to death. As it was, they were cold enough. All night long, a snowstorm raged, thrusting in the sides of the tent and making it impossible to strike a light, so that, besides being deprived of a warm supper, the men were unable to smoke. Each of them realized then, as he lay, hungry, exhausted and numb with cold, that for the sake of the reindeer as well as for themselves, they must find a way out of the wilderness and head towards civilization again while they still had the strength.

Already, the animals were dangerously thin and becoming almost daily thinner, while the men's winter exertions, coming on top of the summer's starvation and grinding toil had reduced them to walking skeletons. Their skins were blotched and yellow with jaundice, their legs and feet perpetually swollen. Latterly, they had suffered from moods of black depression and tasks which a few weeks before had been looked on as mere routine, they now performed with the querulous desperation of men on the verge of collapse.

Next day, after the reindeer in their search for moss had found a path out of the clearing and the men, by dint of their utmost exertions, had succeeded in following them, Anastas gave expression to the common thought.

'Now that the winter's over——'

Semyon gave a mocking laugh.

'Now that the winter's over,' repeated Anastas, 'we must think of getting down into the plain, before the rivers thaw and the last of the snow goes. We shall have to find a place where we can get rid of the hides. Don't forget; we're rich men. . . .'

It took a lot of believing. Perhaps that was why Anastas said it so often: perhaps he did not believe it himself. Divided into four, the sum the furs might fetch would not amount to wealth, and the 'might' was a big one, for between the men and their money lay endless vistas of heart-breaking work, hauling the sledge load, hacking their way back to civilization. And then, the real difficulties would begin: how to persuade the officials at the Hunting Depot to accept furs from men without papers and hence men they would be unable to identify. In the last resort, there was no reason, none at all, why a Party official should have the least hesitation in confiscating their load and putting them back behind bars. But the risk had to be taken, if they were to continue to exist.

Meanwhile, as the weather showed signs of relenting, they

were able to rest while the reindeer were allowed two days' uninterrupted grazing before starting their journey to the plain. It was March now and in the lowland the snows would already be growing less. If they waited longer, the benefits of the rest would be cancelled out by the heavier going for the reindeer when the sledge runners sank into the melting snow.

And so, after two days, feeling weaker, if anything, than when their rest had begun and reluctant as never before to face the perils and hardships of their life, the men struck the tent and prepared to move on—towards the south, said Anastas, but the others thought west would be safer, away from the sea. So it was decided to go westwards.

But first, the reindeer had to be rounded up, and that was left to Grigori. When he started to harness them to the sledge, one of the animals, a stag, sank down on its knees and refused to budge. It was panting heavily and, from time to time, its hind quarters would be gripped with a spasm of pain. As none of the men knew how to treat it, it was clear that the animal would have to be put out of its misery, by a shot through the heart. No one volunteered, but Grigori did not refuse because he was afraid of Anastas, and Anastas ordered him to do the shooting. When the reindeer lay dead at his feet, he burst into tears and he was still weeping long after the others had started to discuss how the heavy load of furs and themselves could best be distributed between the two sledges.

Forell had less right to voice an opinion than Semyon or Anastas and he could do nothing to alter the decision when Anastas finally decreed: 'One man, one sledge, one reindeer —that's no good. If the man ran into trouble, no one could help him. So we'll arrange it like this: Grigori, and Pyotr will ride on the small sledge with the single, unpaired reindeer. All the freight now on the small sledge will be transferred to the big one and Semyon and I will go ahead at a slow speed and wait for you at sundown.'

It was easily said and, of course, it could not be helped that both sledges would now be overloaded, but four animals used to working as a team would have an easier time of it than a single reindeer called upon to draw a sledge with two men immediately after losing its partner. Though Anastas made detours occasionally so that the small sledge following behind should not get stuck, that did not alter the fact that Forell was repeatedly forced to get down and follow the trail on foot until it started to slope downhill again.

'Follow our tracks!' Anastas had said. 'We'll bivouac at nightfall.' In the event, it was long after dark when Grigori and Forell caught up with him.

* * *

At about half-past nine, when it was still twilight, Anastas and Semyon started setting up the tent. To do it properly, erecting the poles and weighting down the sides would take time and they had gone ahead faster than they had promised so as to allow themselves a good half-hour. When the tent was up, they collected food for a fire and then roasted some bear meat. By the time it was cooked, they were too hungry to wait for the others and Anastas started eating straight away.

At the first mouthful he grimaced. 'It needs salt. Where's the bag?'

'Under the hides somewhere, at the bottom of the sledge.'

'I can't search for that now. Semyon, give me some of yours.'

'I haven't got any salt.'

'Well, get Grigori's rucksack—he'll have some.'

'He'll slaughter me if he finds out I've been rummaging in his kit,' said Semyon lugging the rucksack into the firelight.

'Yes, I expect so,' said Anastas calmly. 'He sleeps on it every night. Have you noticed that?'

Semyon was feeling around under the flap. 'Plenty of dirt here, but no salt.'

'Well, pack it up again and put it back on the sledge!'

The next moment, Semyon gave a low whistle. 'Hey! What's this?' He was holding a small oblong in his hand wrapped in grimy wool. 'Come and feel the weight of this!'

Anastas slipped round the fire and tested the weight in his palm. The thing was as heavy as lead. Looking at it closely, he saw that the lengths of woollen material were stitched carefully together along the sides and held in position with two small straps.

'Let's open it up!'

'We can't—without him knowing. . . .'

When Grigori and Forell arrived, they found the other two eating their supper by the fire. 'You've had an easy time of it,' grumbled Forell.

'And what about you?' retorted Semyon. 'We cooked the supper—all you have to do is eat it.'

There was silence. A curious constraint seemed to lie over the four men. It continued until after the late-comers had eaten. Then Anastas handed round the vodka-bottle. Up till now, vodka had only been used on the rarest occasions—to disinfect a wound, or in extreme cases of exhaustion and cold. As a stimulant, it was useless, Anastas had always maintained. It bucked you up and then left you stranded, worse off than you were before. For that reason, it was dangerous.

'But the worst of the danger is over now,' he said cheerfully, passing the bottle.

'Is it?' said Forell. 'I shouldn't have thought so at all!'

'Well, we hope it is,' replied Anastas blandly, and urged everyone to drink. Grigori barely wetted his lips, Semyon refused and Anastas sipped politely. The level in the bottle stayed curiously high. Only Forell drank deep and so failed to realize that there was an object behind Anastas' alleged conversion to vodka, for before long it was little enough of the other men's talk that penetrated his reeling brain. As the evening wore on, the voices around him became more acrimonious. He gathered they were having an argument with Grigori. 'Shut your mouth!' someone yelled. 'What do you know about it?' And a while later, another voice, Semyon's perhaps: 'Have you ever met an honest man? Give me a name, just one single name. . . .' Later still, in a brief interval of lucidity, Forell heard Grigori say:

'You can go without me, then. I'll buy myself a forged *propusk* and go and live like a human being again, fur trading, or something. . . .'

'If you can keep your hands from stealing!' said Anastas.

'Who doesn't steal?' retorted Grigori.

Anastas sounded outraged as he said: 'Nonsense!'

Semyon interposed. 'I agree with Grigori, at any rate as far as the gold-mine was concerned. The overseers were worse than the convicts. Look at the way they cheated us of our bonuses! Anyone finding one of the big nuggets was supposed to get three bottles of vodka, wasn't he? And what did we get? Half a bottle—and half of that was water!'

'Oh yes, you're right there,' said Anastas. 'The men would rather chuck the big stuff away, tip out the gold with the waste than see themselves diddled like that—wouldn't they, Grigori?'

Grigori made no reply. 'I said, wouldn't they?' repeated Anastas.

Wouldn't they . . .? wouldn't they . . .? The words were still sounding in Forell's ears as he fell asleep. It was some time before he learnt what Grigori had already guessed: the others had discovered Grigori's secret, and the object of the vodka bottle was to induce him to reveal it. For Grigori himself had once found a big nugget of gold, and unlike the other men, he had not thrown it away.

Next morning, when Forell and Grigori again set off on the small sledge, Grigori insisted they took their rucksacks with them. That meant adding about eight stone to the load drawn by a single reindeer and the animal had already been limping on the previous day.

'You're crazy, Grigori! We won't get a yard like that!'

'And you're still drunk,' retorted the robber. 'Volka isn't water, you know.'

'But why not leave the rucksacks with the others—they were all right yesterday.'

'Were they . . .?'

Grigori was full of unaccountable suspicion. He said the single reindeer would be finished soon, anyway. He asked Forell what had happened to his Siberian skis—he might need them before long. He wanted to know how much ammunition Forell had on him. And finally, he forecast that if they travelled for a fortnight, they would never catch up with Anastas and Semyon again. But there he was wrong. They followed the tracks of the big sledge all day and came to the bivouac shortly after dark. As on the previous night, the tent had already been set up, the fire had been lit and bear meat was roasting over the flames. They deposited their rucksacks in the tent and then sat round the fire with the others. Anastas and Semyon were in surly mood. They seemed to have been quarrelling all day. Grigori kept glancing at them as he ate his supper, as though trying to read their thoughts. Then as soon as he had finished, he got up and went into the tent. Forell stayed, hoping to discover the reason for the others' ill humour. But they never spoke a word.

Before they set off next morning, Anastas asked Grigori to reconnoitre the route with him for about a quarter of a mile ahead. It was a pretext, obviously, to talk to him alone, but Grigori agreed: talk could never rob him of his gold. Sure enough, as soon as they were out of earshot, Anastas told him bluntly that his secret was out. Grigori already knew that —or so he maintained, when later he gave the German his version of what had transpired.

Anastas had started: 'I've got something to say to you, Grigori.'

'Well, can't you say it in front of the others? We've got no secrets, have we?'

'No, not now, now that we know about the gold.'

'We?'

'Semyon and I.'

First Anastas tried persuasion. 'What do you say to going shares, Grigori?'

'I say no.'

Anastas tried to argue, then asked Grigori to be 'reasonable', to admit the justice of share and share alike. Everything they had, he maintained, was communally owned —between the three of them, of course. The German had no right to anything, except to a share of the winter's hunting bag. 'In any case,' said Anastas, 'he's only a burden on us now. We must get rid of him as soon as possible.'

145

Grigori pointed out that there was a difference between what they had earned as a team—the alluvial gold, for instance, the hides and the equipment they had got out of Lederer—and the personal possessions they had with them when they escaped from the gold mine. He had found the nugget and he had escaped with the nugget, and therefore it was his.

That floored Anastas, so he started threatening. Semyon, he said, was for a drastic solution. 'Now he's smelled gold, he means to have it—if necessary, he'll shoot.'

'And you?' asked Grigori.

Anastas said he wanted the nugget, too. Now he'd seen it, he could not bear the thought of that yellow lump in someone else's possession, the lump that could not be split until it was sold.

'I'm going to sell it,' answered Grigori. 'I'm going to buy myself a new set of papers, so that I can start a new life. The nugget will pay for one set, but not for three.'

Anastas changed his tactics again, suddenly went all limp and weary, leaned dejectedly against a tree and said he was sorry now all three of them had not been swept away in the winter storms. There would be no peace between them now. Grigori had started something terrible—couldn't he see?

'What's so terrible?' said Grigori. 'I'm all right. I'm going to get myself a forged *propusk* with that gold.'

'Not now,' said Anastas, 'now the secret's out; only over Semyon's dead body.'

'All right,' said Grigori finally. 'So be it!'

When Anastas and Grigori returned to the previous night's bivouac, they found the single unpaired reindeer lying dead with its throat cut beside an empty sledge. Semyon, the German, the big sledge, the hides and every single piece of equipment had vanished. So Grigori had already lost his gold. . . . The sight of the deserted camp filled him with rage and he was gripped with an implacable resolve: from now on, he would live for one end—the death of Semyon. As for the German: 'That viper,' snarled Anastas, 'we've nourished him long enough,' and he swore he would shoot him down the moment he set eyes on him again—if he ever did.

At that moment, they heard a shot. They knew it could not be Semyon and, as they told him later, it never occurred to them that it might be Forell. They took it to be a stranger, and they hoped it was. Without tent or sleeping bags, they would be in sore straits when night came, unless they could find help. So they fired an answering shot. Fifteen minutes later came another single shot, this time closer at hand. Again they answered, their spirits rising at the thought of the approachng stranger. Then they saw Forell.

As Forell came staggering and gasping for breath over a hump of ground and saw the two men gazing at him about twenty yards ahead, his first feeling was one of relief. He was afraid they would have gone. He was too exhausted to be more than dimly aware that, a moment later, they raised their rifles and then slowly lowered them again. In fact, they had meant to shoot him dead, there and then, but refrained because they saw he could barely stand.

But Forell was not the only one to be surprised when Grigori suddenly gave a shout of joy and running forward to meet him, flung both arms round his neck. 'Oh, my friend!' he babbled. 'My dear, dear friend!' Then he started to paw Forell's clothes, running his hands over his rucksack. 'Let me help you,' he said breathlessly. 'Let me carry it. I can see, you're all in!' And there was nothing for it, but Forell had to let Grigori shoulder his rucksack. The man seemed to have difficulty in lifting it—he kept fingering the sides, as though doubtful where to take hold. Then, with a broad smile, he hitched it on to his back.

'Well?' said Anastas, who had been watching the panto-mime. 'Are you satisfied?'

Grigori, for one, understood the question, but he evaded it. 'I had to help him,' he said lamely. 'He's all in. . . .'

Anastas turned to Forell. 'What happened?'

'Semyon just drove off and left me standing. He took every damned thing we've got. I shouted, but it was no good—he drove all the faster. Then he threw something out of the sledge, my rucksack.'

'And you ran after him—tried to catch him?'

'Yes. What else should I have done?'

Anastas did not reply. Instead, he gazed grimly at his surroundings and even more grimly at Forell's rucksack now resting securely on Grigori's shoulders. Then Forell saw the small sledge, with the reindeer lying dead beside it. 'The swine! Not content with stealing a sledge, its team and all our equipment, Semyon has to go and murder our last remaining reindeer!'

'That's it, Pyotr,' said Anastas, 'more or less.'

'Why "more or less"?'

But Anastas merely smiled, Then: 'We must get going,' he said.

Anastas and Grigori were in a desperate hurry, not to catch up with Semyon it seemed, but to get as far away from him as possible. The only equipment left to them were their rifles and what ammunition they carried on them. Not a single reindeer skin remained as covering for the night—no tent, no cooking utensils, no tea, no vodka, and at that time of year, the nights were still bitterly cold, with the thermometer many degrees below freezing. Forell had his pack, with one greasy, dirt-caked skin that had lasted him since the early days of his escape; otherwise, he was no better off than the others. Unless they could recover the big sledge, it seemed certain that none of them would last long, and to him, the obvious course was to follow its tracks at once, while they were still fresh and before they were obliterated by further snow.

But the two men were deaf to argument. Not only that, but they threatened to shoot Forell out of hand if he did not fall in with their plans and do as they told him, and Forell had been with them long enough to know that they meant what they said.

'All right, then,' he said. 'What do you want me to do?'

There was no mistaking their relief. They were mortally afraid and they wanted Forell's help. Speed of movement was essential, they said, and without something to enlarge the size of the tread, their feet would get hopelessly stuck in the snow. Snow racquets were the thing—a thin length of sapwood bent into a bow and strung with interwoven strips of reindeer hide.

While Forell took the reins from the small sledge and carefully sliced them into thongs, Anastas and Grigori set about preparing the frames. Inside two hours, the racquets were finished. Still in a feverish hurry, Anastas and Grigori bound theirs to their feet and showed Forell how to do the same. Then, without a moment's pause, Anastas went striding off round the hill-side towards a thick plantation of young birch trees, shouting to Grigori and Forell to follow.

* * *

The racquets prevented the feet from sinking into the soft snow, but that was all that could be said for them. To prevent them overlapping meant walking with splayed legs, or where there was no room to do that, taking giant strides with the feet placed in line. In either case, progress was very tiring, particularly as Anastas had chosen to plunge into a forest of saplings.

Forell was the only one of the three who still had his pack. For a while, he carried it himself, then, strangely enough, Grigori volunteered to take it over, carried it for an hour and passed it on to Anastas. Anastas would not hear of handing it back until late afternoon. Why so helpful, suddenly? Forell wished he knew. . . .

All the time, for as long as daylight remained, Anastas kept up a desperate speed, thrusting his way, whenever he could, between closely-spaced obstacles where Semyon with the sledge could not follow, even jumping on one occasion eight feet down a vertical outcrop of rock. Then he made for cover again as quickly as he could, tunnelling through dense undergrowth, while the others followed, sweating, cursing and, as far as Forell was concerned, becoming more determined with every step to know the reason for this headlong and illogical flight from Semyon and the sledge load of equipment without which, in the long run, they would be unable to exist.

It was night before Forell could demand an answer. When he did so, Anastas merely looked up from the shelter he was trying to make out of branches and twigs and said grimly: 'We are in great danger.' As though to prove it, he decreed that, cold as it was, no fire was to be lit for the bivouac and no game was to be shot for supper, for fear they would give their position away and Semyon would descend and slaughter them while they slept.

It was ludicrous, on the face of it. On the other hand, Anastas and Grigori were used to danger and would never impose such privations on themselves unless convinced of their necessity. That they were convinced became clear when, to cheat his hunger, Anastas broke off a piece of resin oozing from a cleft in a tree and started to chew it where he sat, racked with cold, in a hollow scooped out of the snow. But when Grigori tried to insist that one of them should stand guard over the other two while they slept, Forell finally rebelled. If Grigori liked to make a fool of himself, that was his look-out. He, Forell, proposed to sleep, all night through, without a break, and it would take a better bogey-man than Semyon to stop him.

In answer, Anastas' voice came croaking from the dark. It was the voice of a sick man, speaking with effort.

'German! Listen to me! Do you want to get home?'

'Perhaps.'

'What else do you want?'

'A chance to live.'

'All right. But I'll tell you this: it's not living you need to worry about at the moment but staying alive. That's the situation, and it goes for all of us. And that's not a threat, either—it's a statement of fact.'

'I don't believe it.'

'I'm not asking you to believe it; I'm asking you to act as though you did.'

'Why? Why should Semyon want to kill me? He had his chance this morning, didn't he?'

There was a pause. Then Anastas' voice came again, pleading almost. 'Listen! You've got to trust me. I don't want you to get hurt. Some of us are bound to, but there's no

149

reason why you should. But you will get hurt if you go on asking questions, and refuse to do as I say. . . .'

The voice trailed away and there was silence. Anastas, it seemed, lacked the strength to say more. In asking Forell to trust him, he had sounded sincere. But Anastas was changeable. Later on, equally sincerely, he might let him down.

'Are you going on guard?' said Forell.

The answer was barely audible. 'Of course. . . .'

So then Forell agreed to take his turn—but more to let a sick man sleep for a few hours than because he was convinced there was any danger. Grigori insisted on keeping watch first. When Forell relieved him, he pointed with trembling finger into the darkness. 'That's the direction he'll come from! If he comes, it will be from there. He's dangerous. Watch out!'

The fear was infectious, and if Forell was to keep watch effectively, it was his duty, almost, to be afraid. He was not sorry when, some hours later, Anastas stood, gaunt and shivering, beside him, ready to take over for the last hour before dawn.

The following night, after another day of forced marches in which the only food had been a hare hastily roasted at midday, they kept guard again and once more Forell was condemned to search the night for the first sign, whether rustle or glint, that the enemy was upon them. But no sooner had he gone to sleep than Grigori, who had relieved him, loosed off into the dark. Forell jumped, with beating heart, for his rifle. What was it? Two green eyes watching him, said Grigori, over there, from the bushes. . . . So the bushes were laboriously outflanked and encircled and then the three of them stood, rifles at the ready while Anastas shouted his ultimatum: 'You are surrounded. If you do not surrender, we shall fire.' But the bushes made no reply.

Another day. And another night—fireless, almost foodless and jangling the already overwrought nerves of the pursued, watching in vain, while the pursuer bided his time. Yet another day. And one more night. Still no fire. They tried to eat a squirrel, and they waited for Semyon, but he never came.

On the fifth night, they could stand the cold no longer and they risked a fire. But now, they thought, with the tell-tale glow marking the bivouac, a watch was important as never before. Semyon would be on the look-out for a fire; Semyon would be drawn towards it; tonight, he would come, and then—— But their nerves had reached the limit of their scale and could be screwed no higher—then, how simple everything would be! It would merely be a matter of kill or be killed.

* * *

Next day, shortly before noon, they were working their way down a ravine. The going was rough and with their failing strength they were having to rest every few hundred yards. They were sitting, backs to a rock, out of the wind, and Forell was almost asleep.

'Look. . . .' It was Grigori who had spoken. It was not a shout, not even an exclamation, but merely a sound that escaped his lips as he saw the confirmation of his fears—a thin line of ski tracks on the opposite side of the ravine, starting at the top and running diagonally down across the snow. The tracks disappeared from sight below them, round a spur in the ravine. Grigori gazed at them as though hypnotized. 'Semyon!' he gasped. 'Semyon!' And slowly he shifted his gaze to Forell in limp, terror-stricken appeal.

If it was Semyon, he must have made the skis himself and their rough fashioning would be revealed in uneven tracks. But was it Semyon? Anastas said no. He believed they had given him the slip. He would never have thought it worthwhile to abandon the sledge with its valuable load. They should carry on, said Anastas, along their side of the ravine and ignore the tracks. But in Grigori the tension was now stretched to breaking point and, one way or another, demanded release. Uncertainty was no longer tolerable. He had to know: was Semyon there on the other side of the ravine? Would he have Semyon in the sights? Would it be crisis or anti-climax?

So they started down to investigate the ski-tracks. The wind was blowing across the ravine and the bottom was completely sheltered. The snow had piled up thickly there and the three men had to move cautiously, step by step, to avoid the drifts and the patches of dense undergrowth that lay, partly hidden, beneath. At times, they were up to their waists in snow and then the distance they could see along the bottom of the ravine was reduced to a few yards.

Ahead went Grigori in a steam of sweat, both arms raised, holding his rifle above the snow; then Anastas; and lastly, because of the weight of his pack, Forell. Forell had given up hope of finding sense in the other's behaviour. He was indifferent now to their mania and immune from its contagion. While they thrust noisily on, he was content to amble, shoving a little, stopping from time to time and so unintentionally dropping further and further behind. In that way he had time to look around, ahead at Anastas and his flailing arms, upwards at the sunlit sky, and to the right, at the figure of a man rising about fifty yards away out of the undulating snow. . . .

'Semyon!' thought Forell. 'I've got a bone to pick with you!' And he waved as he had often done when one or other had been returning from the hunt. But Semyon merely stared,

151

then raised his rifle. Forell dropped flat into the snow. At the same moment, Semyon must have fired. Forell heard a crash as the bullet struck splinters from a nearby rock, and felt a searing pain in his leg. He waited face down in a snowdrift, wondering where the next shot would land. Semyon fired again. Forell heard it this time, and the whine of the bullet, and a sudden yell from Anastas or Grigori, a few yards away. Cautiously, Forell lifted his head a little to see what was happening. Semyon was in the act of bringing up his rifle again. Then came a shot from Forell's side and the effect on Semyon was strange. He threw up his arms and his head was suddenly scarlet. Then he toppled backwards into the snow.

Staggering to his feet, Forell heard a yell of triumph and saw Grigori. The man's cap had come off and the long hair hung matted round his face. 'Did you see it?' he yelled. 'Did you see how I fixed him?'

'Where's Anastas?'

'Oh Anastas—he's dead.' And Grigori lurched off to where Semyon lay spreadeagled in the snow and started rifling his pockets. While his hands paddled about in the blood-soaked clothing, his mouth kept up a commentary of threats and incoherent noise. Then suddenly he had it—a little bag, the same as Forell's, containing Semyon's quarter share of the alluvial gold. Grigori tore open the bag and squinted inside. He seemed satisfied. Binding it up carefully, he stuffed it into his cartridge belt. Then he seized the dead man by the shoulders and propping him up against the mound of snow, reloaded his rifle, stepped back a few paces, and raised it, aiming at the shattered head.

'Grigori! Stop. . . !'

'This is not your business, German! You're advised to stay where you are.'

Then Grigori fired.

*   *   *

Grigori was insane. As he talked, Forell had plenty of time to consider the fact, and the probable consequences for himself during the next few days.

At the moment, Grigori was in a communicative mood. After his pent-up emotion had spent itself in a final barbaric act, he had suddenly become calm and lucid. In a detached sort of way, he told how, as soon as Anastas had been killed, he had filched from him, too, his quarter share of the gold. He had three little bags now. Would Forell, by any chance, like to add his, and make it four?

Forell said no.

All right. Forell had earned it, and he could keep it, it was his. But there was something that wasn't his, and he, Grigori, would trouble him to hand it over.

'What?'

'Open your rucksack!'

Forell was intending to do so to find something to bind up the wound in his leg. He took out a shirt and started to tear it into strips. Then Grigori plunged a hand into the rucksack and drew out a short, flat object, about the size of a child's slipper. It had been carefully sewn into a woollen sock. Forell had never seen it before and had no idea how it got there.

Grigori enlightened him. It was gold. Grigori undid the sock and showed him the dirty, pitted surface. Then he scratched it and his nail left a thin gleaming line. Solid gold.

Grigori had stolen the nugget from the gold-mine—the mine one hundred and fifty feet below ground, not the river bed! This wasn't surface gold. Nuggets of that size were pretty rare, even in the lowest strata, where the biggest were usually found. The mines were dug in galleries, nine feet square. An old mine, like the one Grigori had worked in, came to look like a rabbit warren in time and the guards could not be everywhere. If he was clever and knew how to recognize gold in the rough state when it was covered with oxide, a prisoner could often manage to slip a bit under his shirt.

It was easy, almost, to pinch the stuff; the difficulty was to get it out of the mine. That was why Grigori had escaped with Anastas and—— Grigori left the sentence unfinished. And the other two men, asked Forell, had they known nothing about it?

'Why do you think Semyon is lying there,' said Grigori, 'with a bullet through his head? And why do you think we had to stand guard every night? Anastas could have told you. . . .' Then Grigori added with a malicious smile: 'You didn't know you'd been carrying a lump of gold around in your rucksack, did you—for over a week? That was why Semyon came after us. He guessed where it was as soon as he saw it had gone from my baggage. He guessed. Anastas put two and two together. And I knew because I put it there. It looks like you were the sucker!' Still holding the small grey slipper in his hand, Grigori laughed uproariously. Forell eyed the nugget and thought of all the occasions during the past week when he might have made off with it on his own. Now Grigori had got it back, it was too late. Or was it——?

'Can I see it again?' said Forell.

'All right. But only to look at, mind!' Grigori allowed Forell to take the slipper in his hand. Then he raised his rifle. 'Meanwhile, Pyotr, just in case——' And he placed the barrel

153

against Forell's head. The latter held his breath, not daring to move, while he gazed as though hypnotized at the scarred and pitted surface of the gold. If Grigori could have read Forell's thoughts at that moment, he would have pulled the trigger.

'It weighs about two and a half pounds,' he said.

'Really?' Two and a half pounds. . . . Forell remembered stories about men with a 'lust for gold'; now he was experiencing it. He had caught the fever. It was in his bones. Already his outstretched hand was beginning to tremble under the weight of the nugget. 'Here!' he said. 'Take it back.' Grigori slowly lowered his rifle and, taking the slipper, wrapped it again carefully in its rag, then buckled the two small straps. That done, he put the parcel away in an inside pocket, under his furs. He sat eyeing Forell in silence for a moment. Then quite calmly: '*You* want it now, don't you?' he said.

Forell said nothing. As the two men sat on without speaking, they realized that one of them was under sentence of death.

Next day, before they set out to try and recover the sledge abandoned by Semyon, Grigori wanted Forell to empty the magazine of his rifle. Forell agreed, on the condition that Grigori did the same. So they continued for a while, retracing Semyon's ski-tracks, until Grigori stopped and said, perhaps it would be a better arrangement if he carried the ammunition and Forell took the guns. Forell did not demur. But Grigori was not satisfied. He was careful, Forell noticed, to walk behind and was gazing fixedly at his back whenever Forell glanced round. Soon Grigori had another idea. He had been thinking, he said, that it wasn't quite fair on Forell to ask him to carry two heavy guns as well as his pack. Wouldn't he prefer to take all the ammunition and let Grigori have the guns? Forell raised no objection, so Grigori took the guns and only then did he empty his pockets one by one and hand over the ammunition. Forell had no doubt that he had kept a round or two, hidden, probably, under his cap.

That evening, their first alone together, each preferred to go without food rather than trust the other with a cartridge, or a gun. Next morning, when their hunger became unendurable, Grigori was allowed one cartridge. He shot a dove; Forell roasted it and Grigori divided it in half, in case Forell should try to steal more than his share.

Another day passed and on the following morning, the faint line of the skis merged with reindeer tracks. They followed them until dusk and then, slowly because they had to watch each other's movements, they made a fire. Then they sat for a while, neither of them speaking, and then Forell pretended to sleep.

On the morning of the fifth day, they came up with the reindeer and for some hours, then, they had an arduous task, herding the reluctant animals back over the ground they had already grazed. Progress was slow and when they reached the brow of a hill and saw that the downward slope on the other side was steep and rocky they paused to consider whether the reindeer would be able to negotiate it. Forell was thinking it might be better to go back the way they had come and try and work round the base of the hill. Apparently Grigori thought the same, for he was making no move to start the descent. When Forell turned to speak to him, he found Grigori had come up close behind him and was standing at his shoulder.

At that moment Grigori saw the sledge—'Look! Down there, among those trees!'—and he pointed to the base of the hill, about two hundred yards below. Forell could see the trees clearly enough, but not the sledge. He leaned forward to get a better view. In all perhaps a minute had passed since Forell first realized that Grigori was not, as he had thought, some yards away, but was standing close behind him. At any time during that minute he might have saved himself, if only the truth had dawned: Grigori was about to push him over the edge. But it did not, and so when Forell felt a sudden powerful thrust in his back, he was taken by surprise and went plunging helplessly down the slope.

For the first six feet or so, the drop was vertical. Then Forell's shoulder crashed into a rock. The rock spun him round, clutching vainly to stop himself falling. Then he went wheeling, feet over head, pack on to chest, while the long knife caught and levered his legs. Rolling now, scraping a shin, he gathered momentum; crashed into another rock, wrenched a hand—rolled on, caught a foot, and fell, twisting, hip first, into more rocks. Rocks battered his chest, winded him, pounded him, passing him down criss cross like a ball on a pin-table till there came a sudden, shattering blow, a flash like lightning across his eyes—and darkness.

Forell awoke in a globe of pain; at first, one globe, then, as he tried to move, each limb became a separate world of agony. He supposed he had fallen. Where . . . ? How . . . ? Knives stabbed his chest as he breathed. A foot throbbed and twinged. Fingers were broken. Something clawed at his spine. All was weakness, nausea and racking pain.

His eyes opened and he saw sky, with ground sloping up to one corner. On the skyline, high above him, stood a man. At that moment, the man started to move down the slope towards him. The way he moved had something familiar about it.

Then Forell recognized who it was. He tried to stand up, but his legs refused. Instead, he levered himself with his arms and tried to sit upright. As his thigh touched the ground, a shaft of agony streaked through him—and darkness returned.

The first thing he saw when he regained consciousness was a mountain sheep lying not two yards from his side. There was no sign of Grigori. Crawling painfully towards the sheep, Forell found that it had been shot cleanly and skilfully through the heart. Grigori must have stood close by him as he lay unconscious. He had come, probably, for Forell's quarter share of the gold dust, then seeing his victim was still alive, had taken the trouble to shoot and lug the sheep to his side, not so much out of pity for Forell as for his own sake, as a gesture of appeasement to the Fates.

Now Grigori had gone and Forell was alone, lying at the bottom of a rocky slope somewhere in Siberia, facing death from starvation, thirst, exhaustion and cold. To avoid all these still would not give him life, but merely the chance to recover his strength and ultimately, perhaps, struggle onward under suspended sentence of death across thousands of miles towards home. Death was insistent, could be had for less than the asking. But life could only be won at the price of an immediate and unstinting effort of will, and even then, it might elude him. Death promised: Life gave an enigmatic smile.

But Forell had his knife with him as a means of fleecing the sheep and the thin glaze that remained of the winter's snows would suffice to quench his thirst. It seemed he might survive, and the possibility was enough to rouse him. That day, he succeeded in cutting a small piece of meat from the sheep, and in crawling to the fringe of some trees to collect twigs. Little by little, with many pauses, he built a fire, lit it with the aid of the tinder-box fortunately still in his pocket and coaxed the damp wood into flame with cartridge powder. Then he tried to roast the meat tender, but before it was more than singed the fuel ran out and he had not the strength to collect more. So he lay down, exhausted but too cold to sleep, and when the last glimmer had died out of the ashes he shut his eyes against the mocking twinkle of the stars.

Next morning, his back and the injured joints were swollen and rigid and the pain had become more diffused. As soon as he tried to stand, his body folded up as though hinged. Only one arm was usable, the arm on the side opposite the fractured ribs. Nevertheless, he managed to crawl about fifty yards to the spot where his pack had fallen among trees. Having reached it, he was forced to rest for some hours before hauling it on to the foot of a tree where there was wood for a fire and shelter from the wind.

The time that followed left few traces in his memory. Weak and racked with pain, there were long intervals when he was barely conscious. But though often no more than a glimmer in the recesses of his mind, the will to live never left him and each day he struggled to crawl a little further. Fortunately, it was summer time. The nights were still cold, but the days were fine and warm. Each evening at sunset, as the trees stood silhouetted before him and the colours crept darkening up the sky, he selected one of them as the goal for his next day's crawl. Sometimes, he would reach the tree; at others, he would find that he had underestimated the distance and had to give up. But even a few extra yards covered each day gave him a feeling of achievement and a growing sense that he was master of his fate. And justified or not, such confidence was sorely needed, for it was at this time that he discovered that Grigori had not only stolen his gold but his pistol as well.

* * *

Now it was gone, Forell realized what the pistol had meant to him. Deprived of its strength he realized his own weakness, and felt suddenly frightened and appalled. The immense spaces of Siberia looked sinister now, and sunset was no longer welcome as the end of day and toil, for it was also the beginning of night, and with the darkness came fear.

To be afraid of the dark was something new to Forell, and unexpected. He told himself it was because he was weak and hampered in his movements; with returning strength, his fears would go. And slowly, with the passage of time, he did manage to stand upright and then to walk and, as the fractured ribs knit together again, to use both arms. But the fears persisted, growing, if anything, stronger. Even in the daytime, as he lay exhausted after carrying his pack a few hundred yards, his brain would get twisted in a knot of fear and he would find himself gazing back over the way he had come, every nerve in his body clamorous with warnings of danger creeping towards him from behind. He would gaze, then, as though hypnotized, at a shadow, a bush or a dark patch of ground showing through the melting snow, waiting for the first sign of movement, until his eyeballs ached with the strain and the scene before him began to pulse and flicker, repeating the rhythm of his heart. Then he would jerk his head away and start talking to himself, trying to forget he was alone.

The forest lay all around him. Ever since he had started to limp forward again, westwards by the compass, he had been among trees and now they were becoming thicker. Giant firs

157

blocked out the sunlight, so that even at noon, he was in a twilight world where the only sounds were his own muffled foosteps and the sough of the tree-tops stirring in the wind. As the day advanced, the twilight deepened and involuntarily his hand would stray to his side to make sure that the long Siberian knife was still in its sheath.

Then early one morning, just before dawn, he awoke to a curious smell. It seemed to be everywhere, acrid and pene-trating—an animal smell. And suddenly, he was back on a night of bitter frost, standing by a group of reindeer, while three men crept out, their rifles glinting in the moonlight, towards the smell of wolves. The stench in the nostrils was the same; all else was different. Now there was only one man, badly injured and just able to walk, and all he had was a knife. Now it was dark and Forell could see nothing. There was only the wind to hear, chanting through the forest. He drew his knife—it was all he could do—and waited.

He waited, remembering what he had been told. Wolves, it was said, were cautious when attacking men. They liked to surround them noiselessly and take them by surprise. But if the men had rifles, or any sort of firearm, the wolves would know it and silently disappear long before the men had even seen them. With one man, it was different. If he were armed, he might get away with it; if not, then the leader would summon the pack and the wolves would go straight for him, *en masse*, too confident of the kill to bother about tactics or noise.

Still the horrible stench persisted and Forell sat on, unseeing, in the damp hollow where he had made his bivouac. Three saplings stood round it. On one side they screened the view and when it got light, if the wolves chose to attack him from that side, he would be unable to see them. But they had been the first saplings he had come across since entering the forest. Their tops could be drawn together to form a kind of tent, and that was why he had chosen to sleep there.

Slowly the daylight was beginning to penetrate the cavernous forest and it was no imaginary fear now which made Forell strain his eyes to see if he could detect movement among the shadows. He sat motionless, hardly daring to breathe, in case the sound should give him away and the snarling pack descend. Then, on the far side of a clearing among the trees, out of the corner of his eye he saw that the shadows were shifting slightly, close to the ground. The next moment, his spine turned to ice as a solitary howl rose, wild and lamentable—then died, echoing away among the trees.

The howl came from somewhere near the clearing, to his front. It was answered by another howl from behind. Then Forell started to run, oblivious of pain, and despite the fact that hitherto he had barely been able to walk. He was running for dear life towards the only climbable tree he could see, one of a clump of small larches, about thirty yards away, showing a brighter green against the massive trunks of the fir trees. The wolves were in a circle, closing in. He could hear them as he ran and as he reached the tree, one of them came loping out to meet him and an indelible picture was recorded in his mind: a long back, massive, with grizzled fur, and jaws breathing wisps of vapour into the morning air.

He clutched at a branch and tried to draw up his legs. But there was no hold—the boots kept slipping down. He tried from the other side, where the thin trunk sloped away from him, and got up and began to climb. And the first wolf sprang, a streak of grey steel, for his feet, and missed, dropped back, turning as it fell and rebounded in another sinuous and more powerful leap. By now, he was six feet up —almost as high as he could go—and, clinging with his hands, he managed to pull his legs out of reach. Then he hoisted himself up a little further, another three feet at the most, and that was as far as he dared. Already the tree, its trunk no thicker than a flag pole, was swaying under his weight. The branches were too thin to stand on and he was having to cling with the soles of his boots turned in and gripping the trunk like pincers. As the sweat rolled into his eyes and his muscles ached, he knew he could not last long.

Below him the wolf pack snarled, twenty of them, twenty-five, perhaps more—what did it matter how many? They were there. Three had just leapt simultaneously, collided in mid-air and gone head over heels in a snarling, struggling mass, to separate, leap and collide again, savaging each other to get at the victim first. Forell glanced down, saw the shifting, steaming throng. Then, suddenly, the tree began to bend.

Supple as a bow, the trunk arched over under his weight, lowering him gently towards the ground. The wolves waited, jostling one another at the spot where he would land. As he came down, he sprang, like a diver from a board, thrusting himself upwards against a yielding form. The wolf gave a yelp of pain. The trunk reared up, then sagged, cracking, on the other side. The wolves surged round to meet him. Again a desperate thrust. The tree trunk rose a little, then dropped. Crack! A scream of animal pain, a snarling scurry among the wolves. Now he could cling no longer. His fingers were slowly parting. Another, louder crack, and with eyes shut tight, he fell. . . .

Two men muffled in furs were standing over him. When they saw his eyes were open, they broke into cherubic smiles and hastened to help him to his feet. Still smiling, they brushed the snow off his clothes and with noisy good humour started to tell him what had happened. The story lost nothing in the telling, that was obvious, and he gathered they looked on themselves as considerable heroes. As they talked on in some language other than Russian, he had time to look around. With their shot guns the two men had wrought fearful carnage among the wolves. All round the tree the snow was littered with bloody remains, those animals that were injured being attacked and torn to pieces by the others before they, too, succumbed. By the time Forell dropped from the tree, the wolves had already turned on each other and were too absorbed in their own battle to pay much attention to him. So much he could see for himself, but he also gathered that it was no mere chance which had brought the men to his aid—they, too, had had the stench of wolves in their nostrils for days.

Dizzy and panting for breath, Forell started to limp towards his rucksack, lying in the hollow where he had left it—an hour, was it, or a century ago? One on either side, the men went with him, laughing and chattering as though they would never stop. Oh! They wouldn't miss this! This was interesting! Let's see how he's made his bivouac! They inspected it, noted the saplings drawn together over the top to form a tent, and nodded, recognizing a man of experience.

Where had he come from, they wanted to know.

Forell pointed a finger. Really? He must have had hard going!

It hadn't been too easy, at times. . . .

The elder man seemed to think it was time for introductions. 'Kolka,' he said, laying a hand on his chest, meaning: 'Kolka is me!'

The younger man did the same. 'Aljoscha!'

Forell bowed, first in German fashion, then with hand on chest, and said: 'Pyotr.'

Pyotr. That was a respectable name, too. They smiled and, speaking in Russian, told Forell they were Yakutes. (Kolka raised his shotgun, fired once into the trees. A lone wolf on the prowl—cheek!) Yes, Yakutes they were: the Republic was named after the people.

They weren't far from the town, Yakutsk, then?

Kolka laughed. Only six hundred miles!

In which direction?

Oh, over there, somewhere. There was a road up there, running from Yakutsk to the coast.

The sea? And how far was that away?

Not far. . . .

Before Forell could ask more questions, Kolka decided it was his turn. 'You're no Russian!' he said bluntly. 'Where are you from?'

Forell hesitated, wondering what he should say. Would they sell him to the Russians if he told them? They'd find out, anyway, so why not give them the truth, straight—they would respect that—instead of a halfhearted lie?

'I'm a German. *Voenna Plenny.*'

A prisoner-of-war. There was silence. But the men still smiled. Then: 'All right,' said the elder one, quietly. 'We understand.'

Placid and amiable as ever, the strangers surveyed Forell. Then one of them put a hand on his shoulder and said again: 'All right. Good!'

The men busied themselves for a while yet around the scene of their recent battle. They said they had been trailing the wolves for days. There had been a story about a pack getting among the reindeer somewhere—a pack about twice the normal size. But this wasn't the usual place to find wolves. Something must have happened to bring them out here. The men had been hoping for a chance to get at them. They didn't often find a bit of fun like that. . . .

Their chatter stopped abruptly as they caught Forell's expression and guessed his thoughts. 'Yes,' said one of them. 'It's all very well, isn't it, if you happen to be a flying squirrel, or you've got a gun with you?' They went on to explain how they had known that the wolves were after a human being. Kolka traced in the snow the tactics the animals used when they were attacking a sledge team. The pack split, coming up with the reindeer to either side in the form of a U. Then he drew a circle with a dot in the middle. The dot was a man, on foot and unarmed, as Forell had been—a poor devil of a man, stuck there, too slow and too weak to do anything but wait, while the wolves came in. . . . But Forell knew all about that. There was no need to go through that again.

Forell shouldered his pack and followed as the men led the way to the verge of the trees and then across low ground sodden with melting snow. They noticed he was dragging his left foot. At once, they were full of curiosity. Hurt himself? Surely not, falling from a little tree like that? Well, if it wasn't the tree, what was it? A snowdrift? Well, then. . . . Perhaps it was the war? Had he been wounded in the war?

The men prattled on. They were as inquisitive as magpies. Finally Forell had to say something, so he told them: 'I had a fall. My companion abandoned me, he took everything I had.'

As they reached the crest of a ridge, Kolka gave a shout. Immediately, from somewhere below them, came a shrill, yip-yapping chorus and Kolka went hastening down to his sledge team of thirteen huskies, bouncing like indiarubber balls where they stood tethered to the ends of their sledge lines. Each dog was attached separately to the sledge by a long trace, all traces being of equal length so that, when pulling, the dogs spread out fan-wise and each did its share of the work.

Kolka disentangled the traces and gave the huskies their dinner, a quantity of small dried fish which they gulped down at lightning speed, head, backbone and all, and then sat back on their haunches, pink tongues licking black lips, awaiting the signal to start.

The *Furka* or dog-sledge, was small for three people, but they managed to squeeze in with Forell in the middle and Kolka in front, holding the traces, and steering by thrusting alternate heels into the snow and braking with both. It was afternoon by the time they reached the village of seventeen tents and the journey in the quivering nutshell had made Forell look back on reindeer sledges as a luxurious mode of travel.

The Yakutes' tents were of the kind Forell had already met, consisting of arched poles with skins stretched over them and snow piled up round the sides to keep in the warmth and exclude light and air. On their arrival, Kolka, who seemed to be the patriarch of the settlement, called the inhabitants together and harangued them in soap-box style. His audience listened attentively, breaking in from time to time with laughter or questions. Though not one word spoken was Russian, in these swift exchanges Forell kept hearing two sounds which seemed vaguely familiar: 'Freets' and 'Villum'. They were synonyms, apparently, for an object as rare as it was curious, none other than Forell himself, a Fritz, a Wilhelm, a German of unusual size whom the hunters had chanced upon in the forest closely besieged by a pack of wolves.

In that or a similar fashion, Kolka must have broached the subject of the stranger in their midst, for from the start, the Yakutes treated Forell with a friendly respect. But like most easy-going people, they were talkative. Who were their neighbours, Forell wondered, and how close was the nearest Communist listening post, in the shape of a local Soviet or collective farm? How could the Yakutes resist telling the goggling townsfolk about the amiable giant they had found in the forest, the 'Freets', as they called him—yes, because he was German, they would explain. And then they would glance round to make sure everybody was listening and say, 'Don't tell anyone, but he escaped. . . .' The damage would have been done, and in that country, where everything that lived did so on sufferance and not by right, it would only be a matter of days before the rumour reached Communist ears that a biped of Teutonic origin officially denied the right to be treated as a human being had been found by some Yakute tribesmen in the forests beyond the mountains.

The danger to Forell was real enough, but when he tried to point out to Kolka the need for discretion, the latter dismissed it with an airy wave of the hand. He took Forell to his own tent, planted himself by the entrance and said in Russian: 'My house!' Then he invited his guest to enter. His meaning had been clear, and he conveyed it in generous style: 'As long as you are here, you are under my protection.'

As on previous occasions, Forell had to make an effort to overcome his repugnance before entering a native tent. The stench, the fetid, smoke-laden atmosphere, the sense of closely-packed but invisible humanity combined to repel as only the prospect of an enforced intimacy with uncouth strangers can. With hands outstretched, he groped his way inside, sensing with the tips of his fingers when he was about to touch somebody and so avoiding contact with the occupants of the tent. Every inch of ground seemed covered by a human form. An aged crone spoke something in a high-pitched voice—but whether a curse or a greeting Forell could not be sure. Then he saw another woman holding a small bowl with water in it. She laid it ceremoniously on the ground before him and spoke, as though inviting him to perform a rite. Was he expected to drink the water? He put a finger in, to find out if it was hot or cold. As he did so, the onlookers —there seemed to be about six of them—motioned as though with approval from where they were watching, crouched round the sides of the tent. The water was cold, but the bowl was the wrong shape for a drinking vessel. Perhaps he was supposed to wash his hands? Yes, that was it—the onlookers were smiling. The water was to wet his hands and face, as a token that he accepted their hospitality.

Meanwhile, Forell's rucksack had been brought in and placed behind him, sitting cross-legged on the reindeer skins that covered the ground. Kolka, who had eyes only for his guest, invited him to drink from a small earthenware bottle. After four or five sips, Forell got the taste, and found it not unpleasant. He could not see the colour, but the liquid effervesced slightly, like sparkling wine, and it was certainly potent: by the time Kolka told him it was distilled from a mixture of sour reindeer milk and bitches' milk, the news was too late to mar his enjoyment. After he and Kolka between them had eaten a large and superbly cooked fish, Forell was ready to collapse on the half inch of ground designated as his sleeping place.

It was only after two or three nights in the tent, that Forell noticed surprised looks on the faces of the women when he lay down to sleep fully clothed. Their surprise was nothing to his, however, when he saw that the Yakutes slipped naked, two at a time, into their sleeping bags, vanishing inside by stages until finally, no doubt as a concession to modesty, they withdrew their heads, as well.

As Kolka's guest, Forell found a welcome in all seventeen tents in the settlement, and wherever he entered, the earthenware bottle was produced and a state of convivial intoxication followed, to be prolonged by the comforting thought that the supply of liquor was limited only by the willingness of huskies and reindeer to provide the raw materials.

The Yakutes kept a peculiarly small breed of reindeer, mostly for meat and milk. The animals were allowed to graze at will in the area and nobody seemed to know, or care, how many there were. Apparently, their owners were not afraid of them straying and were confident that they could be found when wanted. But, unlike other nationalities whom Forell had met, the Yakutes were not professional reindeer raisers, but earned their living by breeding sabakkis or sledge dogs. Kolka claimed to own several hundred, and certainly there were more than Forell could count when they went together to the vast enclosure where the huskies were kept.

Even dog breeding was being collectivized now, said Kolka. But rather than let the State take over his huskies, he would turn them loose, the whole seven hundred of them, all but a dozen or so for breeding, and the village would migrate into the mountains. . . . Kolka broke off, his voice drowned by the yelps and yowls of his vociferous family. The dogs set up their chorus as soon as they caught sight of him and never ceased as long as he was there, except to bark at the tall stranger whom their master had brought with him.

Kolka's face creased into a grin behind the loosely woven blinkers which he was wearing to protect his eyes from the sun. There was good money in dog breeding, he said. A well-trained team leader was worth a small fortune—or what unpretentious people like himself would think of as such. But the training took time and was arduous, for the trainer as well as the dog. And that reminded him, said Kolka, he would be away for a few days, leaving on the morrow. He was going to show off some of his dogs in the nearest town. Meanwhile, Forell was to stay. He wasn't to go wandering off to Germany while Kolka's back was turned!

'I wish it was as easy as that!' said Forell. 'I shouldn't get far in rags like this, and with no equipment.'

But Kolka's mind was preoccupied and all he said was: 'Oh, you'll manage all right. . . .'

Forell was grateful for the chance to rest for a few more days. The friendliness of the Yakutes and their plentiful food had done much to restore him, but his chest was still painful

164

and he still walked with a heavy limp. How he was going to manage when he was on his own again, he hardly dared to think.

In Kolka's absence, the men took Forell with them when they went fishing and taught him how to lay snares. With the summer thaw far advanced, breaking holes in the ice was a dangerous business, but the risk was matched by the size of the catch, the men hauling up the fish one after the other and apparently without effort as though from an inexhaustible barrel. When they had caught enough for their immediate needs, they hastened to resume their favourite occupation: sitting cross-legged on the floor of their tents while the women worked, sewing garments out of reindeer skins. The men never seemed to tire of talking, smiling, and doing nothing. Only the finest weather would bring them voluntarily into the fresh air and the women, so Forell was told, hardly left the dark, smoky atmosphere of the tent from one year's end to another, with the consequence that many of them had lost their sight.

There were more than three times as many Yakute women as men and polygamy existed in fact, if not in theory. Kolka, for example, seemed to have two wives and the number of children in the settlement showed that the same applied to the other men. There would be yet more children, the Yakutes explained, if so many of them did not die soon after they were born. As it was, their coming and going were events too frequent to arouse surprise, or to disturb the Yakutes' indolent acceptance of fortune good or bad as foreordained.

When a woman was about to give birth, it was only to make more room that the children were sent out of the tent. Men, if they were present, stayed, and it would never have occurred to them to do otherwise. In their attitude to child-birth, the Yakutes were touchingly simple, and horrifyingly ignorant. One afternoon, in the same tent as Forell, a young woman of about thirty folded the fur jacket she was making and sighed. A man said something to her and she nodded. He seemed to be her husband, for he spoke quietly to the children and they left the tent, then to two other women, as though giving them directions. Near the middle of the tent was a wooden post over which a leather belt was placed for the woman to grip with her hands, while closer in to the side, the midwives cleared a space, revealing two shorter stakes for her to press against with her feet. Then the men began to talk loudly amongst themselves and the midwives knelt beside the woman, handing her the belt whenever it slipped from her fingers, their broad backs meeting the husband's anxious glances and screening his wife from view. Soon the woman's groans turned to sharper cries and as they became louder and more frequent, the men forgot to keep up their talk and waited silently, clasping and unclasping their hands. At last, when the child was born, the midwives broke into a hymn of tender admiration—it was a boy.

One of the midwives had picked up a knife from the floor of the tent to cut the umbilical cord and had tied it with a length of greasy thread fished from her pocket. Now, taking a narrow strip of leather, she made a knot in the middle and bound the strip round the infant's body so that the knot pressed in the navel. Each man was allowed a glimpse of the child, before it was carried from the tent, stark naked except for its belly-band.

For two hours, while the mother lay pale and silent in her corner, the men passed round the bottle and all was boisterous merriment. Then the midwife returned with the baby, having washed it, or as the bibulous father asserted, rubbed it with lamb's wool. While the midwife tidied up, making the couch of skins comfortable for her to lie on, the mother stood waiting for her child surrounded by the noisy talk and laughter of the men. Then she took it for the first time to her breast, and as she did so, the men fell silent, awed by her grace and tenderness.

Did the child survive? Forell never knew. But it sickened him to think of its life being needlessly endangered through lazy, fatalistic ignorance and he longed for that child to live, because he had been present at its birth.

It was eleven days before Kolka returned, beaming all over his face. With thirteen of his finest huskies spread out in the fan-hitch, his arrival was an imposing sight and he matched it with an equally impressive gesture of greeting to the women assembled outside his tent. Then he caught sight of Forell, and his contented expression changed to one of dismay. Obviously, although he had expressly invited him to stay, Kolka had expected to find him gone on his return.

Next day, at the huskies' feeding time, Kolka asked his guest to come with him. Kolka's good humour seemed completely restored and in his lisping Russian, with much humming and hawing as he searched for words, he told Forell about his trip. The sledge team had been his travelling advertisement and he had done very good business. The prices were better than in previous years, not for pups, but for properly trained two-year-olds. That was where the money was, that was what people wanted, a dog, a gelding, say, that they could use straight away, and with no surprises after the deal had been settled in the shape of night blindness or distemper. Then Kolka laughed. But could you believe it? People weren't satisfied with a good husky; they wanted Kolka to go in for horse breeding as well! They thought they'd travel faster with a horse. So they might, on a road, but where there weren't even tracks, where you had to make your own —well, they were crazy, stark-staring mad!

Who 'they' were was not clear, but Kolka had not brought Forell with him to talk about the price of huskies; there was something else on his mind. There was silence for a moment, and when Kolka spoke again, it was in a serious tone.

'What was the name of that man who was with you when you had your accident?'

'You mean Grigori?'

'Yes. You hunted together during the winter didn't you?'

'Yes. Why?'

'You seem to have done quite well for yourselves.'

'Why? What do you mean?'

'A sledge-load of furs, and three times their value in gold: the furs from hunting, and the gold by theft!'

'So Grigori is alive! You've been talking to him!'

'No. Grigori is dead, shot, by the Russians. It is the Russians who have told me these things. Grigori confessed, you see. . . .'

Forell had pretended to Kolka that he had fallen over the cliff by accident. Now he told how Grigori had pushed him, how the two of them, with Semyon and Anastas, had spent the summer gold washing, and with what result, and then, as Kolka seemed to believe the tale which the Russians had extracted from Grigori, Forell told him the whole history of the lump of gold, its discovery in Grigori's rucksack, and how two men had died because of it, and very nearly himself, as well.

'And that is the truth,' ended Forell.

'I believe you,' replied Kolka, 'but that doesn't help you very much. It doesn't alter the fact, I'm afraid, that the Russians are on your trail.'

'How do you know?' Forell heard himself ask the question, but the words sounded hollow and remote, like echoes in a far-off cave.

Kolka looked round and then said earnestly: 'Listen. This is what happened. I went in to Ayan, the town on the coast. Of course, I had to show my papers, and when the Russians saw where I came from, they said: "You haven't by any chance come across a German, have you, a tall fellow, about six foot three, probably alone, probably limping, begging for food, or——" "Sorry," I said, "I can't help you. I wish I could." "Well, if ever you do, let us know, there's a good chap, because we want him."'

'Was that all?'

'No. No, that was just the beginning. I thought I'd better find out all they knew so I asked: "Who is this German and what's he doing here? Tell me all about him and then if I see him, I'll recognize him." So then the whole story came out, first about this fellow, Grigori—only that wasn't his real name. . . .'

'I never thought so.'

Kolka smiled. '—Any more than Pyotr is yours!—Anyway, Grigori, or whatever his father called him, behaved like an idiot. After he'd left you for more or less dead, he must have made straight for Ayan with his sledge-load of furs and his gold. "Where's the Hunting Base?" he said to the M.V.D. there. "I want to get my money." And he waved a bit of paper at them, some sort of certificate to the effect that he was a Hunter of the Soviet Union, was to be granted every facility, and one thing and another. Well, when the Russians saw the signature——'

'Lederer's?'

'Yes. When they saw that, they had to smile, because it was the signature of a dead man. Lederer himself was working in the gold mine, sentenced to twenty-five years for assisting an escaped convict.'

'But how——?'

'Don't ask me how his mistake was discovered. But the M.V.D. got Lederer and learned quite a lot about Grigori, and when they got Grigori, they heard even more about you.'

'Mostly lies!'

'Oh, yes, that's what they thought. But not all lies, because they told him he'd get off if he helped them to find you.'

'What did he tell them?'

'I don't know. Where he last saw you, I expect. What you were wearing. What sort of equipment you had. What sort of a state you were in after your—accident.'

'Do the Russians know I am still alive?'

'They think you may be.'

Kolka could be trusted, thought Forell. He would not let him down. But suppose the M.V.D. appeared in the area and started talking to the Yakutes? They would not know the difference between boast and betrayal. Guileless and unsuspecting, they would talk as long as the Russians would listen—of the wolf packs that had been roaming the neighbourhood, of the numbers they themselves had destroyed, and of the tall stranger they had saved, just in the nick of time. . . . One thing, at any rate, was clear:

'I must leave you,' said Forell, 'and the sooner, the better.'

At first, Kolka made no reply. He seemed lost in thought. Then he nodded his head, slowly, several times. 'Yes, I think that would be best.'

It was settled that Forell should start on the day after the morrow, aiming to reach the Manchurian frontier as quickly as he could. Among the Yakutes, meanwhile, the attitude towards him changed to one of sympathy mingled with a vague unease. They would be glad to be rid of him, because they were afraid for themselves, but, having once saved his life, they were sorry to see him risk it again by launching out into the unknown.

As Forell surveyed the tattered remains of his clothing and equipment, he agreed that the risk was not inconsiderable, but, encouraged by the gift of all Forell's remaining ammunition—and he still had upwards of sixty rounds—Kolka came to his aid in generous style, supplying a leather shirt, as cool in summer as it was warm in winter; a pair of long boots with straps for tying above the knees, called *potoki* and made of wonderfully soft and supple leather, and, for food, some flat round cakes, compounded of fish, meat, flour and millet dried hard in the sun. *Palemi* was the name the Yakutes gave to it and it seemed to Forell the ideal food. It was nourishing, tasted good, was light and took up little space. All the same, his rucksack, which the Yakute women had made for him out of skins as thin as parchment, was soon overflowing.

Kolka said he hoped Forell's legs would stand up under the load. When he came to rivers or streams that were too wide to cross with his rucksack—and as the summer advanced, they were getting wider every day—he would just have to wait, that was all, until they were passable.

'But that might be months!' protested Forell.

'Well, what if it is? You'll have to be patient. A man in a hurry never gets far. To hurry isn't normal; it arouses suspicion.'

'What doesn't, in Siberia!'

'We are mistrustful in this country,' said Kolka gravely, 'but we also know the meaning of compassion. We have fitted you out like new, but soon, after you've slept a few nights in the open, you will look the same beggarly wretch as before. And that's all to the good. This is the country of the outcast, and the ragged, half-starved Strafniki will find nothing but kindness here. It is freedom and prosperity that arouse our mistrust. If someone wants to know where you're going and who you are, then tell him you're a convict on your way to work. However evil he may be, the man will let you go then, and if you look at his face, you will see sympathy written there. But never say you're a free man—or you'll find yourself behind bars.'

'Um. . . .' It was a fine speech, thought Forell, and there might be some truth in it. But meanwhile: 'I shall need a new flint for my tinder-box. I must be able to light a fire.'

'Yes, you must. And you must have a hook and line to fish with, some snares to trap game. And when you're asked about yourself, you must have the right answer.'

'I think I have, now,' said Forell. Kolka smiled.

That evening, Kolka gave Forell a new flint and wick for his tinder-box and Aljoscha cut his hair for him and shaved off his beard. Then he produced the broken corner of a mirror and Forell saw his face, clean-shaven for the first time since his escape. His expression as he caught sight of himself must have been comic, because the Yakutes roared with laughter. And so it was, funny, in a way: the face he saw was that of a total stranger.

Early next morning, Aljoscha was ready with a sledge and fifteen huskies to take Forell from the settlement and deposit him far enough away for the Yakutes to be able to deny all knowledge of him, should the M.V.D. one day decide to pay them a visit. The tribesmen, headed by Kolka, stood round with smiles and nods for their departing guest. Kolka eyed the scanty remains of the winter's snow, pursed his lips and said something to Aljoscha. Then he turned to Forell.

'Aljoscha will see you over the river. Where you will cross, no one can follow you, only Yakutes. So with the river at your back, you will be able to look forward without fear. But remember, do not talk too much with people. Your Russian is good, but your accent is a strange one to Siberia. Speak as little as you can. Just look at people, sadly, like you are looking at me now, then they will see that you have suffered enough and will let you go.'

Forell stowed his rucksack in the sledge and climbed in behind Aljoscha. Fifteen bundles of fur—white, cream and silver—fanned out on scampering, skidding paws. With a jerk, the sledge started to move and, sick at heart, Forell waved good-bye to his friends.

That day, they covered about forty miles, a very good distance, considering the state of the ground and the fact that, for most of the way, it was slightly uphill. The team had to slither as best they could over strips of frozen snow, alternating with soft going where they were up to their necks in a deep, feathery carpet. At times, when the gradients were steep, both men had to walk, treading down the snow to find firm ground for the sledge to pass over.

After a night spent in bivouac, they continued on the following morning, descending gently over bare moss and occasional patches of snow. Soon they could see the river running across their front below them and within an hour from their start, they reached it at a point where the waters roared through a deep gorge at least fifty yards across. No, said Aljoscha, not even a Yakute could cross that! Ten miles upstream was the place. There was a pool there and early in the day, before the sun had loosened the ice from the banks, it was usually thick enough for a sledge and two men to cross.

Here, then, was the place known only to the Yakutes. And when they had crossed, Forell was surprised to find himself wishing that they had found the ice gone and his parting with Aljoscha postponed.

They stood on the far bank, surrounded by the huskies, panting and grinning, seemingly, from the excitement of their perilous journey over the river. Forell lifted his rucksack from the sledge, the first lift of many, the first trial of a weight that would be with him, biting into his shoulders, day after day, for as long as his feet would carry him.

'Kolka asked me to give you these.' Aljoscha held out a pair of hunter's skis, light as a feather, each weighing less than a pound. 'And something else. . . .' And he bent down to where the huskies' traces were attached to the bow of the sledge and unhooked the line of the dog that pulled in the centre of the fan, on the leader's left. 'Kolka would like you to have someone to talk to, a companion and a friend, someone who will warn you in good time of approaching danger. Don't be dismayed. You eat the fish and give him the head and backbone, that's all he'll want.'

Aljoscha said something to the dog, telling him to stay with Forell. Then he unhitched another dog from the team so as to restore the odd number, settled it in the sledge behind him and turned to re-cross the river. '—And Kolka wishes you good luck!' he called. Forell said, 'Thank you,' and watched him go. Ten minutes later, the sledge had disappeared from view on the far side of the river, but Forell still stayed, listening, for as long as he could hear them, to Aljoscha's shouts of encouragement to his team. Then, when all around him was silence, he looked at his dog, and decided to call him 'Willem.'

* * *

Summer, 1951. As a first step towards his distant goal, Forell turned to the sublimely confident Willem and made his acquaintance. On closer examination, Willem proved to be a fine example of the Mendelian Law of Independent Assortment, one of those embarrassing anomalies that spring sometimes even from respectable parents. He should have been a Chuchi, but wasn't, and the fault was not in himself, or in his parents, but in their chromosomes. The shading of dark fur which should have adorned his face cropped up instead like a saddle on his back. His ears, which generations of forebears had borne broadly based in the form of an equilateral triangle would barely have passed as even isosceles, while in the show ring, his size might have earned him a place among the St Bernards, but hardly with the breed to which he claimed to belong.

But these shortcomings meant nothing to Forell, though no doubt they helped to explain why Kolka had been prepared to part with the dog. From now on, Forell and Willem journeyed together, the man aiming slightly south of west and the dog revolving round him. At any particular moment, the direction of the march depended on what landmarks were nearest to the chosen compass bearing, but as far as possible, Forell went in a straight line and avoided detours. Willem found that boring. While his master trudged slowly ahead, he scuttered purposefully to and fro, intent on some mysterious business of his own.

Willem seemed to have inexhaustible energy and he squandered it, perhaps because he missed the other huskies and the continual turmoil of the Yakute settlement. Whenever Forell stopped, Willem would prance about, yapping for him to be off again. Then Forell would stretch out a hand and start scratching his head in the hope of calming him down, but caresses merely made Willem sneeze. 'Pah!' he went, spluttering with impatience, and dodged away to go crashing through the undergrowth, determined to find something, if only a beetle, on which to vent his rage.

On the evening of their first day together, Forell and Willem sat under the spreading branches of a larch tree. Forell took a small piece of *palemi*, broke it in half and gave one portion to Willem, who swallowed it at a gulp and then sat on his haunches, staring sphinx-like into the setting sun. Aching and exhausted as he was from the unaccustomed weight of the rucksack, Forell nevertheless forced himself to go out again with Willem to lay a few snares in the vicinity. Beside each one, he pushed a stick into the ground as a marker, for the snares were easily lost. Then he slept, too tired to feel oppressed by the forlorn immensities of earth and sky.

Unless he managed to catch some game, Forell could not last long on *palemi* alone, and next morning, his first thought on waking was for the snares. He found them untouched and empty. After a mouthful each of the Yakutes' iron ration, man and dog set out for the day's march. Before long, Willem, who had been exploring ahead, began frenziedly barking and, coming up with him, Forell found a polecat, lying crippled from some previous fight, defending itself savagely with tooth and claw. Part of its spine was protruding and most of its body was paralysed. Willem was snarling horribly, but took good care not to venture too close and it seemed unlikely that he would be able to despatch the animal alone. Holding off the dog with one hand, Forell seized his stick with the other and slayed the polecat with a blow on the back of the head. But even Willem preferred hunger to its fetid flesh.

That evening, Forell again put out the snares—and awoke in the early hours of the following morning to see the stars glinting sharp and clear against a velvet sky. It promised to be a hot day and, rather than march under the burning sun at noon, he decided to start at once, so giving himself time to rest later. But first, the snares. One by one, he picked them up, and, for the second time in succession, all were empty. Postponing breakfast, Forell shouldered his rucksack and calling to Willem, set off slowly westwards.

This was the time of year when the young steppe grass was beginning to shoot up between the previous season's growth. Already the plains, stretching like a tawny ocean between the mountain ranges, would be tinged, later become suffused, and finally be flooded by the emerald tide. Siberia, that in winter turned all life to stone, had now become a gigantic forcing ground. After days of scorching sun, the last snows had almost vanished and before long, the soil would be as dry as the withered steppe grass that meanwhile shielded the new growth and prevented the ground from losing its humidity. With each step that Forell took, the tall blades swished against his legs, rustling like tissue paper.

Soon, the stars began to fade and the sky to lighten, the veils of night dissolving, one by one. As prelude to the dawn, a band of violet appeared on the horizon, glowed for a moment, then diffused and lost its intensity, drawing a broader band of purple after it. Still invisible, the sunlight, diffracted by the distant, snow-capped mountains, then sent a lilac ribbon to succeed the purple, while all climbed upwards, decking the sky with a vast and many-coloured robe. Lilac strengthened to green, through blue. Saffron followed, grew brighter, gleaming, shadowless as polished brass; then a lurid, baleful flush of burning sulphur, and the furnace burst upon the world. In an instant, Forell, wide-eyed with terror, saw the dried-up tinder of the steppe grass take fire and the vast plain as far as he could see leap skyward in one seething mass of flame.

Long afterwards, Forell still bore the marks of his finger-nails where he had thrust them deep into his palms under the shock of that moment. He took a long step back, as though the yard would save him from destruction. For a second, his breathing and, as he believes, the very circulation of his blood were halted by the terror of the scene. And then he saw his shadow and breathed again. Willem's tail wagged reassurance. The blood drained from the sky. Smiling, Forell stood, while the sun spoke his reprieve.

But a dog knows no false alarms, and Willem meanwhile had been concentrating on other things. When Forell looked down, a hare was lying at his feet.

Man and dog journeyed on over the shifting sea of steppe grass, crossing a series of plateaux that descended, one below another, towards the plain. On the following day Forell had again set out before dawn, so that he could watch and enjoy to the full the spectacle of the sunrise. Then came days of broiling heat, when massive thunder clouds crept slowly along the mountain ridges, to break with shattering suddenness in torrential rain. To be caught in such a deluge was to jump head-first into a swimming bath and after his first soaking, Forell was careful to have his shelter ready, made of poles trimmed from the nearest branches with his leather sleeping bag laid over the top as roof.

The rains made progress slower and for days at a time brought it to a stop. Streams that before would have been small enough to wade or jump swelled to roaring torrents and, when faced with water obstacles, Forell soon discovered that there was no longer any point in exploring upstream in the hope of finding somewhere to cross; if they were impassable at one point, they would be so along their entire length. Nevertheless, he chose to keep on the move, stopping only to fish at suitable places and usually going downstream towards the lowlands.

Meanwhile, Willem had successfully crossed the No-Dog's-Land that lay between detachment from his old master and devotion to the new. From now on, Forell had an emperor's bodyguard, and one that seemingly never slept. In the night, sometimes, when all was apparently peaceful, a cold nose would jerk into his face—'Ssst! Wake up!' A touch of the hand and Willem would cease his burrowing to sit motionless close by Forell with senses focused on the point of danger. Often enough, Forell could hear and see nothing and only the dog's ears, cocked and swivelling, and the twitching of his nose would betray the direction from which the invisible life approached. Then, after a while, Willem would relax and sink slowly down, to lie full length on the ground and make his first comment on the night's alarm, a faint 'Humf. . . .', but whether of disappointment or relief, Forell could never be sure.

It was about this time that, reaching the top of a wooded slope, he saw buildings in the valley below him—sixteen compact-looking houses and two sheds, or barns. But it was not these that riveted his attention so much as the appearance of the surrounding fields. For the first time since his escape, he was looking at green grass, 'real' grass, and grazing cows. It was a glimpse of home in a foreign land, the more poignant for being unexpected. Even the sounds were familiar—farm dogs barking monotonously, more in boredom than alarm. There was no sign of a human being. The place seemed deserted. Forell was about to draw back out of sight before starting on a detour, when, lower down nearer the houses, he noticed some more fields cultivated in ridges. Along the top of each row ran a line of green foliage—beans, perhaps? Of course! No, they were potatoes! It was so long since he had seen potatoes growing, that he had failed to recognize them. The mere thought of them made his mouth water. Potatoes filled the stomach without seeming to overload it. They killed hunger like nothing else. They were the one food which prisoners never forgot, and always yearned for. Forell made up his mind to have some. He would wait until nightfall and then help himself.

It was not quite dark when Forell and Willem started down the slope. The dogs at the farm were still barking inter-mittently, but for the time being Willem ignored them and trotted silently behind his master. They reached the field without incident and Forell saw that the potato tops were only a few inches high. He presumed they were seed potatoes for lifting later in the autumn. By then, they would be unfit for human consumption, turning black and watery as soon as they were cooked. Were they edible still, or not? Forell thrust his hands into the ground beneath the nearest plant and felt about until he found a potato. The tuber was still firm, so he proceeded to turn up a stretch of twenty feet or so, stuffing the potatoes into his sleeping bag as he went. Then, while the farm people obligingly stayed behind their lighted windows, he went staggering back with his haul. Halfway to his bivouac, he suddenly remembered Willem and stopped to look round. Willem was there, at his heels. Perhaps it was Forell's own guilty conscience, and it was too dark, really, to be sure, but he could have sworn the shameless animal was grinning from ear to ear. . . .

Next morning, Forell sought out a spot on the reverse side of the slope where he could make a fire without the smoke giving him away and bake some of the potatoes under the ashes. He and Willem spent the rest of the day eating, the whole of the night dreaming of potatoes and the next day, eating potatoes again. By then, they were beginning to regret the whole adventure, and were certainly in no mood for a repetition that night. But Forell thought the opportunity to replenish his food supplies too good to miss and throughout the day, he had kept the farm buildings under observation to find out which were inhabited, where the tools and farm machinery were kept and which of the two barns was most likely to be the food store.

At nightfall Forell and Willem again descended, heading for the far end of the nearest barn. This time, Willem was in argumentative mood and at the first sign of life from the farm dogs went flying into their midst. Immediately, there was a pandemonium of squeals, yaps and scampering feet while pursuer and pursued gyrated, head to tail, like horses on a merry-go-round. Somewhere on the ground floor of one of the houses a window was flung open and a voice shouted to the dogs—with the result that they continued their performance at the back instead of the front.

In the din, Forell was able to slip unheard into the barn. Sacks of what seemed to be flour were stacked near the door and, seeing he had come to the right place, he unshouldered his rucksack so as to have more freedom to explore. The barn was divided into sections and on his left was another door which he guessed led to the food store. He tried the latch, but could not move it. Perhaps he could lever it up with the long blade of his Siberian knife. He was feeling for the sheath, when an inrush of cold air told him that the main door to the barn had been silently opened again. Side-stepping into a corner, he was just in time to see the figure of a man come hurrying up to the partition and stop within a yard of his elbow. Facing the self-same door that Forell had just tried to open, the man put an arm under a projecting board and holding the latch with his other hand, lifted the whole door upwards on its hinges. It swung open and he disappeared inside. A moment later, a rushlight burned up beyond the partition and creeping closer, Forell saw that the man was peering at the contents of the store, as though uncertain what to choose—bacon, butter, cheese, barrels of fish, onions, tea, tobacco, bread . . . the man gazed, then dipped two fingers into a butter jar and carried them to his mouth. A common thief! Indignant, Forell took a step forward, then remembered. . . .

Meanwhile, the man had collected an armful of assorted goods. Now he sensed the other's presence and turning, saw the tall figure in the doorway.

'Good evening,' said Forell, not knowing what to say. The man merely stared and clutched his haul closer to his bosom. Taught by the cringing attitude of the thief, Forell decided to act the policeman. 'Helping yourself, I see!'

The thief was visibly quaking. A couple of tins slipped from his embrace and clanked on to the floor.

'Do you make a habit of this?'

'Y-yes, Gospodin. I mean—no, Gospodin!'

'Gospodin!' The man must be really frightened; otherwise he would have said 'Tovarisch'. 'Do you live here?'

'No, sir.'

'I suppose you work here?'

'Just now, sir, yes. Not all the time. Depends on where they send us.'

'Us?'

'The road gang.'

'You're a prisoner?'

'Yes, your Honour.'

For a second, Forell was tempted to declare his one-time membership of the same exclusive club; then the shivering Strafniki whined, 'Mercy, your Honour!' and destroyed the impulse to fraternize.

'Put that stuff down!'

The man bent forward and let the loaves, the jar of butter slide to the ground. Then he stood limp and uncertain, one eye winking convulsively. Forell relented. 'All right, since you're here, you can take one loaf!' The fellow hovered, fearful there might be a trick, then, when Forell told him again, plucked up courage and quickly snatched a loaf from the floor.

'Where do you sleep?'

'In the barrack by the tractor shed.'

'How many of you?'

'Forty.'

'Why did you choose tonight to pinch the stuff? Are you moving somewhere?'

'No, it was just the dogs. They seemed to be busy, so I thought I'd take my chance. Something's upset them tonight —another dog, I'd say. . . .'

'Yes, mine. He's going the rounds with me. Now push off before he sees you.'

But the man did not move. He stood, looking at Forell, and suddenly a clever smile came over his face and he said: 'You're a German, aren't you?'

'That's none of your business. Now get out!'

'I thought so. A foreign Communist, eh? Well, how do you like your new masters—any better than the old?'

Forell took a step forward.

'All right, German. I'm going. And since you've been decent to me, I'll wish you luck. There's no harm in wishing, is there?'

And taking his time, the Russian picked up the other two loaves and the jar of butter and was gone. The door to the barn closed softly. Forell was alone. He had played his part with conviction and it was a few moments before he returned from make-believe to reality. But the rushlight was still burn-

177

ing and the sight of the crowded shelves in the food store helped to speed the transition. Then, for the second time that evening, loaves of bread, butter, and anything light and compact enough to be carried, fulfilled their economic destiny by reaching the hands of the consumer. For the second time, the barn door opened, a heavily-encumbered figure emerged and closed the door softly behind him. At that point, history preferred novelty to repetition. Waiting for Forell with a strangely coy expression on his face was Willem, backed by a whole army of canine friends.

Forell decided it would be prudent to leave by a different route and though the risk of meeting someone was greater, he set off down the path leading to the tractor station and the bridge beyond it that his daylight observations had shown would take him over the valley stream. As he went, Willem bade a reluctant farewell to his friends, shedding them one by one until the last had dropped behind. For the rest of the way, he clung to Forell's heels, making up for bad behaviour in expectation of favours to come.

For three days, Forell never stirred from his bivouac, while the sight, the taste and the comforting proximity of long forgotten foods lay over him like an enchantment.

On the fourth day, when what remained of the plunder was not too bulky to be carried in the rucksack, Forell roused himself and slowly, feeling weak in all his limbs, continued his journey. As he had found before, the daily distance covered increased with his hunger, though from now on, the distance was never great, owing to geographical and climatic conditions. The scenery was much more picturesque than any he had yet come across, but the luxuriant vegetation hindered progress and at times stopped it altogether. Dense forest, in which all kinds of trees seemed to be intermingled, concealed precipitous crags and defiles among the foothills of an irregular mountain range, and even in valleys, where there were marshes and peat bogs, the trees continued in endless variety.

Forell still kept on principle to a compass bearing whenever he could and headed south-west. He knew that the Manchurian frontier lay further to the south; but what with the marshes, the summer rains and the obstacles, every day more formidable, which Nature threw in his path, there was often no choice of route open to him, but only one on which it was possible to make progress at all, and that was eastwards, following the watercourses towards the sea. So, when he could, Forell went south-west, and when he had to, east. The result, he hoped, would be a slow, snaking progress southwards.

Apart from his bitter experiences in the preceding six months, Forell avoided going higher towards the mountains because, unarmed as he was, he would be unable to find enough to eat there. In the lowlands, on the other hand, where the rivers and streams flowed more slowly, fish were plentiful and easy to catch and the dog, Willem, could find hares and other small animals to contribute to the diet.

The days of blissful surfeit were a distant memory and the plunder had long since vanished from his rucksack, when, making his way across a strip of marsh land, Forell saw ahead a gang of men working a pile-driver. Standing apart, presumably supervising, was a figure in uniform and, to one side, the outline of foundations for a new road. Before the men had a chance to see him, Forell dropped back behind some trees. Then he made a wide detour round the marsh, reaching a wood on the far side.

New roads were often built in unconnected sections and gangs might be working anywhere along the projected route, and so it was that, emerging from a line of trees where they ended abruptly in a clearing, Forell suddenly found himself in the midst of another bunch of swarthy, close-cropped labourers.

He nodded and raised a hand in greeting. Hail—and farewell. Willem, you idiot! Why didn't you warn me? Surely you could have smelt them a mile away?

Then came a shout. 'Hoi! You there! Where are you going?'

Oh, just right ahead. . . .

'The road isn't built yet, you know!'

That's supposed to be funny and isn't worth answering.

'The way you're going won't get you anywhere!'

And whose business is that?

'Look, where do you *think* you're going?'

'Chita,' said Forell.

Now the *Natschalnik,* the foreman, took a hand. 'Chita? Do you know how far that is?'

'Yes, I know, but——'

'You're going by rail, I suppose?'

'Rail?'

The foreman looked towards the head of the valley. 'The railroad, up yonder, that's where you're heading is it?' He spoke patiently, as though to a child. Forell nodded hastily. Yes, he was heading up yonder.

'Travelling on duty?'

What had Kolka said? 'If people ask, tell them you're a convict.' Would that work? Who were these men? Would they be sympathetic? They looked like lumbermen.

'Well, if you must know,' said Forell slowly, 'I've just finished an eight-year term of forced labour. I've been discharged officially, but now I've got to report to the Rayon

Chief of the M.V.D. in Chita. That's why I'm going there. Once a prisoner, they never let you go. . . .'

'Then of course you must go by rail,' said the foreman, all solicitude.

Kolka was a wise man. Nowhere did Forell receive so kindly a welcome as from these Russian foresters. Lower down in the valley, about twenty minutes from where they were cutting and stacking timber, was their home, a sizeable and well-equipped block-house, containing plentiful supplies of food. Having taken Forell's arrival as an excuse to knock off early, they led him to the block-house and entertained him royally. That evening, they told him about themselves. No, they weren't Strafnikis, they had signed a voluntary engagement to work in the area for two years—voluntary in the official sense, that was, which meant, either you sign, or you don't —you're free to choose. But if you don't, then you must take the consequences. So they had signed. They had not been too keen on the work to start with, but the pay was good and at the end of the two years would amount to a fair-sized sum. After that, they would probably be asked to sign on for another two years—'asked', or 'told', it came to the same thing. . . .

'What sort of work were you on, Pyotr Jakubovitsch?'

'Road work.'

'Ah-ha. . . .'

'It wasn't too bad.'

'Um. . . . What part of the country do you come from—I mean, were you born in?'

'I wasn't born in this country.'

'I didn't think you were. You don't speak like a Russian.'

'I come from Riga.'

'Latvia! Ah! That explains it!' And turning to his comrades, the Russian said innocently: 'Latvian! That's what it is; that's his accent. I thought so all along.'

Forell was a Latvian, they all agreed on that. Friendly and unsuspecting, they only wanted to help him. All the same, he had to be on his guard. At any moment in the conversation he might find himself poised on the brink of an abyss. To return to safer topics, he asked how the timber they felled was transported from the site. He seemed to have hit on the right subject, for the foreman smiled knowingly, said 'Ah! You'd never think it possible, would you?' wriggled, lifted his shoulders and, with many dramatic pauses, delivered a lecture on his favourite theme. On the far side of the clearing, no distance from the site, ran a tributary of the mighty Amur. The timber was floated down-river for about twenty miles and there transferred to a saw-mill to be processed. Then came the great problem: how to get the timber away from the saw-mill. For that purpose, a special branch line had been built, westwards to the Trans-Siberian Railroad. Fifty miles of line, just completed, to the junction, and another seven hundred and fifty miles from there via the Trans-Siberian as far as Chita—eight hundred miles in all by rail, not counting the twenty down-river: Forell was not so far from his goal, after all! Why! He could be there in four days!

Forell began to feel uneasy. 'That's a bit too quick!' he said, attempting to grin. In four days' time, if he went by rail, he might be stepping straight from the train into the arms of the M.V.D. Apart from that little difficulty, he could not get there fast enough.

Um. . . . Yes, the foresters could see the point—or they thought they could. Of course, once in Chita, the discharged prisoner's brief interlude of freedom would be at an end. There could be only one reason why he had been summoned to report to the Rayon Headquarters of the M.V.D., and that was, to be saddled with a further period of forced labour. They could see why he was in no hurry to start that. Still, he had to put in an appearance some day. Then the foreman had a bright idea. Why not go to Chita unofficially, not by passenger, but by goods train? The Timber Control Officer would be coming to take over a consignment in a few days. The foreman would suggest he send Pyotr as escort with the first train-load that left the saw-mill.

Here was the second abyss. Forell could not dissuade the friendly foreman without destroying his own story, so he had to concur, and at the same time prepare to vanish before the Timber Control Officer arrived.

Unfortunately, as is often the way with senior officials, the officer had decided to spring a surprise and he turned up two days before he was expected. On the eve of Forell's intended departure, the door to the block-house suddenly opened, and there he was, scattering sparks in all directions.

'Who is this man and what is he doing here?'

The foreman was not to be intimidated. 'This is Pyotr Jakubovitsch, just completed a sentence of eight years forced labour and ordered to report to the Rayon H.Q. of the M.V.D. at Chita on his discharge. We thought you might be able to use him as escort for a timber consignment, so he could get there quicker.'

'Why should he? And why should I?' said the official briefly.

The foreman tried a different approach, 'We know, sir, that it's unusual to send anyone with the timber, and the railways always maintain they can look after it themselves, but there's rather a lot this time, and——'

'How much?'

'In the creek up there and on its way down river, in all, ninety-eight standards.'

'A very creditable achievement,' said the Timber Control Officer, thawing slightly. 'There might be something in your suggestion.'

He turned to Forell. 'What's your name?'

'Pyotr Jakubovitsch, sir.'

'And your family name?'

Nobody had asked for that before. Forell said the first conceivable Latvian name that came to his mind. 'Lemengin.'

'You're not a Russian from the sound of you. Let's have a look at your papers.'

'No, sir. Latvian.'

'Well, that's no reason why you shouldn't speak Russian properly. In eight years, you've had plenty of time to learn. Your papers, please.'

The answer which came to Forell's lips was not the product of reflection; he was far too agitated to think. In his desperation the only valid excuse dropped ready-made into his mind. 'When I was discharged, they took all my papers so that they could be sure of not losing me. I was told the papers would be forwarded direct to Chita.'

'Hm. . . . Well. . . . What were you sent to prison for?'

'My offence, you mean? I was sent to prison because I was in Riga, young and fit to work, when the Soviet Troops marched in in 1939.'

The Control Officer seemed about to say something, but instead he surveyed the room in silence for a moment. Then he turned to the foreman and said briskly: 'See this man is fed and gets somewhere to sleep. Your suggestion is a good one.'

Next day, the man of iron condescended to relax and become more human. Beneath his forbidding exterior, beat a heart of warm and generous impulse, a heart that loved. The Timber Control Officer loved a motor boat. The craft was highly unorthodox in appearance, but it went and it was his, for use in official trips along the river. After he had inspected the imposing mass of timber and official duties were over, he led the way past the spot where the Wonder Boat was moored. The party stopped and, standing next to the owner, Forell could not restrain a sigh of envious admiration, little knowing that the sound went straight to the great man's heart. Every detail of the craft was now explained to the attentive bystanders. Then Forell was invited to step aboard and pull the string that started the motor, being careful to note the ease of operation, the immediate surge of power. Finally, the owner described trips past and those that were still to come. One day, he said, he was going to sail right up through the

Bering Sea and into the Arctic Ocean, so that he could say he had seen the easternmost point of all the Soviet territories—— Could anyone tell him what that was?

No. No one could tell him.

It was East Cape, Cape Deschnev, in the Chukchi Peninsula. Well. . . . Fancy that . . . just fancy. . . . And suddenly, Forell was glad of the chance to go westwards by train. The sooner he reached Chita, the sooner his ordeal would be over. Chita was only a short distance from the frontier.

That evening the vodka bottle was produced and the Comrade Superviser became decorously drunk. Forell, on the other hand, as was only appropriate to the convict, Pyotr Lemengin, disappeared from view at an early stage to hold a private conversation under the table with his dog, Willem. When the party finally broke up, the men left him there in a besotted daze, talking earnestly in a language which, fortunately for him, they failed to recognize as German.

Next morning, Forell felt as light as a feather, cheerful, but alarmingly empty headed. Life seemed to flow past him like a dream that he saw, but in which he had no share. The Timber Officer's motor boat took him down-river to a landing stage by the saw-mill, where the floating timber was held at a grille placed across the river and hauled ashore to be cut up by six band-saws and loaded on to a railway truck in an adjacent siding.

The processing and loading of the timber took several days. At midnight on the last day, a goods train came up the branch line and after a noisy altercation between the railwaymen and the foresters, it was decided to put the lumber wagons in the middle.

Forell was issued with a travel permit and given his instructions. He was to occupy the brakeman's cabin on the last of the twelve lumber wagons and his duties would be, at the longer stops, to check the stanchion chains holding the timber in place and, whenever the train stopped between stations, to make sure that none of the timber was stolen. And his dog? Not a bad thing, thought the railwaymen, to have a dog with you, especially one that had a touch of the wolf in him. The sight of a dog would keep thieves away better than any pistol. Yes, let the dog go too. What was his name? Willem? Willem would want something to eat on the journey, though, wouldn't he? And the railwaymen conjured up bones, fish, meat—all that a dog travelling on duty could ask for.

Forell's travel permit was made out for Chita, but the train itself, with the lumber wagons, was going on to Ulan Ude. The name sounded vaguely familiar. Perhaps if he saw it in writing, he would remember where it was. He went to a truck standing under an arc-lamp and looked at the card fixed in the metal slots at the side. Unloading Point: Ulan Ude. Hm. . . . He knew it so well, had heard it and seen it dozens of times, but though he racked his brains, he could not visualize the map, or remember even roughly where the town was in relation to Chita, or the frontier. It could not be east, surely? It must be west of Chita. What had happened to his memory? Why, instead of thoughts and pictures, was there nothing but a bare wall in his head? What else couldn't he remember? His name. What had he said? Lemen—Oh God! He could not remember that now. What was the matter with him? What had happened?

Somehow, the story of the Strafniki and the vodka bottle had got about till now everyone seemed to know that Pyotr Jakubovitsch Lemengin had spent his last night at the blockhouse stretched, dead drunk, on the floor. And who could blame him? After eight years' forced labour, it was only natural, a man went straight for the bottle. And so, days afterwards, no one was surprised to see Forell wander about on the siding, frowning and muttering to himself. It was a wonder the man could stand upright. It was a very creditable achievement. The lumber men slapped Forell on the back and said: 'Cheer up! You've four days to get over it!' Yes, and four days to remember where Ulan Ude was, and decide whether to try and reach it by train.

At last, the wagons were hitched, as the railwaymen wanted them, in the middle of the train, and it was ready to leave. With eight-syllable imprecations, the tottering Strafniki and his dog were hustled into the brake cabin, and the train went creaking slowly westwards.

* * *

The train was scheduled to reach Chita in three days. It took five. The sight of the town shocked Forell's memory into life. There, beyond the station, lay the bleak expanse of the marshalling yard where, six years before, the slave train had finally stopped. Nearer at hand, he could see the level crossing, with its rotting, soot-caked boards, where those who had survived the journey left the railway for the vaunted jail, the Osmita, from which it was said no prisoner had ever escaped. And there, in their pit of misery and cold they had been visited by new horrors, the convoy soldiers came, whip in hand, to stretch the limit of their suffering. A bright red roof, that memory told him he had seen before, now caught Forell's eye, rekindling despair. All was the same. Nothing had changed. Chita was the hub round which the intervening years had revolved. Chita was the sum of all his sufferings. Now he would break the vicious circle and go westwards, to Ulan Ude.

The train was to be made up afresh before continuing its journey. The engine hauled the leading trucks to the goods yard to be unloaded and, with a thrust from another engine, the lumber wagons and the tail of the train were sent rolling down the line to a siding. Forell decided to sit tight and await developments. He knew that the M.V.D. seldom checked the personnel on goods trains and it was unlikely that anyone would demand to see his papers. But if they did, and wanted to know why he was still in the train, he would act the simple backwoodsman and ask when the train was due to reach Chita. Meanwhile, it was no good trying to hide in the cabin. It would only arouse suspicion if he were found, and, in any case, the truck setters would want to get at the brake wheel. He must be seen, leaning out of the cabin door, ready and waiting at his place of duty. Willem should be seen, too, to distract attention from his master.

As the wagons were stopping Forell pushed his head out of the door. Running up the line towards him came a bunch of truck setters.

'What are you doing up there?'

'Timber escort, travelling to Ulan Ude.'

'And the dog?'

'He's to stop people pinching the stuff.'

'Let your brake off then, will you? We're coupling up.'

The truck setters ran on towards the engine now backing slowly on to the head of the train. When they came back, the same man stopped again.

'What's that you're wearing, fancy dress?'

'Um?'

'That get-up of yours, it looks sort of funny to me.'

'Have you ever worked in the forest?'

The man laughed. 'So that's why you look like a tree!' Then he glanced at the sky, suddenly overcast with leaden thunder clouds. 'You'd better shut that door of yours, if you don't want to drown!'

As the train moved out, the first drops began to fall. The next moment, the rain was drumming on the wooden sides of the brake cabin, blotting out the noise of the train so that only the familiar shudder-and-shift told Forell that he had left Chita behind. The truck seemed to be thrusting through a wall of water and on either side, cascades streamed past the windows.

After a while, the rain stopped as suddenly as it began. Forell opened the door a crack to get some fresh air, but instead received a pailful of water on his head. Away behind him, the thunder clouds lay lowering over Chita, while ahead, to the west, the sky was clear. Then, as on the journey to Chita, the sun burned down on the roof of the cabin till the temperature inside, even when the door was open, rose to over a hundred degrees Fahrenheit. Forell dozed throughout most of the days, sitting on his perch by the brake wheel, while Willem lay in a torpor at his feet. Whenever the train stopped for the engine to take on water, man and dog drank greedily and Forell refilled the skin that would have to last him until the next halt, perhaps twenty-four hours later. The nights were cool and he slept soundly then, waking with parched mouth and aching limbs when the heat returned.

It was night-time when they reached Ulan Ude and Forell was asleep. He awoke as the cabin door opened and someone looked in, said, 'All right,' and shut it again. Forell slept on. When he finally awoke, it was broad daylight and voices were yelling outside. It seemed the lumber wagons had been taken off the train and the altercation concerned them rather than the gawky stranger peering from his box.

'You can send the whole lot back!' someone was bawling. 'I'm not accepting any of it!'

'It's going to be difficult,' said another voice, 'the stuff's consigned to us, and we shall have to——'

'But look at the ticket, man!' came the first voice again, rising a semi-tone. 'Have you seen the ticket? "Carriage Forward!" Do you think I'm going to pay a six-hundred verst freight charge on this stuff when we've got timber on our own doorstep, waiting to be picked up for nothing? It's time they were taught a lesson, those fatheads in Timber Control. It's sabotage, that's what——'

'Sssh!' came the agonized whisper. 'Not so loud!'

'I don't care who hears me!' trumpeted the voice. 'It's a senseless waste of timber and rolling stock! It's sabotage, that's what it is. . . .'

Forell leaned further out of the brake cabin to get a better view of the speaker, a small, tubby little man with bald head —comic to look at, but obviously a man with authority. The second voice belonged to a tall, stooping fellow who was clearly a subordinate.

'They want smoking out, some of these bureaucrats,' continued the first. Then he saw Forell. 'Who's this? A stowaway, heh?' The man planted himself before the brake cabin and glared furiously at Forell.

'Him? Oh, he came with the timber.'

'With it? Or in it?'

Then Forell spoke up. 'I'm here to see it doesn't get stolen.'

'Huh! Can you beat that!' said the little man to his junior. 'Not only do they send the timber to the wrong place, but somebody has to go with it to see it gets there!'

186

While the mutterings continued like a retreating thunder storm, Forell looked at his surroundings. The wagons were standing in the siding of a factory that seemed large enough to deal with twenty times that amount of timber.

The little man with the big voice was concluding the argument. ' . . . We'll take it if we can use it. Otherwise, back it goes!' That was that. Now for this half-witted lumberjack.

'Well, come on, then! Are you going to spend the rest of the day up there?'

Forell dropped his jaw and gaped like a simpleton. 'Is this where we get out?'

'Are they all as bright as you in Timber Control?'

'Have we got to Chita, then? Are we there?'

'Chita?' The boss had to laugh. After all, he was only human, and what townsman wouldn't laugh at this gangling oaf from the forest in his homespun get-up? Now. What did his papers say? Chita, that was where he was supposed to have gone. Ah well. . . . He was probably illiterate—couldn't read the name on the platform, of course, though the letters were six foot high. They'd have to send him back again, that's all there was to it. Just endorse his ticket . . . feed him . . . wash him. . . .

Forell, with his dog and his rucksack, was taken to a gigantic administrative building. On the way, the fat little man made a point of showing off his find to all the passers-by—a gift from the Forestry Department, a genuine troll, minus the supernatural powers! It was good for morale—nothing like a real prize specimen from another Department to raise the output of your own workers!

The factory made rolling stock for the railways and was a model of its kind. There was a huge welfare department that catered for every human need. Taking their tip from the Comrade Director's attitude of amused benevolence, the white overalled staff accepted the challenge of the bearded, dirt-caked nomad and steered him with capable hands through the process that would transform him into a clean and self-respecting Soviet citizen. This way, please . . . !

Clinging to his mask of imbecility, Forell was led to the shower baths. What did it matter if he spoke with a peculiar accent? Everything about him was odd. The luxury of a hot shower was almost too good to believe, but, of course, he had to conceal his joy and back away like a frightened horse—the attendants seemed to expect that. Once under the shower, once the pigwidgeon had got over his fear of the water, then, as they all expected, he soaped himself ten times over from head to foot, wanted to stay there half an hour, refused to budge till they turned off the water—— Meanwhile, his clothes were being deloused. They were returned to him without his leather shirt. What had happened to it? It had been burnt, on grounds of hygiene. That was his cue to raise a fearful howl, and to go on howling even when he got two cotton shirts instead—and the protest was not all play acting, either.

From the shower Forell was taken to the barber's. His beard was clipped, his hair cropped and then he was given a clean shave. Then he was fed, and then, owing to the vigilance of the shower-bath attendants who had noted his scarred and wasted frame, a doctor came to see him and Forell had to strip once more. The doctor examined him, saw the badly knit fractures, the bruises and the wasting from long years of starvation, and Forell sensed the suspicion as it dawned in his mind. Those were the marks of a convict. Was this man supposed to be at liberty?

Before long, Forell was being questioned by a whole posse of M.V.D. men, men who were used to sifting truth from falsehood and who would not be satisfied with glib stories, or with a repeat performance of the village idiot act. So Forell varied it and instead of a simple mind, paraded a simple heart. Discharged on completing his term of eight years penal servitude, he said, he had been ordered to report to the Rayon Headquarters of the M.V.D.—a pure formality, so he had been told, that was necessary in order for him to enjoy the status of a free, honest Soviet citizen. Could the gentlemen wonder that he was heart-broken to find he was passed through Chita and gone on, by mistake, to Ulan Ude? His one wish was to get back there as quickly as he could and start the new life that awaited him.

The gentlemen of the M.V.D. scrutinized his papers. The papers said nothing about his past, but merely that he was escorting the timber as far as Chita, where he was to report to the M.V.D. Had he been a convict or not? Where had he worked? In a gold mine, Forell told them, and described the conditions as Anastas, Grigori and Semyon had done the year before. It was a hard life, there was no doubt about it, but—and Forell, with his simple trusting heart—gave a happy smile—all that was over now, or would be, if only they would help him to get to Chita.

There was silence, while the senior of the M.V.D. men rolled himself a cigarette. It was a horrible moment. A telephone call to the M.V.D. at Chita and Forell's escape would have been in vain. His story would be exploded and the bitter road to East Cape would face him again. The interrogator shut his tobacco tin with a click and put it back in his pocket. 'We will help you,' he said. Even the M.V.D. could not but feel sorry for a mutt like that . . . the convict who had served his term and thought that therefore he was free.

As soon as the crisis was past and Forell knew that the M.V.D. had accepted his story, he began to feel impatient. After all, what had he gained? Permission to return to Chita, that was all! But he did not want to go to Chita. He wanted to stay where he was and await a chance to get further west.

And now, two burly M.V.D. men, with the green cap covers of hateful memory, were conducting him to the station, and their very helpfulness made him want to spring at their throats. Why were they so good humoured, so courteous? Because they thought they were shepherding a sheep to the slaughter and the surprise that awaited him at Chita when he reported to the Rayon H.Q. filled them with sadistic delight. And still, he was compelled to play the booby and smile back at them, taking their courtesy at its face value.

'I won't have to change, will I, before I get to Chita?' He was sitting in a shed reserved for military personnel, spooning a bowl of soup. The M.V.D. had spoken to the station superviser before they left and, as a result, Forell had been put in charge of a soldier who would see him into the train. The man was friendly and had brought Forell to his canteen. Willem, too, had his plate of soup—a new Willem energetically 'de-flead' by the Railways Welfare Department.

'Change?' said the soldier. 'No. It goes straight through.'

A pity! thought Forell. If he had had to change trains, there might have been a chance of getting back to Ulan Ude again, without ever going to Chita. He felt no desire to see that town again. There was a map of the area on the wall of the canteen just behind him. All he had been able to see so far was a green line to the south of it, marking the frontier with Mongolia. The frontier! He could not be far from it now. And suddenly, it was all he could do to go on eating his soup and restrain the impulse to thrust his way out of the canteen and set off there and then to cover the last few miles.

Forell awaited a chance to glance at the map again. It came when he had finished his soup. He stood up, then, to hand back the bowl and while the soldier was returning it to the counter, he remained standing, ostensibly talking to Willem, who sat close to the wall. Yes, there was Ulan Ude, about a hundred and fifty miles from the frontier. And Chita? Chita was off the map. Railways? Yes, there was a line, southward—to where? Quickly, the place! Ky—— Ky—— what? The soldiers was coming back. . . . Kyakhta. . . .

'Sitting makes my legs stiff!'

The soldier grunted. Forell repeated the name to himself. Ky-ak-ta. . . . Ky-ak. . . .

'Tell me when it's time to go to the train, won't you?'

'Yes, yes, of course. . . .'

The soldier turned to speak to someone. Forell sat down again and began stroking Willem. What were the soldier's instructions? Most likely, he had been told to put Forell in the train to Chita, and if he hadn't, what platform did the trains to the frontier go from, and would there be a chance to get to it?

The soldier had come back to Forell again. 'A nice dog! What's his name?'

'Willem. There's no possibility, is there, of me landing up in the wrong place again?'

'No. None at all. You can't go wrong. I'll come with you to the platform. I'll see you into the train, and the first time it stops, you get out. That's all there is to it!'

'Thank you very much. . . . I'm not used to going by train. It's rather—well, it upsets you, you know. It gets you all hot and bothered.'

'Yes, you look it. You want to calm down a bit.'

Calm down! And at the next platform, perhaps, when he was leaving for Chita, there'd be another train starting for the frontier. . . . And he couldn't get to it because of this godammed oaf. . . . Three thousand miles he'd come, and now he couldn't go three yards. . . ! Forell was trembling from the effort to control his rage.

The soldier laughed. 'Come on! What are you so scared about? I've told you, I'll see you to the train!'

'That's very good of you. . . .'

There was a wooden bench running round all four sides of the carriage, with hinged sections by the doors. The carriage was already crowded when Forell and his escort arrived and the last minute incursion of yet another passenger, not to mention his dog, provoked sour looks. Forell kept up his yokel act to the bitter end and in different circumstances the soldier's painstaking reassurances that, this time, he could not fail to reach Chita would have been comic. But now the train was about to leave for Chita, Forell's simmering fury returned and while the other passengers heard him speak a polite good-bye and noted, perhaps, his rigid, imbecile expression, Forell was gazing with murder in his heart at the man's retreating back. Perhaps the soldier sensed it, for as the train was moving out, he suddenly turned, and Forell caught a glimpse of a puzzled face. . . .

During the whole of the twelve-hour journey to Chita, Forell exchanged not one word with his fellow passengers. Not that he was afraid to betray his foreign accent, but the prospect of becoming involved in pleasantries was intolerable to him. Seeing his master's mood, Willem flung himself into the social whirl with gusto. Men from the locomotive works at Ulan Ude, women from the glass factories, a couple of children—he talked to them all, and in return, they petted him, fed him and told him he was a wonderful dog. Willem agreed.

*　　*　　*

Next day Forell was back in Ulan Ude.

The trains had stood alongside in Chita station and he had simply got out of one and into the other. It was some hours before the train left and he had plenty of time to think over what would happen if the M.V.D. decided to check on the passengers and asked for his papers. It was quite simple. They would see that he had no identity card. They would telephone their Rayon Headquarters at Chita and discover his whole story was a lie. His accent would tell them he was a German; his broken body, that he was a convict; his exhaustion, that he had escaped. Finally, if his photograph had been circulated from East Cape, they would know that he was Clemens Forell. What more could they ask? What better excuse would the M.V.D. ever have had to put a man up against a wall and shoot him? Now that he was so close to the frontier, the dangerous situation he was in combined with his impatience and physical exhaustion to make him a desperate man. From now on, if anyone tried to stop him, Forell swore he would draw his knife across the Russian's throat from ear to ear.

When he got out of the train at Ulan Ude, the desperate mood was still on him, but his luck still held. No one had questioned him during the journey and nobody paid any attention to him now. His only thought was to get away from the station and out into the open where he could find a place to sleep. Too weak to care whether he was seen or not, unable to think, he went staggering across the rails, promising to murder whoever stood in his way. Once, a voice shouted at him, but he never looked round. At length he came to the outskirts of the town and some ruined buildings. All seemed deserted. 'Lie down, Willem,' he said, and slipping the rucksack from his shoulders, he collapsed asleep, by a wall.

When he awoke, Willem was gazing at him, swishing his tail as he sat, couched like a lion on a patch of grass. Forell made up his mind to reach the frontier by road, aiming for Kyakhta, the frontier town. He set off southwards, wandering through dusty streets. He could see more of Ulan Ude now, enough to recognize above the modern, flat-roofed houses, a jagged skyline typical of industrial towns—factories, chimneys, water-towers and wisps of smoke or steam.

Forell plodded on, indifferent to the stares of passers-by, until he came to a sign board. As he was studying it, a voice beside him said: 'I see you're a stranger. Where do you want to get to?'

'To Kyakhta.'

'Come from the other side, have you?'

'Yes. . . .'

'You want the motor road, then. You're not going on foot, are you? It's a long way.'

'No, I—don't expect so.'

Forell's memory retained no picture of the man who put him on the road to Kyakhta. The traffic was heavy and whenever a likely-looking truck came towards him, he thumbed for a lift. Three went straight past, but the fourth stopped. He remembered it was the fourth, because it struck him at the time that the people here were about twice as considerate as wartime German drivers. Then he remembered eight or nine trucks passing him before finally one stopped and gave him a lift.

Now, a Chinaman was grinning down at him. 'Kyakhta?' 'Get in!' Beside the driver there was just room for Forell and his dog. To Forell, the man was Chinese because he had slit eyes and a yellow face, and his truck was a 'tin lizzy' because it was old and rattled like a canful of marbles. But it went, and maintained the furious pace that its driver decreed until, on a steep gradient, a cloud of steam spurted from the radiator and they had to wait till it cooled. The Chinaman, however, did not allow such technical necessities to destroy his good humour—they were all part of the fun, and he was just as happy poking about under the bonnet, mopping water out of the magneto, as he was twirling his steering wheel with a foot clamped hard down on the accelerator. And not only his antique bone-shaker but everything they passed on the road was apparently a never-ending source of joy to him. The Chinaman was, as medical men would say, in a state of euphoria. The winding hilly road, the parched, sandy waste that lay on either side, the lakes dotted about in the valleys—the whole scenery was of absorbing interest and made him screw up his face like a contented child. But to Forell, his greatest recommendation was that he spoke Russian even worse than he did himself and after the umpteenth attempt to understand each other had ended in the driver's chortling laughter, Forell was almost aggrieved to find that his sullen and desperate mood of recent days was beginning to thaw.

Some hours later, the Chinaman stopped the truck and, courteous as ever, invited Forell to get down. Kyakhta? And where was that? Forell could see nothing but bare sandy hills with, here and there, clumps of what looked like fir trees. Where was the town? The Chinaman smiled and nodded and said something about another man joining him to share in the driving. Had he genuinely failed to understand the question, or was he merely pretending? The town could not be far away and probably he was anxious not to have Forell with him when he entered it. At any rate, he was adamant that he would take his passenger no further, so there was no more to be said except 'thank you', followed by an incomprehensible phrase from the Chinaman of which he was clearly very proud. It sounded like: 'Bolchi rekommandantura', and judging by the solemn expression on his face, he, too, seemed not to have the faintest idea what it meant. The next moment, he was grinning again as the engine roared to the opened throttle and the truck rattled off, trailing clouds of black smoke.

The Chinaman's very friendliness had made Forell suspicious and because the man had advised following the road to the left, he took, instead, the first turning to the right, determined to find his own way to the frontier. The country was open steppe, undulating and bare except for fir trees, coarse reeds, growing in low ground and a thin covering of parched steppe grass. Prospects of crossing the frontier unseen were slender.

The steppe lay parched under a burning sun. Forell had a little food in his rucksack, but no water and the landscape was as dry and arid as a bone. Soon the branch road he had been following began to peter out in the sandy waste, leaving only the outline of a track winding over the dunes. There was no sound, no sign of life and no hint of where the line of the frontier ran. Not even a landmark was visible by which to check his direction or the distance covered. The undulations of the steppe ran east and west, and stretched indefinitely, like a vast corrugated roof, towards the south. As Forell went down into the troughs and up to the ridges beyond, he was hoping to get an extended view of the countryside, but each time the horizon was limited by the succeeding ridge, lying no more than a mile away. Sometime, in a few hours perhaps, today, or tomorrow, he would come to a ridge that offered a different prospect, a ridge that confronted him with—what? Barbed wire? Frontier posts? Or another stretch of innocent-looking desert that sprang to life only when someone tried to cross it and came within range of hidden machine-guns with intersecting arcs of fire? Forell had no idea how he would recognize the frontier when he reached it. Only one thing was certain. He would never get across unchallenged.

For a long time he trudged on with every nerve in his body keyed for a sudden crisis. Then gradually the sense of urgency became blunted. Thirst, weariness, and the slumbering torpor that lay over the steppe drew his mind inward, cutting off reality and wrapping him in a soft blanket of indifference. He had lived too long as a hunted animal to project his thoughts far ahead or to let tomorrow's dangers disturb tonight's sleep. Once again, as so often before when daylight had begun to fade, he was content not to know where he was or what the future would bring, so long as he could find a sheltered spot to sleep in and accept the truce that twilight offered to his sufferings.

In the morning, both man and dog were suffering torments of thirst. Forell copied Willem and licked the heavy dew from the steppe grass. At least it moistened the tongue.

So far there had not been a sign of a human being or of any man-made structure since the Chinaman had deposited them by the roadside on the previous day. Now, Forell's caution returned and on each slight elevation he paused to gaze out over the sun-drenched sand. But the Siberian snows had combined with under-nourishment to weaken his eyesight and it was Willem who saw them first, and stopped dead in his tracks. They had reached a place where the steppe began to fall away towards the plain. Topping the hills that stretched to right and left below them were a series of rectangular towers, obviously sited so as to overlook the whole of the surrounding countryside. Four were visible from the point Forell had reached and the nearest was no more than half a mile away. The platform of the tower was surrounded with open boarding and on it, just visible, was the figure of a man. Forell dropped hastily to the ground. He was far too near for safety and if it had not been for Willem he would have been nearer still and probably spotted.

Examining the area carefully, Forell could see now a double row of posts running in a continuous line between the towers—the line of the frontier. Each post was about twelve foot high and though the barbed wire was invisible at that distance, his memory supplied it clearly enough from an occasion ten years before, when he had lain, clicking his way through just such a double apron fence on a frontier in another continent. Between the two rows of posts, now as then, would be a no-man's land. While he watched, the guards in the towers were relieved and then a party of soldiers marched into the palisade and dispersed along a section of its length, while an equal number emerged and formed up on the far side. So there were troops stationed in the no-man's-land. . . .

As long as it was day, Forell did not dare to move and hour after hour he lay with Willem beside him, watching the unhurried progress of the sun. To go forward by day or night and try to get past the watch towers would be suicide, and he had no intention of ending his two-year pilgrimage from East

Cape lying pinned to a fence on the Mongolian frontier like a butterfly on a board.

When night came, Forell waited until it was completely dark and then, with great caution in case at some point the frontier curve further northwards, he crept back several miles until he judged he was in safety again.

The following day, he came to a broad river. When man and dog had satisfied their thirst, Forell sat for a while bathing his swollen feet in the water and admiring the freshness of the trees and bushes that grew along the banks—'admiring', that is, in the limited sense appropriate to a man faced with grim alternatives. For Forell had now to make up his mind either to accept defeat and the end of all his hopes, or else to creep up at nightfall and attempt the formidable palisade. He chose the latter.

The river flowed northwards from its source in Mongolia and Forell had approached it from the east. His only hope of getting past the frontier defences alive was to find a weak spot somewhere along their length to westward, the portion he had not yet seen. That meant he would have to cross the river. Somewhere, he supposed there might be a bridge, lower down the valley, perhaps towards the motor road. It would be worth the detour if he could find one and get across dry-shod. The danger from the people he might meet would have to be accepted. As a last resort, if there was no bridge and nothing in the way of a raft, he would have to swim, but apart from the exertion involved—where he was standing now the river was about a hundred and fifty yard across—to be seen swimming a river, pushing his clothes in front of him on a bundle of sticks would be bound to arouse the suspicions of anyone who saw him, and as long as he was in the water, he could do nothing to avoid recapture, even if the whole of the M.V.D. were lined up, waiting for him on the opposite bank.

For three hours or so, Forell followed the east bank of the river downstream towards the north, without finding any means of crossing on foot. Then, as the river seemed to be getting continually broader, he gave up the search and resigned himself to the necessity of swimming. But first, he wanted to get some food inside him and feed Willem, as well. In the valley, the soil was more humid and a lush pastoral scene opened before him, at first, only a faint green among the sunburnt grass with flocks of grazing sheep; then, progressively, a thicker carpet of meadow grass and increasing signs on either bank of ordered cultivation. Cattle browsed contentedly, knee-deep in green; gardens of vegetables appeared adjoining white, box-like houses. All was peaceful and homely, and dragged at the wanderer's heart—until he began to think of where he might steal some food. He would have to wait for darkness again, but it would be worth it if he could steal a lamb, say, or some potatoes. But when the time came and he headed towards some farm buildings selected in daylight for their isolation, he was set upon by watch dogs and the net result of the raid was a torn ear for Willem.

And now Forell had to wait until daylight before he could swim the river. Any spot would do, so long as it was away from houses and the banks were not too steep. Next day he cut some brushwood and tied it into a bundle to serve as a float to carry his clothes and rucksack. Having strapped them on, he waded out and started to swim, pushing the float in front of him and calling Willem to follow. But Willem had other ideas. Seen from the bank, his master was not enjoying himself. What exactly he was trying to do was not clear, but it evidently called for strenuous exertion. Sometimes the man disappeared altogether, except for the top of his head, then he came up again, spluttering and making horrible faces. Perhaps he was having a drink. Perhaps he was thirsty. Well, Willem wasn't—not that much, anyway, and he leaned forward over the bank and started to bark with short, staccato yaps, loud enough to be heard in Mongolia. Forell swam back and had to talk to the dog long and earnestly before he could coax him into the water. By that time, the float with his clothes was twenty yards away down-stream. Swimming frantically to head it off, followed by the agonized Willem, Forell had just managed to recapture his bundle and was in almost mid-stream when a shadow caught his eye and turning he saw a ship bearing down on him. It might have been a pleasure boat of the kind that takes about two hundred passengers for Sunday trips on the Rhine. At any rate, there was little enough room for it to pass. Forell began to race for the bank, still pushing his precious bundle before him. The ship gave a toot with its siren and altered course to avoid him. As it passed, a crowd of people on the upper deck leaned over, roaring with laughter at the naked swimmer afloat with all his goods and chattels, including his dog. It was Willem's fault, Willem who somehow set the seal on the comic picture of a man committed to the waves with all his worldly possessions around him. But it was Forell who felt more foolish than ever in his life, before or since. As the stern wave of the ship struck him, he clung desperately to his bundle of clothes to prevent it capsizing. Whatever happened, he could not afford to let them get soaked. As he was clambering up the west bank of the river, hauling his clothes after him, the steamer's siren gave a farewell 'blip!' Was that Siberia's way, Forell wondered, of expressing compassion on the shivering skeleton of a man who had nearly drowned?

While his clothes dried in the sun, Forell sat fishing on the river bank; and he caught a fish, a splendid one to look at, but sweet tasting and horrible to eat, as he ate it, raw, for fear a fire might attract unwelcome visitors. Willem, on the other hand, found it delectable. With the raw fish inside him, Forell suddenly succumbed to a mood of delirious good cheer, and the fact that he had nothing to feel cheerful about merely heightened it. Next day, he managed to steal some melons, gherkins and raw maize from a farm garden and the same night, partly to find something to eat for Willem who by that time was in pathetic straits, he plundered an outhouse at the same farm, carrying away a rucksack full of food. Then he went in search of the frontier.

Further to the south, the countryside was idyllic—open woodland gradually closing in as he progressed until he found himself among ancient, densely packed firs. All seemed deserted. The only sound was a distant tapping of the kind he remembered hearing in those far-off summers before the war, when timber was being felled in the forests at home —that, and the sound of birds calling among the branches overhead. Here and there the trees thinned again, revealing bushes covered with berries, plump and rubicund as country faces, under a segment of glittering sky. After a while—the peacefulness and solitude still unbroken—he began to think he might already have crossed the frontier unawares and be treading now on Mongolian soil.

Yet the idyll was a lie—he knew that, and soon it began to appear sinister, the very innocence of the scene striking terror into his heart, hardened though it was against imaginary fears.

He came to a clearing and stepped out into the sunlight. He ought to have paused, of course, before leaving the cover of the trees and to this day he cannot explain why he did not. As it was, he had taken three or four steps before he realized that this was no natural clearing, but a broad strip cut clean through the forest and shaved of the last blade of vegetation. Then he stopped dead. The nearest watch-tower was fifty yards away, planted in the middle of the no-man's land, and there were others spaced at intervals throughout its length. He could see at least three. A stone's throw away to the right, the sentry on his platform was gazing southwards towards Mongolia. In a moment he would turn and move round the platform. Now was the time to vanish.

Keeping his eyes fixed on the sentry, Forell made to step back—then found he could not move. He was paralysed. His legs would not budge. He was helpless.

Now the sentry was straightening his back—yawning—shuffling round the platform towards him. The leather, thought Forell, that's what he'll see, the pale chamois leather lining

197

the open jacket. . . . Willem? No sound. Willem stood motionless, hypnotized.

The sentry was gazing straight at Forell.

The sentry's head was drooping with boredom. Now it was turning—away—and now his body—and his feet now, moving —one-two-three—slowly across the platform—and round, to the far side.

Then Willem growled. Forell glanced down, saw the bared fangs and bristling neck, and then another sentry with a huge hound, a mastiff, about two hundreds yards away to his left, coming down the clearing towards him.

The guard dog leapt forward and at the same moment, Willem dashed out, snarling savagely. They met in the middle of no-man's land. Forell saw the huge animal try to seize Willem by the throat and Willem, undaunted, twisting and somer-saulting round it. The next moment, a machine-gun stuttered and from the nearby watch-tower, a hail of bullets swept up the clearing. The spell was broken. Forell leapt back, reached the cover of the trees, turned—and saw both dogs lying dead with the sentry bending over them, not ten yards from the spot where he had been standing.

That was the last Forell saw before panic sent him stumbling back through the forest, away from the frontier and the giant sleuth hounds that would soon be set on his trail. He was convinced he had been seen. The first dog was dead. How long would it take to summon the pack? An hour, possibly, certainly no more—probably less.

An hour.

Forell ran for dear life. The terror at his back lifted him forward, propelling him, holding him up. There was no time to fall. He was barely conscious of effort. He ran—in whatever direction the trees were thinnest.

An hour. If the hounds caught up with him, he would be finished. One, perhaps, he could deal with, but the whole pack —they were trained to kill—went straight for the throat—the Siberian knife would be useless.

An hour—or less even than that. He ran on. A branch lashed his face. He stumbled, lurched, and kept running. Now the forest was thinning out. He came to an open space, never paused, ran across, and then down, saw a stream and was in up to his knees and wading before it dawned: here was salvation. Water would destroy his scent.

As he scrambled on, the fast-flowing stream lifted his feet, speeding him forward. But the cold and the weight of water in his clothes quickly tired him. Inside a minute, he was soaked from head to foot. Still he went on, stumbling over rocks, slithering, slipping, sliding, with the terror howling through his brain—on through evening, and past sunset and into the night, until at last the thought filtered into his mind that now he might stop, certain that the dogs could no longer follow.

There were trees growing beside the stream. Mechanically, unaware of what he was doing, he searched for one that was easy to climb and had strong, spreading branches with plenty of foliage to conceal him from view. Hauling the rucksack after him, he worked his way up until he came to a fork where he could sit with his back to the tree trunk. Out of his sodden pack he dragged all the straps and cords he could find, tying them together and binding himself to the tree so that when asleep he would not fall out. Food? He couldn't be bothered. Cold? He was too exhausted to feel it. And tomorrow? Tomorrow, he told himself, he would make absolutely sure of putting the dogs off the scent and wade a little further down the bed of the stream. And with that, the fear inside him relaxed and allowed him to sleep.

He awoke, rigid with cold, at an early hour. He fetched a sodden strip of bacon from his rucksack and caught himself tearing off a piece for Willem. But Willem was dead. He would miss his dog, as he missed those other friends whom Fate had snatched from him, one by one, year after year, as though it were decreed that this man should fight and suffer alone, to the end of his days.

*   *   *

Forell had only one thought now—to get as far from the frontier as he could in the shortest possible time. For eleven days he tramped on, heading for the wilds. The country was the most rugged and awe-inspiring of any since he had left East Cape. Enormous sandstone cliffs, topped with dark pines and cedars, hung menacingly over cavernous ravines. Spurred on by the fear of pursuit, he struggled on up steep and thickly wooded slopes, squandering his energies, indifferent to discomfort or natural dangers, so long as he could find a place remote enough to promise him safety. After eleven days he felt he could risk meeting people again without fear of being recognized.

The first men he encountered were rangers. They asked him where he had come from and where he was going. Though their questions were friendly, they were difficult to answer for a man who had no idea where he was. Forell said he had been taken on for forest work, but on account of sickness had not been able to start at the appointed time. Now he had to find his own way to the site. He had a feeling he had gone wrong somewhere; the route given him had been rather vague. . . .

'Which brigade do you want?' asked the older of the two men confronting him.

'Oblenov,' said Forell, for the sake of a name.

'Oblenov? Never heard of it! Orsay perhaps?'

Forell drew out the papers supplied by the M.V.D. to convey him to Chita. 'Yes, Orsay. That's right. That's what it says here.' And he stowed them away before the men could look over his shoulder.

'To get to the Orsay brigade will take you another day, at least. Why didn't they send you with the funicular? It would have taken you straight there.'

The rangers gave Forell his directions. It was about twelve miles to the site where the timber was being felled. But Forell was all-in. He was near to collapse. Could he spend the night with the rangers and go on next day? Of course, they said, but not next day, the day after. Tomorrow was Sunday.

Forell found himself in a sizeable log cabin, preparing to take a sauna bath. The rangers had built themselves a sauna adjoining. The stove was heated and a young man in his twenties, Mihail by name, fetched buckets of water and poured them on the hot tiles.

Forell stripped and stood in the steam.

'You don't look too good to me,' said Mihail. 'Been slimming, have you?'

'I've been ill.'

'You won't get far in that state.'

'What do you mean, "far"?'

'Just that. . . .'

The rangers gave Forell plenty of food with some extra for his rucksack. Then, as the following day was Sunday, they let him sleep for as long as he liked.

On Monday morning they told him again how to get to the gang known as the Orsay brigade, and Mihail offered to put him on his way. They had been going for about a quarter of an hour and Forell was wondering how to get rid of the man when Mihail stopped and, laying a hand on Forell's arm, said:

'Let me give you some advice. You want to be careful.'

Forell felt his heart constrict. 'What do you mean?'

'Just that. . . .'

They continued in silence for a while. As the man showed no inclination to turn back, Forell tried to give him a hint. 'I'm sure I can find the way from here. Thank you very much.'

Mihail smiled broadly and said: 'Yes, I'm sure you could —if you wanted to.'

Forell felt he ought to get angry, but there was obviously no point. The man was leading up to something. Then it came. 'Listen. You can't fool me. You're no Russian. Shall I tell you what you are? You're a German. South German. Probably Austrian.'

It was not a guess. The man knew it. 'Yes, my family came from the Tyrol. What about it?' said Forell.

'Only this: my father was born in Wiener-Neustadt.'

'Vienna? So we're compatriots?' Mihail nodded, smiling. 'What are you doing here?' asked Forell.

'Not trying to escape, like you are. You're an escaped prisoner, aren't you—originally a prisoner-of-war? And it's the Mongolian frontier that hovers before your mind—am I right?'

'It did—once.'

'Where did you try to cross?'

'Near Kyakhta.'

'You're crazy. You deserve to be dead by now. Did you bother to think what would happen if you had got over? The Mongolians would have handed you back, that's all.'

Mihail was not encouraging. He said it was impossible to get out of the Soviet Union, so Forell might as well give up trying. But when he heard that Forell had come from East Cape and not from a prison camp on the shores of Lake Baikal, a couple of hundred miles away, as he had assumed, he quickly changed his tune. If Forell had come that far, he could go a bit further. Had he heard of a town called Abakan? No? It was a moderate-sized place up in the mountains, to the west. It was a long way away, over six hundred miles, but if Forell ever got there——

And for the first time since his escape, Forell was given the name and address of someone who would help him—Leopold Messmer, manager of a bakery, Abakan, Street of the October Revolution. The shop had simply *Pekarniya*, 'Bakers', over the doorway. The man was Mihail's own father. 'You'll like him,' added his son, 'and you'll have something in common. He's just as home-sick as you are, you for Innsbruck, or wherever it is, and he for Vienna. He didn't want to leave any more than you probably did. But he had to. You ask him to tell you the story. . . .'

Forell went west-north-west, keeping to tracks, as Mihail had advised him, so as not to get hopelessly lost in the precipitous mountain country. He crossed under the rope railway that one of the rangers had mentioned and skirted a site where lumbermen had been at work. Amongst the felled timber he had the luck to find an axe. Next day, he ran into a forced labour camp for women. Through the barbed-wire fence he saw about forty women chopping wood under the supervision of two guards. The prisoners were dressed exactly like men, in threadbare trousers and lumber jackets. They were being made to work hard, but they never ceased chattering, and for hours Forell watched and listened from the cover of some undergrowth, fascinated, yet hardly knowing why. Once, a comic incident occurred provoking peals of feminine laughter. What did it matter whose voices they were? To Forell they opened the door to a whole world of grace and enchantment, a world that he had lost, but still hoped to regain.

Evening came. The prisoners were herded indoors. Their chatter ebbed, then rose again when the lights went on in their huts, and still Forell stayed, waiting for the night. When all was quiet in the camp and the darkness universal, he crept under the fence and, going to a window that he had already marked down, eased it out of its frame with his axe and took some food. Then he made off into the night and, weak as he was, kept marching until it was light enough to select a place for his bivouac, a hollow, sheltered and secure, where sleep would cover his loneliness.

*   *   *

By the time Forell reached the plain, the first snows were falling. Below him lay pleasant, undulating country, and about half a mile away he could see a village nestling in a hollow. It was a relief, after weeks of grim forest and harsh mountain defiles, to come upon a tamer, more domesticated scene. Here, in summer, cattle would be browsing, and the wheat would spread like a yellow sea, and in the evenings the sound of crickets would pulse in the still, warm air.

But now it was October, and already the village lay silent under a thin white shroud, awaiting its winter burial. From where he was standing among dwarf pines, Forell counted the houses—thirty or so small wooden huts clustered at random by a stream and a couple of longer sheds. It was getting towards midday and the people all seemed to be indoors. The men were probably working in one of the sheds and would come out in a moment and go home to dinner. Children would be sent to fetch water from the stream, a woman calling after them from a doorway to hurry up. Forell watched, pleased to be close to humanity again. The place was too isolated to be dangerous, for throughout his journey, wherever people had been free to express their natural feelings, they had proved to be friendly.

Forell waited a while, then, still seeing no sign of life in the village, decided to go down and inspect. There would be some simple explanation, of course, for the lack of activity. Perhaps the inhabitants were out of sight somewhere, working in the open. . . . He sauntered down the bare hillside in the uncomfortable knowledge that he could be seen for miles, certainly from every corner of the village. But nothing stirred. No smoke rose from the chimneys and the only sound, as he came to the first hut, was the low murmuring of the nearby stream. He knocked. No answer. Seeing the door was ajar, he gave it a push and it swung wide open, creaking on rusty hinges. The place was empty and looked as though it had not been lived in for a considerable time. From the remains of furniture lying about, he could see that one of the two rooms had been used for sleeping. The other had a wooden bench along one wall and the remains of an iron stove. Obviously, the hut had been no mere temporary shelter, for harvesters, say, in summertime, but had been a permanent home.

The hut was typical of the whole village. There was not a living soul anywhere. Apparently, the people had gone, not in an orderly way, taking all their possessions with them, but in haste, for besides the larger furniture, they had left behind small possessions which they would never have willingly abandoned. The whole place was now infested with rats, attracted by the food and fodder which the inhabitants had been unable to take with them. The floors of the sheds were inches deep in mouldering debris. Forell found a hut that was reasonably free from vermin and for the sake of a fire and a roof over his head, decided to spend the night there. He lit the stove with bits of furniture, hung his rucksack from straps tied to a hook on the ceiling so that the rats should not get at his food, and then lay down full length on a bench. But the place seemed to be full of noises and sleep was difficult. Outside the wind moaned thinly round the building, rats scuttered about inspecting the intruder and before long, after they had bitten through the straps, the rucksack suddenly crashed to the floor. Forell left before dawn.

The country was open and he was concerned to see that the snow was now deep enough to take the stamp of his footprints. The scene had now lost its charm and Forell was glad to get away from the mysteriously deserted village. As he went, he wondered what the fate of the inhabitants had been. During the war, he had seen how civilians caught in the tide of battle would cling on to their possessions, even beds and heavy pieces of furniture, to the very last moment. Women tottering with heavy chairs on their backs, or coal scuttles and umbrella stands, had been no uncommon sight. Every human instinct seemed to rise up against the thought of abandoning the hard-won accumulation of years. It must have been the same with these people in the village. Something other than their own free will must have put them to headlong flight, stripped of almost everything they possessed, and that something could only have been fear—but of what? Forell himself began to hasten his steps, conscious of a vague unease. He headed towards a valley, knowing that if there were people anywhere, that would be the most likely place. In the valley was another village. That too, had been abandoned.

This time, he had no desire, or need, to go into every hut. The appearance of the place was already familiar. As before, the doors were open, the furniture was still in the rooms; dust, cobwebs and rats were everywhere. The only difference was the size of the village. This was larger and on the outskirts stood an enormous shed, big enough to hold a hundred head of cattle. But the cattle had gone.

Forell was gazing into the empty shed when round a corner a man suddenly appeared. His hair and beard were grey and caked with dirt and he was in rags. 'What do you want?' It was the voice of senility, and the eyes were those of a madman. Forell said he had lost his way.

'Who are you? Who sent you? Where do you come from?' The old man hobbled forward, shrill with rage, or fear.

'I'm on my way to Abakan.'

The man lowered his head and repeated the word, trying to remember. Then it suddenly dawned. 'Oh! Abakan! Yes. . . . Um. . . . Yes. . . . Well, good-bye. . . .' And he turned away. Then he stopped dead, while a sound that to the younger man had once been all too familiar hovered in the air and grew rapidly stronger—the hum of aircraft. Forell was standing, wondering what their errand could be, when the old man seized hold of him and, in the last stages of terror, dragged him under cover of the shed. As the planes roared down, doing a sweep over the village, he clung, cowering, to a wall and it was not until the last faint throb of the engines had died away over the plain, that he came slowly out from his hiding place, wide-eyed and trembling in every limb. There was no thought of good-bye now; he was obviously glad of Forell's company.

'They come over every other day,' he quavered.

'But what for?'

'To make sure that no one's come back.'

'Why?'

'Because it's not allowed. It's forbidden.'

Bit by bit, Forell got at least part of the story. The inhabitants of the village, the entire population, had been forcibly removed elsewhere—where, the old man did not know, but they had travelled a great distance. But he had escaped on the journey and come back. The old man grinned inanely. A while ago, he said, the planes had spotted his sheep and tried to bomb them. He led the way to a hut and, pushing

204

open the door, showed Forell four sheep in what had once been the living-room. Hearing movement overhead, Forell looked up and met the haughty gaze of umpteen chickens, perched on a beam.

The old man was delighted to see his surprise.

'They think there's no one here!' he chortled. 'But you can see, can't you? I was the only one to get back, and I mean to stay!'

He raised a quaking finger and pointed upwards. 'They won't drive me out. I'm not afraid of them!'

Forell asked him again why the people had been taken away, but the man made a lunatic gesture, clapping his hand over his mouth so that no word should escape him. When Forell persisted, he frowned and muttered evasively: 'I don't know. Don't ask me. The villages are empty, all empty.' Then, as though in explanation, he added: 'Tannu Tuva——!'

Forell dimly remembered seeing the name on a map. 'Why, what——?' But the old man interrupted him, repeating like a sorrowful chant: 'Tannu Tuva. . . . Tannu Tuva. . . .' And he would say no more.

The fellow gave Forell three or four hard-boiled eggs, some sheep's milk cheese and told him, as well as he could remember, how to get to Abakan. Then, seeing he preferred to be alone, Forell left him. During the next two days, he came upon two more abandoned villages, making four in all.

*   *   *

It was three hundred miles or more to Abakan. The country was mountainous and it might take six weeks to get there. Earth, rivers, the sky—all was sickening towards winter. The nights were bitterly cold, and the food in his rucksack was almost exhausted. Why go on? What hope was there of ever reaching a frontier? It was over two years since his escape from the lead mine and now he was in the very centre of Asia. The nearest frontier opening on to freedom was by the Caspian Sea, and that was—Oh! Thousands of miles, thousands of years away, somewhere beyond the moon. . . .

But Forell went on, to start with because he was desperate for food, and the sight of mountain sheep tempted him to pursue them, following laboriously by circuitous paths where they led, nimbly scaling crags and perilous escarpments. For a whole day, the chase continued. The sheep were agile, but starvation taught Forell cunning. He worked his way up the mountainside until he was looking down on them where they stood on a rocky terrace. He loosened some boulders and rolled them down towards the animals, knocking them off their perch so that they fell hundreds of feet and were killed on the rocks below. It was too late then to go in search of the bodies, but when he came to them next day, most of the meat had already been eaten by wild animals.

As soon as he came to inhabited areas again, Forell managed to keep alive by stealing food from isolated farms, and that was easier than tracking wild sheep among the mountains. But it had its dangers, and the chief of them was that he might succumb to the temptation to sit down and eat within sight, almost, of the place he had raided, or—as it was usually impossible to creep up unseen before nightfall —that sleep might overcome him before he had gone far enough to elude pursuit. The least danger of all was that he might be caught in the act of stealing, for by now Forell was a professional vagabond and the one instinct which was sharpened rather than dulled by undernourishment was the instinct that warned him of approaching danger. Fear, in the form of vague, unspecified anxiety concerning himself and the future had gone, leaving him free to take life as it came.

Whereas formerly the mere sight of a railway line would have sent him plunging off into the wilds, now he made straight for it, to walk calmly between the rails in defiance of all who might try to stop him. If a plate-layer spoke to him, he barely deigned to reply. If the man had become tiresome, he would have had no compunction in seizing his big spanner and striking him down, for the mere thought of opposition was enough to kindle his smouldering rage. Conscience would not have stayed his hand, only the calculation that if, as seemed probable, he was forced to remain in the U.S.S.R., then he could not afford to start a new life burdened with guilt. As it was, it would have little enough resemblance of life as he understood the word.

'Hey! You! How far is it to Abakan?'

'A couple of miles. It's on the other side of the river. There's a ferry will get you across.'

Forell climbed into the flat-bottomed boat that was waiting, moored to a landing stage. As the ferryman steered across the river, Forell sat in silence with his back to an icy wind. When they reached the far bank, he learned that the man expected payment. He still had some of Doctor Stauffer's notes in his rucksack. He fumbled around and fetched out the smallest he could find.

'What's this supposed to be?'

'Take it. There's your money.'

But the note had long since ceased to be legal tender. The ferryman looked at Forell, saw the gaunt figure, the sunken eyes—and said: 'Go on, I don't want any payment from you.'

Abakan. Nothing much of a town, but it looked as if it

were going to be, some day. Roads half-finished, buildings in process of construction, piles of sand and cement mixers—everything seemed upside-down. Perhaps that was why no one asked Forell for his *propusk*.

'Leopold Messmer, Street of the October Revolution, a shop marked simply *Pekarniya*, "Bakers".' And Leopold Messmer was at home, a grey-faced little man who could surely be no relation of the strapping Mihail.

'What is it?' came an anxious voice from beyond the half-opened door.

'I met your son Mihail a while ago and he asked me to look you up.'

'Come in.'

Leopold Messmer hustled Forell inside and shut the door. 'Tyrol, is it? Or Bavaria? I knew it was one or the other as soon as you spoke.'

'Both—and half-and-half. To come to the point, Herr Messmer. . . .'

'You escaped?'

'That's right.'

'Where from?'

'East Cape.'

'Why?'

'Because I wanted to get home.'

The baker laughed. 'So did I. I was taken prisoner by the Russians in 1914, before you were born. After the Revolution, I tried to get back to Wiener-Neustadt, to my bakery, but it was no good. Who cared about prisoners of the Tsarist Army? Tsarism was dead. That was in 1919. In '21, Nansen and his people tried to find out how many German ex-prisoners were still left in Siberia. I gave them my name. But nothing happened. Meanwhile, I had got work, lumbering. One day, Albrecht—you know, the German Forestry Super-viser, he came and inspected us. I wormed my way towards him and said: "*Herr Forstkommissar, hören Sie mal——*" Of course, when he heard me speak German, he wanted my whole story. At the finish, he said: "Don't worry, I'll get you home. As soon as I return to Moscow——", and so on, and so forth. Well, two years later, when still nothing had happened, I thought I'd better apply for Soviet citizenship, and inside six months, I got it. Exactly a year after that, I had a letter from Moscow telling me that my repatriation had been arranged, I could go home. Ah! But the Soviet Union was my home now, not Austria! It didn't matter what I did —I moved heaven and earth—I explained why I'd taken out Soviet citizenship, I argued, I pleaded. It made not a bit of difference. I had changed my nationality and I had to stay where I was. And so here I am. . . .'

The timid little man spread his hands, as though he felt he was lucky to be anywhere above ground. 'But keep all that to yourself, won't you? I don't want any trouble. I only told you so that you can see you haven't a hope of getting home. If I couldn't get away thirty years ago, when things here were all upside-down, then you won't now.'

Not even the distance Forell had already come would impress the baker. He was afraid to help him, so he made up his mind that help would be wasted. Even so, he found he had to do something to get rid of him, and he fitted Forell out with a complete set of his son's winter clothes. That would pacify Forell and at the same time, perhaps, persuade Fate to allow the baker to continue in his own state of moderate prosperity.

'Which frontier should I aim for, and how do I get there?'

'You may as well try for Iran.'

'Good. Then I——'

'No. Don't tell me!' said the baker hurriedly. 'I don't want to know where you're going! I don't want to be your accomplice. Now, I'm sorry but I'm afraid you can't stay here any longer. You'll have to be on your way. It's too risky. . . .'

And the baker would not even allow Forell to stay the night, the miserable little man!

* * *

Iran. Well, why not? It was something to aim for. Forell himself had ceased to care how his journey ended, but it had to continue. If he had been in any other country but the Soviet Union, he might by now have taken half a dozen different jobs and settled down to enjoy three square meals a day, a weekly pay packet and the prospect of becoming an honoured member of a community where men knew how to respect a hard worker. But in Russia, a man was as good as his papers, and if he had no papers, he was good for nothing except jail. So of necessity Forell was a vagabond, what people blessed with a *propusk* would call a shameless beggar, an incorrigible thief. And so he was, quite shameless in taking the living that Siberia owed to him, if to any man.

But it was suspicion and fear he encountered now more often than kindness. Only an old man and his wife had the goodness to offer more than he was about to ask. They lived in a small hut on the outskirts of a village and one night, he knocked on their window. Without a moment's hesitation they took him in, fed him and offered him a place between them where they slept on a rack above the stove. Next morning,

when he was about to leave, they asked their first question:
'Are you a *Cilny*, a convict?'

'No. A prisoner-of-war.'

'Our son is working in the gold fields as a convict. God be with him, and with you, and bring you safely home.'

* * *

Forell plodded on, a beggar now with all the beggarly tricks. Dragging his rucksack behind him on a hand-made sledge, he stole by night and cadged by day, a whining, shuffling nobody, whom no one bothered to challenge or question. Destitution, he found, was better than any *propusk.*

He was meeting six-wheeler lorries now on the open road, going in both directions. If one of them slowed up, his foot would be on the running-board and the door half open before the driver had time to say no. But if he said no, and meant it, then at least he could spare a cigarette, couldn't he? Not that Forell wanted the cigarette, but it gave him pleasure to browbeat a man and see him give in. Those drivers that gave him a lift were ill repaid for their kindness. It was cold riding in the back of an open lorry and by the time he got down, Forell would be numbed right through. But before his fingers froze, he took good care to poke round among the goods nearest to hand and stuff into his rucksack whatever he thought might come in useful.

So much for the daytime. At night, Forell had long since given up sleeping in the open. When he came to a hut or building, he knocked and asked for shelter. If it was refused, he proceeded to settle himself in an outhouse, whether the owner liked it or not.

On Christmas Day 1951, he reached the town of Rubtsovsk, four hundred miles south-west of Abakan, and slept the night in a cow-shed. From there, he thumbed a lift in a meat truck on its way to Semipalatinsk. He remembered that town, not for its size or modernity, but for the smell of tanning which hung over it and for his failure to pocket some fruit from a market stall. Another fortnight, and he had hitch-hiked as far as Uspenski, on the way catching his first glimpse of a camel train, undulating slowly across the desert-steppe, and later and more important, in the town itself, a glimpse of a map, which told him that Novo-Kasalinsk, lying to the east of the Aral Sea, was the next town to head for. The map also showed the distance, in a straight line, to be about six hundred miles and the country to be arid desert. But there was a railway line running westwards from Uspenski to within two hundred miles of his goal. Forell decided that his only hope of reaching it would be to jump a goods train.

* * *

Somewhere west of Uspenski, Forell was standing in a heavy snowstorm outside a small railway station. Hunger had forced him to jump off the goods train about a mile back when it had been moving slowly up a gradient. Now he was looking for a chance to steal some food. In the driving snow, the lighted windows of the station building were just visible, twenty yards away. The time was nearly midnight.

For ten minutes or so, he waited to make sure no one was about. Then he crept up to a window. Three of the railway staff were closing up the goods office. One of them was counting bank notes and coin into a metal cash box. When he had finished, the man put the box into a briefcase. Forell saw him nod to the others, and go out through the door on to the platform, carrying the briefcase in his hand. Dropping back from the lighted window, Forell hurried to a corner of the building from where he could see the platform. The man was coming along it towards him, walking fast and turning up his coat collar as he went. Forell caught a glimpse of a pale face and a waxed moustache before the man stepped down the ramp at the end of the platform and disappeared along a path flanking the permanent way. Forell counted twenty seconds and then made after him. As soon as he found the path he crossed to the other side of the rails and ran along them for some distance until he judged he was well ahead. Then he crossed back on to the path and waited for the man to come up with him. He was about half a mile from the station, at a point where the railway, with the path beside it, ran along the top of an embankment. In his right hand, Forell held the knobbed stick that he used for walking. He would have about ten seconds to wait.

He had intended to knock the man unconscious with a blow on the temple, but he did not strike hard enough and the man started bawling for help. So Forell sent him rolling down the side of the embankment and made off, clutching the briefcase, before the man could climb up and see which way he went. Forell ran along the permanent way in the direction the man had been going, taking two sleepers at a time in giant strides. 'Help Thief! Ho-o-o!' yelled the voice behind him. So as to be able to move faster, Forell tore off his rucksack and pitched it over the embankment. Then he saw lights gleaming dully ahead of him—a train! He lurched off the track, then saw that the train had stopped. He crept down the embankment and worked his way along past the engine until he could see that it was a goods train. Two minutes later, he was clambering into an open truck and crawling, still with the briefcase, under a tarpaulin that covered some machinery. Soon afterwards, the train clanked into the station. The place was in an uproar. From where he was hiding, Forell could hear his victim's shrill description of the attack. The man must have just got back and be standing on the platform. 'No. No, it was too dark,' he was saying. '—A terrific size! A giant! That's all I saw. What——? Yes, I slipped. Otherwise I'd have floored him!' Then feet were running past the truck. 'Merkulov! The police are on the telephone. . . .' Another voice: 'We'd all better stay. . . .' A roar from the engine blowing off steam. A shout: 'Baikonur . . . yes . . . two hours late already. . . .' A whistle shrilled. Beyond the station, the scream of motor tyres. A jerk. The engine snorted as the wheels skidded on the icy rails. Then slowly the train moved out, with Forell under his tarpaulin wondering how much money he had got in return for the loss of his rucksack and all it contained.

* * *

Three weeks later, with eleven hundred roubles in his pocket, but minus his Siberian knife, tinder-box, sleeping-bag, and all his spare clothing, Forell was in Novo-Kasalinsk. He had stayed on the train until cold and hunger forced him to descend, and that was shortly before the train reached the terminus at Baikonur. There he had stolen food and then he hitch-hiked in stages to his destination, restraining the temptation to offer payment to drivers who proved reluctant to give him a lift.

In Novo-Kasalinsk, he wandered about the bazaar, buying food, a little at a time, producing small change and keeping the rest of the money hidden away. He stood himself a tot of vodka and was in the act of swallowing it down when a voice behind him said in German:

'Du, Deutscher! Komm mit!'

Forell finished his drink and put back the glass on the stall. Then he turned, slowly, as though to look round the bazaar. Behind him stood a man in civilian clothes with a few purchases under his arm.

'Ja, dich meine ich. Komm nur mit!'

Forell saw a pair of penetrating blue eyes and noticed the man was a Jew. 'I'm sorry,' he said in Russian. 'I don't speak your language.'

'It's German, the same as yours,' said the Jew calmly.

'What do you want?'

'I want to help you.'

A Jew offering help to a German? It seemed unlikely.

'I don't happen to need any help,' said Forell, again in Russian.

But the Jew persisted. 'Well, we can talk about that,' he said. 'But not here. Better at my house.'

Rather than draw attention to himself by arguing in the crowded bazaar, Forell followed as the Jew led the way towards the outskirts of the town. After all, he was twice the other man's size and the Jew did not seem to be armed.

It was a good twenty minutes before the Jew stopped in front of a small, flat-roofed building huddled amongst an assortment of dilapidated suburban houses. 'This is my home. Come in, please'.

The place was as clean inside as its exterior was shabby. And the rooms were luxuriously furnished. Carpets on the walls and floors, brass and copper everywhere. . . .

'As you have already guessed perhaps, I am an Armenian Jew. Do not ask me why I want to help you, or how it is I am in a position to do so. It is not about myself that I wish to talk, but about you.' The Jew spoke quietly and rather pedantically, but his manner was sympathetic and not without humour. He broke off, while a housekeeper laid the table and brought food. 'Please eat what you like and as much as you like. You are my guest.'

When the woman had closed the door behind her, the Jew continued, in German. 'You speak Russian with a German accent. My German is half Yiddish. Right?'

Forell nodded, his mouth full of food.

'Good. That is how I recognized you. Now. I will say this in the form of a statement—I think that will be easier.' The Jew smiled, but without malice or condescension. 'I will say that you have one wish, and one only: to get home. That wish I can help you to fulfil. But first, you need some rest, a long rest. Then I will explain what you must do.'

For ten days, Forell stayed in the house of the Armenian Jew, resting and eating, in spite of himself, for at the back of his mind was the urge to be gone. At the end of that time, he looked a different man and after he had been fitted out in a new suit of clothes, almost a respectable Soviet citizen. His host was delighted with his changed appearance. 'You'll do,' he said briefly. Then he initiated Forell into his plans and told him enough, almost, for the latter to begin to believe that this man might, after all, be able to help him across the frontier.

Had Forell heard of the Kulaki movement? He hadn't. Well, never mind, so much the better. All he need know was that its members were there to help him, and others in a like predicament. The next person Forell should visit lived in Uralsk. Uralsk was eight hundred miles away and he would have to go by train.

'But—eight hundred miles! And where is this place?'

'North of the Caspian Sea.'

'But I'm heading for the Iranian frontier!'

'I know. But it is in two sections. There is an easterly section bordering on Turkmen, then come the southern shores of the Caspian Sea, and then the westerly section, bordering on the Caucasus Mountains—all that forms the northern frontier of Iran. You must take my word for it that the only possible way to cross is to the west, over the Caucasus. But first, as I can't charter you a steamer, you have got to get round the Caspian Sea. Hence I am sending you to Uralsk.'

Forell was not the man to be 'sent' anywhere. And he was not going two thousand miles out of his way simply on the word of an Armenian Jew. What proof was there that the man knew what he was talking about?

Unaware of the effect of his last remarks, Forell's host continued: 'Now this is the address you must go to in Uralsk. Memorize it, please. Do not on any account write it down. "Mihail Ivanovitsch Slatin, Uralsk, Uliza Stranskaja 42." Can you remember? Mihail Ivanovitsch Slatin. . . . And your code word is: "Starschoy".'

Next day, Forell took leave of his host and started his journey. He was glad to be fending for himself again, and glad to get away from the 'Penny Dreadful' atmosphere, complete with underground movement, code words and the rest of the claptrap. He had never believed a word of it and never had any intention of going to Uralsk. Instead, he struck out southwards, heading for the easternly section of the Iranian frontier, the part that was 'impossible to cross'.

That was in February, 1952.

At the beginning of June, he was back again in Novo-Kasalinsk, knocking at the house of the Armenian Jew. The owner was out, but the housekeeper recognized him and let him in. The same evening, his former host gazed at Forell, his blue eyes wide with surprise—not that he had returned, but at the state he was in. 'I'd say you were nearer to death than the frontier,' he remarked soberly. 'Sit down, man, before you fall down.' Forell was a skeleton, draped in tatters. He began to tell his story, but the Jew stopped him. 'I don't want to hear it, and I don't suppose you want to tell it.'

'Yes, I do,' came the hollow voice.

'Because you feel you owe it to me, after not taking my advice? Not at all. I had a feeling you wouldn't accept my word. And why should you? Let's have no explanations. But let's get you fit again.'

And for three weeks, the housekeeper nursed Forell until he was strong enough to set out once more. And this time, he went to Uralsk. The first hundred miles, he hitch-hiked by road. Then he jumped a train and stayed with it until he was just short of Alga. From there to beyond Aktyubinsk, by road again; on foot to Martuk; two hundred miles in a lumber wagon in burning heat, and the last stretch to Uralsk he walked, reaching the town sometime in August.

Though the Jew's kindness had put him to shame, Forell could not restrain a feeling of unease as he sought out the next link in the mysterious Kulaki fellowship. He passed the house marked 42 in Stranskaya Street at least five times before he could bring himself to go to the door and knock. It was opened by a surly-looking female. Could he speak to Comrade Slatin, please? 'Wait here,' he was told, and the woman pointed to a rickety chair in the dark entrance corridor. The place smelled of garlic and sweat.

It was some time before Comrade Slatin arrived and when he saw a visitor, he made no attempt to conceal his annoyance. 'What is it?'

'I've come from Comrade Igor. The word is "Starschoy".'

'Well?'

'I'm a German prisoner-of-war, or was. I've escaped and am trying to reach the frontier.'

'And what am I supposed to do about it?' The man took Forell into an inner room and proceeded to question him. The man cared nothing about grammar or subtle turns of phrase. All he was after was Forell's bona fides. When at last he was satisfied, he told him to go a hundred and fifty miles south-west, to the town of Aleksandrov-Gay. Just before the town, the roads forked. On the right, lay the Klara Zetkin vegetable farm. The son of the overseer was Filip Bonin. The word was the same, 'Starschoy'.

Mihail Slatin did his duty, but no more. He allowed Forell to sleep the night, and next morning his wife bought him food from the market. The prices were so high. . . . Forell took the hint and paid for all she had brought. On his way out of the town, he could not resist visiting the market himself. He bought some matches, and from that moment on, he knew he was being followed.

Try as he might, he could not shake the woman off. He dived through the crowd round the market stalls, but when he emerged, he found her still there, just behind him. He cut up one street and down the next, to see her ten paces away, following along the pavement. He crossed the road, and she crossed the road. He went into a doorway and lit himself a

214

cigarette. She walked close past and stared into a shop window. Finally he went towards her, and immediately she started walking towards him.

What was the matter with the woman? Was she blind? She would bump straight into him unless he——

'*Oh, Verzeihung!*'

'*Bitte.*' Too late Forell realized he had fallen into the trap and answered in German. Now she was standing there, mimicking him. '"I beg your pardon! Don't mention it!" I thought so! Somehow I knew you were German—not because of your accent when you were buying the matches, but—well, I've got a knack, that's all.'

Forell stared, but said nothing.

'You're not going to deny it, now, after your swift retort?'

'I neither deny nor confirm. What does it matter to you, anyway?'

The girl was pretty, but her errand was not the obvious one. Her clothes were not the right sort, and her tone of voice was too serious as she said: 'Look. I don't want to get you into danger and it's dangerous for you, I know, to be seen too much about the streets. Will you be very patient with me, and if you have the time, walk with me a little way, somewhere where it's not so crowded?'

'What for?'

'Please . . . please. . . .'

To his horror, Forell saw the girl was almost in tears. He walked silently beside her until, in a back street somewhere, she took out a key and, opening a door in one of the houses, led him to her room. 'I'm sorry it's so small,' she said, apparently for something to say. Forell had to bend to avoid hitting the ceiling.

'I won't keep you long,' she said, 'It's this. Do you recognize this photograph?' From a drawer she had taken out a snapshot. Forell found himself looking at a figure in German uniform. A handsome young man, somewhere in the twenties. A sergeant in the medical corps. The photograph was an old one.

'I—don't—think so,' he said slowly, and was about to hand back the photograph.

'Are you sure? Please make sure.'

Her tone was almost pleading and he looked again.

'It's very difficult to be absolutely certain, but I can't say "yes".'

'That is Franz,' she said. 'We met in the war. I am a Russian, of course, but somehow, it didn't seem to matter. We didn't see very much of each other. We met in Kharkov and then he was taken prisoner and I saw him in the prisoner-

215

of-war cage, after the city was recaptured. I tried to find out where the prisoners were going. Nobody knew. I thought perhaps you might have seen him.'

Forell looked at her. Kharkov, that was in 1943. Nine years. She must have been about nineteen, then. Now she was waiting for his answer, as eagerly as if Kharkov had been yesterday. He shook his head. 'But that doesn't mean your friend is not alive.'

'No, of course not,' she said briskly. 'Thank you. Now I expect you'd like something to eat.'

The Russian girl did not speak of Franz again, though of every German she came across in Uralsk she tried to ask the same question that she put to Forell. Not all, apparently, were as patient as he had been.

After they had eaten, the girl encouraged Forell to talk. As he told her his story, her interest grew. What seemed to strike her particularly was that he had succeeded in entering and leaving large towns without a *propusk*. The difficulties were obviously well known to her—better, as it appeared, than to Forell himself. She congratulated him on his luck and skill in evading arrest, and added:

'Have you thought what you are going to do without any papers when you get to the oilfields west of the Caspian?'

'Trust to luck, I suppose.'

She thought for a moment. Then she asked if he would mind staying in Uralsk another night. If not, her room was at his disposal, there was plenty of food and no one would disturb him. Forell gratefully accepted and she left him, saying she would be back the following evening about seven.

Next evening, she returned with an official Travel Permit made out for Pyotr Jakubovitsch Ulyanov, the names which Forell had told her were his. She apologized for not getting him a *propusk* as well, but that required a photograph, whereas the Travel Permit did not. Officials seldom bothered to look at both, and if his luck held, the Permit should be enough. It entitled him to travel anywhere within a radius of five hundred and thirty miles of the place of issue, and it had been issued that same morning in the State Security Office in Uralsk. Forell stared at it, amazed. Date and office stamps, the paper, everything looked perfect. The girl saw his expression and must have guessed what was in his mind. 'It's genuine, not a forgery,' she said.

Forell refrained from asking how she had managed to get hold of the Permit, but said he knew she must have taken serious risks.

'That is my business,' she said and smiled.

As Forell was leaving the house after thanking her as

adequately as he could, it suddenly occurred to him: was the accent on 'my'? Or was it on 'business'?

* * *

From Uralsk Forell followed the links of the Kulaki chain to Aleksandrov-Gay, from there to Urda, from Urda to Grozny and from Grozny to Makhachkala, on the western shore of the Caspian Sea—in all, a distance of seven hundred and fifty miles. With every mile he went, the danger increased. At Urda he said good-bye to the virgin expanses of Asia, the huge empty regions that at first had frightened and repelled, but later attracted him and at last had been his friend, allowing him a respite from inquisitive eyes, sudden questions, the never ending need to be on his guard.

South-west of Urda lay the River Volga and after that came the teeming menace and oppression of modern industry, oilfields, refineries, blocks of ferro-concrete skyscrapers, the hoot and surge of motor traffic and crowds. In every corner of the huge, artificial, roaring nightmare seemed to lurk the agents of the M.V.D. To Forell, the transition from back-woods to shop window was terrifyingly abrupt and the necessity of appearing unconcerned in so strange an atmosphere redoubled the strain. Without the aid of his anonymous helpers, he would never have survived.

By November, 1952, he was approaching the last formidable obstacle, the Caucasus Mountains. With a genie to guide him mysteriously conjured into being by the open-sesame 'Stars-choy', Forell entered the eastern foot-hills with dread in his heart. All he had been through in the previous three years now lay heaped on the table, his stake for the last throw—win-all or lose-all. They climbed, and bivouacked, and froze and climbed again, for two whole weeks, until Forell was con-vinced of treachery. Then, at a rendezvous high in the mountains, four men appeared and invited Forell to go with them. His solitary guide disappeared.

At any other time, Forell would have felt at home with the four desperadoes—smugglers, they were, and proud of it. Cloth, rum, currency and men alive or dead, they guaranteed to get them across, north to south and back again, at any season of the year in return for the usual arrangement. . . . How much could Forell pay? How much did they want? They laughed and took all he had got. For days he was with them, until one morning, as they were wading across a fast-flowing river in single file and they were up to their waists in icy water, the leader turned and said over his shoulder to Forell: 'You're crossing the frontier now.'

217

When they reached the far bank, they climbed up one by one and, still in single file, walked on at a faster rate to dry out their clothes. The smugglers were exercising more caution, if anything, than before. No one spoke and Forell noticed that the leader had drawn a pistol. Any open ground they avoided. Once, for some unknown reason, they went back about a quarter of a mile and then forward again, by a different route. Then the leader stopped and said to Forell: 'We would have left you at the river, only our job's to see you into safety, not just over the frontier. Anywhere ten miles on either side, you may bump into Russian patrols. You've got to keep going for three days before you can risk being seen. But you're over the worst now, and you'll be all right if you're just careful and patient. Have you got enough food?'

The men gave Forell bread and a bladder of fat. He said he could not pay.

The smugglers laughed. 'We don't want any payment. Good luck!' they said, grinning. 'Good luck, and good-bye!'

As he watched them go, Forell was suddenly gripped with dread. Why had they laughed? Why so cheerful? Was it an ironic 'good luck'? A trap? Had they waited to see him safely into Russian hands?

It was three days, as the smugglers had said, before Forell came to the first sign of normal life, with people going about openly, as though in freedom. On the fourth day, he summoned his courage, straightened his back and walked with them, following the drift of traffic and pedestrians to a town. He was gaining confidence, beginning to believe that at last—— When there, on the first large building he came to, was a huge hammer-and-sickle above the Cyrillic letters CCCP.[1] Panic seized him. He bawled at the first person he saw: 'What's the name of this town?' The man did not understand. Forell started to run. He ran aimlessly until ahead he saw a portico guarded by sentries. The uniforms were strange, so were the caps. 'Police!' Forell was shouting even before he was through the doorway. 'Police!' He was in an echoing hall. 'Police? In there!' A man pointed to a door. Forell irrupted. The door banged. A tall police officer in impeccable uniform rose smoothly from his chair.

'Ich bitte um Asyl Herr——!'

The man raised his eyebrows. Forell tried in Russian: 'I ask you for asylum.'

The officer said: *'Sprechen Sie Deutsch. Ich verstehe.'*

Again in German, Forell said: 'I'm asking you for asylum. I escaped from Siberia three years ago. I've just got over the frontier.'

'Repeat that more slowly, please.'

[1] i.e., U.S.S.R. (Soyuz Sovetskikh Sotsialisticheskikh Respublik)

'I was a German prisoner-of-war, in Eastern Siberia. I escaped three years ago and have just crossed the frontier into your country illegally, without passport or papers.'

'Do you know that this is a police headquarters?'

'Yes. I came because I saw the hammer-and-sickle on that building outside. Don't hand me back . . . please, grant me . . .'

The officer was not edified. In slow, pedantic German, after Forell had explained several times who he was and why he had come, he summarized the situation as it affected the Persian police. If Forell was speaking the truth, then he could rest assured he would not be handed back to the Russians. If, as seemed probable, he was a Soviet agent, the authorities would make doubly sure that he did not return. Meanwhile, until the matter was clarified, he was under arrest.

Forell was allowed food and a bath and then he was shown to a cell. Which particular town the cell was in seemed to him of minor importance, but he discovered it was Tabriz.

Four days later, after being called upon to repeat his story innumerable times, he was summoned to prepare himself for a journey. It had apparently been established beyond doubt that he was a Soviet spy. In a closed van, handcuffed and with an armed guard he was driven for nine hours to Teheran. As he was being taken to the police cells, he caught sight of the Turkish flag flying over a neighbouring building.

In Teheran he was interrogated four or five times daily, over a period of several weeks. The chief interrogator was a Colonel of Police, invariably courteous, invariably suave but adamant, despite all Forell's protestations, that he was a Soviet citizen bent on dangerous espionage. At last, Forell became exhausted and succumbed to renal colic. His requests for a doctor remained unanswered until one night, in desperation, he yelled the place down until a doctor was brought. The man was a German-speaking Turk and throughout his examination, a Persian officer remained in the cell for security reasons. A Turkish doctor—the Turkish flag—Ankara —and suddenly Forell remembered.

An uncle of his, Uncle—what was his name?—Erich! Yes, Uncle Erich was a civil engineer, had gone to live in Ankara before the war. . . .

Though his pain was genuine enough, Forell exaggerated it so as to arouse the doctor's sympathy. Then he asked him if next morning he would have the kindness to go to the Turkish Embassy and request that a certain Herr Erich Baudrexel, a German employed in the Highways Section of the Ministry of Communications in Ankara, be asked to come at once to Teheran to identify his nephew, Clemens Forell.

The Persian officer became suspicious at Forell's long

speech and asked the doctor a question. The two then conversed in undertones, the officer finally nodding as though giving the doctor permission to act as Forell had asked.

For six days, nothing happened, while the conviction grew in Forell's mind that his uncle could no longer be alive. He had last seen him in 1936 and had little news of him during the war. Then, one morning, a police officer came to the cell and told Forell he was to undergo further interrogation. He was taken to the same room in which the previous hearings had been held. In the centre, behind a table, sat the Colonel of Police, on his right, a man in civilian clothes whom Forell did not recognize and lastly, a woman interpreter. On the other side, reclining in a decorative attitude and busily filing his nails, sat a dandified young officer who appeared to be holding himself in reserve to take over any or all of the others' functions.

'Sit down, please,' said the Colonel through the interpreter to Forell. Then Herr Baudrexel was ushered into the room. He looked none too pleased at having been hauled exactly one thousand miles at the behest of some ruffian claiming to be his nephew.

'That is the man,' said the Colonel, after Herr Baudrexel had surveyed the room to no purpose. Uncle Erich gazed long and earnestly at Forell, then said in a severe tone: 'I have received the somewhat curious request to identify you as my nephew. I take it that the request came from you?' Forell was nonplussed. His uncle must be playing some sort of game. 'Yes, it came from me!'

'I have here an album of photographs, snapshots of the family to which you claim to belong.' Uncle Erich paused, clearly expecting Forell to cave in and admit his imposture. When nothing happened, he opened the album at random and holding it out to Forell, pointed to a family group. 'Who are these people and what are their names?' Forell identified his father, mother, brother, sister and a three-year-old boy, himself.

The interpreter translated what both had said. Then Forell's uncle pointed to more snapshots and after Forell had identified them all, he produced letters, reading out passages referring to family matters which Forell was then called upon to elucidate. Still unconvinced, he returned to the photographs, pointing to one of Forell himself taken at the beginning of the war. 'Do you recognize that face?'

Forell laughed. 'Obviously *you* don't!' The Colonel said something to the interpreter, who explained what the laugh was about. 'May I see?' said the Colonel. He took the album and looked up and down from Forell to the snapshot and back again. Finally he shook his head, meaning, 'I don't see the faintest resemblance'.

Grim-faced, Uncle Erich continued. 'What is the uniform that young man is wearing? What regiment? What rank?' Neither could be seen from the photograph, but that much Forell could remember. '*Gebirgsjägerregiment* 100. The rank is that of *Gefreiter*.'[1] A pause for interpreting. 'Was he right?' asked the Colonel. Uncle Erich stammered something and then said, 'I'm sorry, I ought not to have asked that question, I'm afraid I can't remember.' The Colonel pulled a face and smiled at Forell. The latter seized his chance. 'That is my mother's album, isn't it? If you take out that photograph, you will find written on the back, in my handwriting, the date of her birthday. There was only one print of that photograph and I gave it to her on 18th October, 1939.'

Herr Baudrexel, took out the snapshot and turned it over. He looked at it and then handed it to the Colonel. While the interpreter translated in an undertone, Uncle Erich said slowly: 'So you are, after all, my nephew Clemens! I didn't recognize you and I still don't, even now, as you stand there before me. But that doesn't matter, that doesn't alter the fact that you are who you claim to be.' He turned to the Colonel. 'I am completely satisfied that this man is my nephew.'

The Persian Colonel, the interpreter and the other two men conferred in the background. Then the Colonel shook Forell by the hand, and apologized for the delay and inconvenience caused by the necessary precaution of placing him under arrest. Finally he said: 'You may return to Germany whenever you like. Congratulations and best wishes for your future.'

Forell looked at the Colonel and tried to speak. He tried to, but could not. At long last, he was free.

A barber was fetched and in the cell, because there was no other place available, Forell had his hair cut and his beard trimmed down to the relic which he intended to preserve. On his uncle's order, a complete outfit of civilian clothes was delivered to the prison for him so that when, in just under three hours, he finally emerged, he looked once more the civilized man-about-Europe. He looked it, but when they transferred to a hotel, he found he had forgotten how to use a knife and fork. . . .

Uncle Erich gazed at the haggard face beside him. 'I can recognize the Tyrolean accent now, but not the face—no, not the face!'

Four days later, after passport formalities had been completed, the two men went by air to Ankara, and then Forell continued alone, flying to Munich via Istanbul, Athens and

---
[1] Lance-Corporal.

Rome. At Rome he had intended to send his wife a telegram asking her to met him at Munich airport, but he refrained, so that she should not suffer in public the shock of his changed appearance.

Forell reached Munich on the morning of 22nd December 1952. Soon after, he wrote to Frau Stauffer in Magdeburg, conveying the message which Doctor Stauffer had entrusted to him three years and two months before.

THE END